BASEBALL CHATTER

*Favorite baseball stories
from the game's insiders*

Credits

The stories that appear in *Baseball Chatter* were gathered by writers who have covered the game for many years, writers/editors who conducted personal interviews expressly for the book and researchers who gleaned many anecdotes from past issues of *Sporting News*.

Ron Smith handled most of the research, rewriting and editing responsibilities and interviewed players, former players, umpires and broadcasters. Dick Kaegel, Mike Kilduff and Ken Rosenthal provided more than 100 stories, and other major contributions were made by Stan McNeal, Tracy Ringolsby, Dennis Dillon, John Rawlings and Albert Dickson.

Contributing editors include McNeal, Chris Bergeron, Dave Bukovich, Sue Dorn, Carlyn Foster, Tom Gatto, Kathy Sheldon and Dave Sloan.

Design work was handled by Michael Behrens, Russ Carr and prepress director Bob Parajon.

ISBN: 0-89204-739-9

BASEBALL CHATTER

Contents

MANAGERIAL SPLENDOR

Jack McKeon, at the tender age of 72, finally hit postseason pay-dirt as manager of the World Series-champion Florida Marlins in 2003. But the best stories about this half century-plus baseball veteran reflect back to a different generation, when McKeon was catching, managing and using his vivid imagination to liven things up in the more colorful minor leagues.

"I've never told this (story) to anybody who believed me the first time," McKeon told a writer for *The Sporting News* in 1973, "but I swear the whole thing is true."

McKeon was catching in Missoula (Mont.) of the Class C Pioneer League in the late 1950s, one of 17 career stops he made at the minor league level. An opposing player hit a home run, but McKeon protested that he never touched the plate.

"The umpire's name was Joe Ring," McKeon said. "The runner really did touch the plate, but I'm arguing that he didn't and finally Ring agrees with me. The manager of the other team is Stan Wasiak, and of course he comes over to argue.

"We have a big discussion and finally Joe Ring says, 'All right, I'll tell you what we're gonna do. I'm gonna put this baserunner back up the line, say about 20 to 25 feet. Then I'm gonna give the ball to the pitcher. When I holler, 'Play ball,' the runner breaks for the plate and the pitcher tries to throw him out.'

"Now I can't believe this is happening, but I swear it did. I also can't believe that Wasiak is going for it. While they're arguing, I'm playing catch with the pitcher and I keep the ball. Joe Ring says, 'Play ball,' the runner starts coming down the line, my pitcher goes into his windup and makes like he has thrown the ball to the plate. I make like I'm catching it and I slap the tag on the guy.

"Joe Ring hollers, 'You're out again, podnah!' "

McKeon also told a story about the young Cuban player, Juan Vistuer, he "shot down" during his double role as manager-third base coach at Wilson of the Carolina League in the early 1960s.

"He ran through my stop sign at third, so I pulled him aside and explained to him that he had to stop," McKeon recalled. "Next night, the same thing, right through my sign and he's out by 40 feet. The following night, he does it again. I pull him aside and tell him that the next time he does it, I'm gonna shoot his rear end.

"I went down to a novelty shop and bought two (starter's) pistols and blank cartridges. I carried 'em in my two back pockets and I had to carry them for two weeks. Finally the night came. Vistuer comes running through third and goes right by me.

"I let him get about halfway down the line and I whipped out these two pistols and fired 'em. He took one leap, slid in head first and knocked the ball loose. And he laid there face down with his hands over his head."

On another occasion, manager McKeon discovered a cure for daydreaming outfielders. One of his players, a youngster named Chuck Weatherspoon, could not seem to keep his mind on the game, a problem that sometimes cost his team runs. So McKeon had rubber snakes strategically placed in the outfield grass.

"I found out he was afraid, deadly afraid, of snakes," McKeon said. "I told the other team's outfielder that when they passed each other changing sides to tell Weatherspoon to look out for snakes. You never saw such a changed player in your life."

When Don Zimmer was managing the Chicago Cubs from 1988-91, he didn't need guns or snakes to enhance his unpredictable, sometimes-zany reputation. The rotund Zim, with cheeks puffed out by that ever-present wad of tobacco, might hit and run with the bases loaded, try to steal third with two out—anything and everything opponents might not suspect. "I ain't got no book," he liked to tell reporters when answering questions about game strategy.

So it was somewhat comforting early in the '91 season, after Zimmer was fired, to see new manager Jim Essian bring a familiar brand of Zimmerism to Chicago. In his second game as manager, with the score tied 3-3 in the top of the ninth inning against the New York Mets, Essian tried to squeeze baserunner Shawon Dunston home from third base.

Doug Dascenzo, unfortunately, fouled off the 3-1 pitch from reliever John Franco, and Dunston had to return to third. But Essian shocked everybody by calling for the squeeze again on the next pitch, an unconventional move that worked to perfection with Dascenzo driving home the winning run.

"He's going to think this is easy," said Ron Schueler, the general manager of the cross-town White Sox and a former teammate of Essian.

But, alas, it wasn't. Essian posted a 59-63 record over the remainder of the season and was replaced in 1992 by Jim Lefebvre.

When former major league righthander Larry Bearnarth was the minor league pitching coach for the Montreal Expos in the early 1970s, he told about a memorable appearance he made for

Casey Stengel's New York Mets in 1964. Bearnarth worked seven scoreless innings (the eighth through 14th) in the second game of a doubleheader against the San Francisco Giants that day—a contest that would not be decided until the 23rd frame.

In his final inning, Bearnarth surrendered a leadoff single to Jesus Alou and walked Willie Mays, prompting a slow walk to the mound by a scowling Stengel as slugger Orlando Cepeda prepared to step into the box. "Thank God," Bearnarth thought to himself, "he's going to take me out of my misery, get me out of here so I can go take a shower."

But when Stengel reached the mound, he looked Bearnarth in the eyes and said, "Tra-la-la-la-la." He turned and left his pitcher standing in stunned silence as he slowly trudged back to the dugout.

Cepeda, as Bearnarth had feared, hit a blistering line drive up the middle. But Mets shortstop Roy McMillan, positioned perfectly, picked the ball off, stepped on second to double Alou and threw to first to retire Mays and end the threat. Bearnarth went back to the dugout, walked over to Stengel and asked, "What in the hell did you mean by 'Tra-la-la-la-la?' "

"Triple play, you dumb bastard," Stengel replied.

Former New York Yankees shortstop and longtime NBC broadcaster Tony Kubek told this spring training story about the irascible Stengel:

"Casey Stengel would always hold court in the (Soreno) hotel lobby at St. Petersburg until 3 in the morning and he'd also be kind of watching for players as they came in. So Mickey (Mantle), Whitey (Ford) and Billy (Martin) go down the alley and find an open window.

"It's a high window so Billy decides that since Mickey is the biggest guy, he should hoist Whitey on his shoulders and Billy would climb over them. So Billy gets in the window and Mantle boosts Whitey up and Billy pulls him in behind him.

"So now Mantle's left standing there, and Billy and Whitey are looking down at him and laughing. They take off for their rooms, and Mickey has to go through the lobby past Casey."

◆ ◆ ◆

Tony Muser's first day as manager of the Kansas City Royals was crazy. He took over from Bob Boone after the All-Star break in 1997.

That the team had lost eight straight games was a major concern, of course, but Muser arrived to find a clubhouse in chaos. He was taken aback by the number of players on the disabled list (why weren't they off somewhere rehabbing?) and besieged by coaches who were unsure of their status and beat a quick path to his office. One wanted to resign and another pleaded his case for staying. Muser assured everyone no immediate changes would be made.

Finally, things settled down and he was about to manage his first major league game against the Chicago White Sox.

As the team lined up on the dugout steps for the playing of the national anthem, Muser found himself standing next to Jeff King. A powerful hitter and a slick fielder, the first baseman always seemed to lack confidence in his ability.

As the flag waved in the July breeze over Kauffman Stadium and the anthem proceeded, King groaned: "Every time they play this song, I have a bad day."

Muser knew his bad day might get worse. And sure enough, the White Sox won, 6-3.

But King? He had two hits, two RBIs and handled 11 chances flawlessly. Muser didn't take King's self-doubts too seriously after that.

Muser's final day as Royals manager was even more bizarre.

The media wolves had been howling for his firing all through the 2001 season, but general manager Allard Baird remained a staunch supporter and Muser returned for 2002. The manager's seat only got hotter when the club staggered to a 7-15 start.

Muser's pain was eased temporarily on April 29 when Royals righthander Jeff Suppan pitched the game of his life—a two-hit, 4-0 shutout of the Detroit Tigers. As the manager enjoyed cocktails at the posh Ritz Carlton Hotel in Dearborn, Mich., with the TV production crew and others in the traveling party, things got frantic at Comerica Park.

Reporters from the *Kansas City Star* were packing up when an editor called with some hot news—a Kansas City television station was reporting Muser would be fired the next day. The TV sportscaster had close ties with George Brett, a club vice president, so a leak was possible.

The two *Star* reporters jumped into a car and dashed to the Ritz Carlton. Their final deadline was imminent and one of them passed the news to Muser.

"I better go find Allard," he said as the news sank in.

He did and Baird fired him immediately, instead of waiting until the next day as he had planned.

Muser returned to the table, told everyone he had been fired and finished his drink.

The *Star* made its deadline.

And Muser's in-between days were not always a cakewalk, either. Like the June 2, 1998, game in which Muser tried to do the right thing—and earned an eight-game suspension.

That was the day the Royals had a bang-up brawl with the Anaheim Angels. It began in the seventh inning when K.C. pitcher Jim Pittsley plunked Phil Nevin with a pitch and Nevin charged the mound, only to be body-slammed to the ground. Quickly, there was bedlam.

Before the evening was over, the scorecard showed two fights, five hit batters and 12 ejections. In the aftermath, American League president Gene Budig suspended or fined 14 individuals and doled out eight-game suspensions to Muser and Angels manager Terry Collins—the most severe punishment against managers in more than two decades.

The second brawl came after a ninth-inning brushback pitch and was accelerated when Royals infielder Felix Martinez clobbered Angels infielder Frank Bolick in a sneak attack. Muser was so incensed by the sucker punch that he grabbed Martinez, threw him into the dugout and dragged him up the runway toward the clubhouse. The next day, Martinez was shipped off to Class AAA Omaha.

And Muser, despite his efforts, was suspended for not controlling his players.

"I'm going to be a lost soul for eight days," he said. Muser was allowed to supervise pregame practice, but he had to watch games from a TV truck in the parking lot.

"The hardest part is physically leaving the stadium, walking out when everybody else is walking in," Muser said. "Saying goodbye to people who are coming in the ballpark—that's a very strange feeling."

◆　◆　◆

Muser's first day as a big-league manager might have been a little unsettling, but Gene Mauch's first minutes in that role were downright embarrassing.

Mauch was in Homestead, Fla., in the spring of 1960, getting ready to head north with the Class AAA Minneapolis Millers team he had managed the previous two seasons. The team, which included a major league wannabe named Carl Yastrzemski, was staying at a little motel, waiting to play its final spring training game.

"But the Phillies had lost opening day," Mauch recalled, "and Eddie Sawyer resigned (as manager). When they asked him why he resigned, he said, 'I'm 49 years old and I'd really like to live to be 50.'"

Philadelphia's general manager, John Quinn, decided he wanted Mauch to take over for Sawyer and tracked him down in Homestead.

"About 10:30 or 11 o'clock," Mauch said, "I get this rap on the door at this little dinky old motel. 'You're wanted on the phone, Mr. Mauch,' a voice said. And I said, 'Where's the nearest phone?' The voice answered, 'Well, right down there in the men's restroom, there's one.'

"The office was quite a ways away so I went into the restroom and the phone was right there over the commode. So I sat there on the commode and accepted my first major league managing job."

Then Mauch smiled.

"That should have told me something," he said.

◆ ◆ ◆

Whitey Herzog's big-league managerial career started with the lowly Texas Rangers in 1973, when he replaced Hall of Famer Ted Williams. It skidded to a temporary halt a few months later when, after being described publicly by Rangers owner Bob Short as "the best damn manager in baseball," he was fired with less than a month remaining in the season.

Things started unraveling for Herzog in late summer when general manager Joe Burke left Texas for the same job in Kansas City. Then things got complicated on September 2 when Billy Martin was fired as Detroit manager. Herzog said he should have suspected what was coming when Short asked him if he had any interest in the vacant G.M. position.

Herzog did not. And a few days later, he was dismissed by the Rangers with a 47-91 record. Martin was quickly hired as his replacement.

"Well, Billy Martin got fired in Detroit," Herzog said. "Short had told me the night before I was the best manager he ever had. When Martin got fired, he said, 'I'll fire my grandmother to hire Billy Martin.'

"Well, I was the grandmother. From being the smartest manager he ever had on Monday, I was the dumbest manager he ever had by Thursday."

In the long run, the move was only a glitch in a successful managing career. Burke hired Herzog to manage the Royals in 1975, succeeding Jack McKeon, and he later enjoyed a successful run as manager of the St. Louis Cardinals.

◆ ◆ ◆

The sometimes-edgy relationship between Baltimore manager Earl Weaver and pitcher Jim Palmer was always entertaining, if not constructive. Orioles players and coaches watched with fascination as the manager and his ace righthander sniped relentlessly at each other, only to go about their business with no lingering effects.

"They're like father and son, husband and wife," said longtime Orioles player and coach Elrod Hendricks. "You go in and say something about it to them the next day and they've already made up like it never happened. Now, everyone just leaves 'em alone when they start."

But not without a few laughs and knowing smiles.

"They're like two guys on the Matterhorn ride at Disneyland," said pitcher Mike Flanagan. "First, they're back in the tunnel, then they're out, then they're back in again. I'm just like a kid having fun watching them.

"Those two are so much alike they don't want to admit it. They're both very opinionated. Neither one is about to back off from the other. When we hear 'em going at it, we say, 'Oh, it's just those two again.'"

One colorful exchange took place during 1981 spring training after Palmer suggested he might not be the Orioles' opening day starter.

"I might sit here in 10 days and tell you Jim's pitching opening day," Weaver told reporters. "But Palmer won't let me. He's already announced the opening day pairings—(Steve) Stone against (Kansas City's) Larry Gura. It used to be he only managed my team; now he's managing the team we're playing, too."

Weaver then picked up a scrapbook and found pictures of himself when he was managing in the minor leagues.

"See that one?" he asked, pointing to a youthful-looking Weaver. "That was in 1966. Then the next year I met Palmer, and look at me now."

In another typical Palmer-Weaver exchange, the manager mentions, within earshot of his pitcher, how many games Palmer has won. Palmer hears Weaver's low figure and corrects him.

"I'm only counting the ones you won since I've been here,"

Weaver says. "The others don't count."

Palmer shrugs and says, "I can only repeat what Dave McNally once said about Earl. That is, 'The only thing he knows about pitching is that he couldn't hit it.' "

Weaver looks at his watch, smiles and fires back, "The Chinese tell time by the Year of the Dragon and the Year of the Horse. I tell time by Palmer—the Year of the Shoulder, the Year of the Elbow, the Year of the Ulna Nerve."

And so it went. ...

Weaver and Jim Russo spent most of their careers together with the Baltimore Orioles—Weaver as manager, Russo as scout. Although they generally got along, there was the occasional, shall we say, difference of opinion.

One such argument took place at the bar of the Netherlands Hilton Hotel in Cincinnati, the night before the 1970 All-Star Game. Weaver, the manager of the American League team, had selected Jim Palmer, Catfish Hunter, Sam McDowell, Jim Perry, Mike Cuellar, Dave McNally, Clyde Wright, Fritz Peterson and Mel Stottlemyre—all starters—for his pitching staff. Russo challenged that decision.

"Earl, you can't do that," said Russo.

"As long as I manage an All-Star team," said Weaver, "there won't be any relievers."

"You're ignoring the special man. You're telling all the relievers in our league, 'I don't need you.' You had to pick Sparky Lyle and at least three relievers.

"You're trying to tell me Clyde Wright can't do a good job? Wright may be a starter, but he can come in and do as good a job as Lyle."

Round and round they went. Finally, around 3 a.m., Russo had had enough. "Go to hell, Earl," he said. "I'm going to bed."

The next night, Weaver looked like a mastermind—for eight innings. Behind Palmer (3IP, 1H, 3Ks), McDowell (3IP, 1H, 3Ks) and Perry (2IP, 1H, 3Ks), the American League took a 4-1 lead into the bottom of the ninth. That's when Weaver called on Hunter to finish off the N.L. and snap the A.L.'s seven-game losing streak.

But Hunter gave up three runs on three hits and the game went into extra innings. Then, in the bottom of the 12th, Jim Hickman's single drove in Pete Rose, whose infamous collision with catcher Ray Fosse jarred the ball loose and gave the N.L. a 5-4 win. The losing pitcher? Clyde Wright.

A couple days later, American League president Lee MacPhail announced that, henceforth, the A.L. All-Star teams would include relief pitchers.

◆　◆　◆

The always-entertaining Weaver was, in the opinion of many observers, the game's umpire-baiting master. But the Earl of Baltimore begged to differ.

"(Houk's) the best in the league," Weaver acknowledged in 1975, deferring to Detroit boss Ralph Houk. "I've learned a lot from Ralph."

Weaver had just witnessed an "Academy Award-worthy" Houk performance after umpire Jim McKean called pinch-runner John Knox out at the plate in an April 28 game at Baltimore's Memorial Stadium. It started with a few choice words, escalated into a typical dirt-kicking routine and culminated with a tossed cap that hit McKean in the back of the head after he had ejected the Tigers boss.

"It must have slipped out of my hand," Houk said. "I couldn't imagine why he kicked me out."

As Houk was reenacting his version of the argument for reporters after the game, he lost his balance and almost toppled over.

"I had my new spikes on and I caught them in the mud," Houk said. "I'm glad I didn't pull a muscle so that I had to be helped off the field. That would have been something."

◆　◆　◆

John McNamara's first major league managerial stop was Oakland, where he posted an 89-73 record for Charlie Finley—the best mark in his first decade as owner.

"The way I got fired," said McNamara, "was like this:

"It was October 1, my wedding anniversary. He offered me congratulations. The season had just ended and we had won 89 games, more than any team of Athletics since 1932, the year I was born. He congratulated me on that.

" 'But we've got to make a change,' he said. Just like that. It came so smoothly and so easily that all I could think of was to agree with him. He said I was too nice."

Finley, of course, hired Dick Williams, who guided the A's to three straight A.L. West titles and World Series championships in 1972 and '73. McNamara went on to manage for 19 years.

"(Finley) was good to me—he brought me to the majors," he said. "I wouldn't have had this opportunity today but not for Finley. He made it all possible."

◆　◆　◆

Baseball reporting can be hazardous to your health. For years, one of the most shown television videotapes was the wobbly but revealing footage of Kansas City manager Hal McRae going into a rage in April 1993.

What started it all?

One radio reporter, hovering over McRae's desk, wanted to know if he had considered pinch hitting George Brett for Keith Miller in the seventh inning of a game against Detroit with the bases loaded and two out. Miller popped out. Brett was used as a pinch hitter in the ninth, but the Royals lost a tough 5-3 decision to the Tigers.

"Don't ask me such stupid (bleeping) questions," said the steaming McRae. "That's it. Everybody out. It's over."

McRae, warming to his sudden tantrum, made more loud remarks about reporters' questions, then swept everything off his desk. A television set went over, a glass bottle smashed. Then he began throwing everything within reach.

Some object—no one was certain if it was an ashtray, a telephone or something else—opened a gash on the cheek of *Topeka Capital Journal* reporter Alan Eskew.

Was McRae really a madman?

"I don't think I'm perceived that way," he said in the following spring training. "People know what I'm capable of doing, but I think I'm perceived as a kind of mild-mannered person, which I am."

McRae, in fact, seemed to enjoy his daily give-and-take with reporters—laughing, gabbing and having a good time. But he loved to win even more.

And that's what he did with the Royals in 1994, reeling off 14 straight victories at one point and charging after the Chicago White Sox in a tight A.L. Central race. Then the players' strike ended the season—and McRae's job with it.

That fateful night in 1993, a TV cameraman kept grinding out footage, catching McRae toward the end of his tirade holding a broken vodka bottle in his hand. It wasn't a pretty picture, one that no doubt contributed to his firing in '94 and kept him from getting another managerial job until 2001 with Tampa Bay.

◆   ◆   ◆

There were two of them. Two Bill Rigneys stood side by side behind a batting cage at Kansas City's Municipal Stadium. Both wore sunglasses, both walked with that distinctive Rigney swagger and both talked with hands moving in ceaseless gesticulations.

But there was one difference. The real Bill Rigney wore a California Angels jersey with No. 18. The fake one wore Angels jersey No. 18½. And the real Angels manager was laughing uncontrollably at impersonator Jim Fregosi's lighthearted charade.

Rigney got into the spirit of the moment by handing the lineup card for the September 24, 1967, game to his flamboyant shortstop, who had been given the day off. Fregosi delivered the lineup, then spent the entire game wandering along the top step of the dugout, dispatching a steady stream of semaphores to his players and coaches.

The Angels responded with a 2-1 victory over the Athletics and Fregosi retired as the American League's only undefeated manager. After the game, he capped his unusual day by walking into Rigney's office, removing the shirt with the makeshift 18½ and tucking it into the real skipper's traveling bag.

"That's how I treat my men," Fregosi cracked. "I give them the shirt off my back."

◆ ◆ ◆

Sparky Anderson, completing his first season as a major league manager in Game 5 of the 1970 World Series, provided an inside look at what a manager might say to a struggling pitcher when he visits the mound. Anderson had agreed to wear a microphone to record key moments for the annual World Series films.

The following conversation with Cincinnati starter Jim Merritt, a 20-game winner, was recorded in the second inning after the Baltimore Orioles had already scored four runs off the lefthander en route to a Series-clinching 9-3 victory:

Anderson: "Badger, I know you feel fine and I know. ..."

Merritt: "I'm OK, Spark, really."

Anderson: "I know that, Badger, but I'm going to have to make a decision and I'm going to make it like I always make it."

Merritt: "Well, Sparky, I'm. ..."

Anderson: "I know you feel good and I appreciate you going out here today, believe me. But I know this. For you to stay out here over four or five innings today isn't going to do you any good. I appreciate you going out."

Merritt: "It's been 11 days and I think I can still get it together."

Anderson: "I know that, Jimmy. Don't think I don't know it."

(Merritt departs and Sparky turns to catcher Johnny Bench.)

Anderson: "He didn't have nothing, did he, John?"

So you want to be a big-league manager. Well, you better be prepared to be on call at all times, even at your daughter's wedding reception.

Anderson was a long way from the baseball field the day his daughter Shirlee got married. He was the father of the bride, a doting parent who simply wanted to enjoy the festivities—the laughter, the music and the tears—like everyone else, without any sports talk.

"Everyone was great about it," said Anderson, who had led the Tigers to a World Series championship in the previous 1984 season. "I thought I might get through the entire evening without having to talk baseball. But I couldn't. I guess it will never happen."

Anderson couldn't remember exactly what he was doing when a guest approached him and asked, "What do you think your chances of repeating are this year, Spark?" He could have excused himself politely, but ever the diplomat, Anderson answered.

"What a mistake," he said. "Then I couldn't get rid of the guy."

◆ ◆ ◆

Willie Wilson, it was said, could make it from first base to third faster than any player in history. He also could make his manager turn gray just as fast.

On one early April day in 1988, the Kansas City Royals were taking batting practice at old Exhibition Stadium in Toronto. Snow swirled over the ballpark and the 34-degree chill was most unbaseball-like. All of a sudden, Wilson rapped a ball into the dirt. ... or was it his toe? Wilson went down like a sack of bricks. He hobbled out of the batting cage and hunkered down next to it.

Oddly, no one paid any attention. Not manager John Wathan, not the trainers, not the other players. Wilson was left to moan without sympathy.

Wilson led off the game, hobbling to the plate, and struck out quickly, an at-bat marked by unenthusiastic swings. He seemed to be asking out of this icy affair. Wathan, though, kept him on the field until the eighth inning. The Royals were blown out by the Blue Jays that day and if Wathan had to suffer, then Wilson could do the same.

◆ ◆ ◆

Go to a game today and watch both players and coaches dispense balls freely to the crowd, a gesture of good will and connection with the fans. Thousands are tossed into the stands as souvenirs over a 162-game season.

That was not the case in 1952, when Leo Durocher was managing the New York Giants. Durocher, coaching third base in a game at Brooklyn's Ebbets Field, retrieved four foul balls and tossed them into the stands—to the dismay of Dodgers vice president Buzzie Bavasi.

"Mr. Durocher will pay at the rate of $5 per ball," Bavasi announced the next day. "Payment will come in the form of a deduction from our check to the Giants."

Bavasi backed off from the "deduction" threat when informed it might be a violation of National League rules, but he remained adamant payment would be collected. Durocher responded that Bavasi should be happy that he only tossed four of the six balls he fielded.

The commotion traced back to Durocher's defection from Brooklyn, where he managed eight-plus years, to the hated Giants in 1948. And the part he played in New York's shocking pennant-playoff victory over the Dodgers in 1951.

Durocher said he was simply reacting to the two balls Dodgers third baseman Billy Cox threw into the stands during a game at the Polo Grounds. He warned at the time he would double Cox's generosity the next time the Giants played at Ebbets Field. And so Bavasi decided to double the cost of the $2.50 balls in the form of an invoice.

"Let him try to collect," Durocher said.

Among Durocher's considerable talents was the ability to conduct a press briefing while conversing with a friend at the same time. The friend in this case was actor Danny Kaye, who had slipped into the office of the New York Giants manager with the inquisitive media types after a game.

Writer: "Who pitches tomorrow?"

Kaye: "Do you want to make it 21 (a dinner spot)?"

Durocher: "(Jim) Hearn. It doesn't matter to me."

Writer: "Does that mean you will open with him against Brooklyn?"

Kaye: "Well, I'll have to go home and put on a tie."

Durocher: "Dunno yet. Why not make it Lum Fong's (another dinner spot)?"

Writer: "What do you hear about (third baseman Hank) Thompson—can he play tomorrow?"

Kaye: "It doesn't matter to me. I'll leave it to you."

Durocher: "Why not go out and talk to the little woman (Durocher's wife Laraine)? She's out in the car. Thompson—Doc says in a day or two."

Red Schoendienst, who managed the St. Louis Cardinals for a record 12 seasons plus two interim stints, was never known for colorful quotes.

On occasion, however, he did exhibit a dry wit. He was usually at his best when a player made an excuse for a bonehead mistake.

One day outfielder Bake McBride, explaining why he ran into an easy out, said he was trying to "surprise the other team."

"Surprises," Schoendienst observed, "are for Cracker Jack boxes."

The Seattle Mariners won an American League record 116 games in 2001, a mark that could stand for a long time. According to outfielder Jay Buhner, who played only 19 games in that magical season because of injury problems, early signs did not presage such dominance for a franchise that had won only two division titles since its inception in 1977.

"When you talk about how the season started for the Mariners, you have to talk about how spring training ended," he said. "We struggled all spring. In fact, we stunk. Granted, in spring training a lot of veteran guys come into camp just to work on specific things. That's how you do it. You work on taking pitches, seeing pitches, working the count, trying to see if you can hit with two strikes. Pitchers are throwing nothing but fastballs some days, and so they might get their brains beat in. There are just a lot of different things to work on.

"So the first couple of weeks went by and we were doing that. Then we were using a lot of young kids late in the games, and we were losing. (Manager) Lou Piniella, being the competitive guy he is, doesn't like to lose. I don't care if it's against a Little League team or if it's in spring training or what it is, he just does not like to lose.

"Toward the end of spring training, he was starting to cut the roster down. We were down to about 30 guys, but we were still losing some close ballgames. He was getting a little ticked off. I'll never forget this. Lou finally said, 'Guys, we need to pick it up. The season is a week away. I don't know what you've got to do, but let's get this thing turned around. Let's get started and get ready for the season.'

"I don't know how it happened after that. I don't know what button these guys pushed or what light they switched on or whatever it was. But from that point on, we proceeded to spill a 55-gallon can of whup-ass on people."

◆ ◆ ◆

There was little "whup-ass" going on during Maury Wills' brief-but-eventful tenure as manager of the Mariners. Hired the first week of August 1980, he was fired the first week of May 1981. One of his more memorable moments came in mid-September 1980.

The Mariners were playing a Saturday night game at Milwaukee. Two batters into the seventh inning, Wills went to the mound and signaled for a lefthander to relieve Manny Sarmiento.

Veteran lefty Dave Roberts took off his heavy coat, grabbed his glove and headed from the bullpen to the mound.

Wills was irate when Roberts arrived.

"Why are you here?" Roberts recalled his manager demanding.

"Well," Roberts answered, "you didn't have anybody warming up. I figured you didn't want to jeopardize the kid's (Shane Rawley) arm, so you must have wanted me."

Wills slammed the ball into Roberts' glove and stormed off the mound.

Wills had a reputation for being easily confused. When he attended a January 1981 news conference to announce the purchase of the team by George Argyros, the manager agreed to an impromptu session with the media during which he suggested Leon Roberts could be the team's opening day center fielder.

"Have you asked the Texas Rangers about that," Wills was asked.

"What difference does it make to them?" he asked.

Roberts, he was told, was part of an 11-player trade with Texas at the winter meetings in December. He no longer belonged to the Mariners.

When Bob Lemon managed the Seattle Angels to the Pacific Coast League championship in 1966, the former Cleveland Indians pitcher displayed equal parts intensity, patience and good humor. All three of those qualities were tested in a May 11 game at Vancouver when Mounties player Santiago Rosario hit Seattle's Merritt Ranew on the head during a brawl.

"If that so-and-so comes to the plate again, he better have a helmet that reaches his ankles," the irate manager was heard to yell. "He'll get it."

When word of the threat got to PCL president Dewey Soriano, he held a hearing and fined Lemon $100. Lemon was ready the next time he encountered the *Seattle Times* writer who had reported the incident.

"You not only cost me 100 bucks, you misquoted me," he said.

The reporter asked him to be more specific.

"Yes, you misquoted me," Lemon reiterated. "I called Rosario something a lot stronger than a so-and-so."

♦ ♦ ♦

In 1988, outfielder Jeff Stone became a symbol of the hapless 0-21 Baltimore Orioles. Acquired to be the team's new leadoff hitter, he began the season 1-for-32 and cost the Orioles a game by losing a ball in the left field lights.

Stone was terribly naive, once declining a shrimp cocktail in a restaurant because he said he did not drink. But he also was a sincere guy, impossible not to like. The problem was, manager Frank Robinson began to lose patience with him as the streak continued to build.

When Stone dislocated his finger, club officials finally had an out. Asked if Stone would need to go on the disabled list, Robinson told reporters, "I don't know. But I hope so."

◆ ◆ ◆

No one today catches like Tony Pena did over his 18-year major league career. From a squat, Pena would keep one leg in the catcher's crouch and extend the other straight out to the side—at such an angle that a batter venturing too far out of the box could have tripped over it.

The style worked for Pena, who developed it on his own while playing in the minors. He won four Gold Gloves and never suffered from the knee pain that plagues many catchers who spend countless hours squatting behind home plate. And umpires never tried to lean on him.

"Eric Gregg told me that I made him feel naked behind the plate when I was catching," Pena said. "I told him, don't worry. You won't get hurt. And he never did."

The Pena leg extension, however, will not become a trademark for any of the catchers he now mentors as manager of the Kansas City Royals.

Pena will not allow them even to try it. Early in his career, Pena tried to emulate another Latin catcher, Manny Sanguillen, who squatted so low his butt almost scraped the ground. But Sanguillen set him straight, telling Pena to catch like Tony Pena, not Manny Sanguillen.

"He told me to just do the things I'm capable of doing," Pena said.

◆ ◆ ◆

Ted Turner built a television empire, became a billionaire, made waves in the yachting world, married actress Jane Fonda and engaged in numerous other activities in-between. One of those "other activities" came in 1977, when the unpredictable Turner managed the Atlanta Braves—a team he just happened to own.

Baseball history remembers Connie Mack as the owner/manager of the Philadelphia Athletics for 50 years. Most baseball purists have tried to forget Turner's one-game stint as owner/manager of the Braves.

After watching his 1977 team lose 16 straight games, Turner sent manager Dave Bristol away on a scouting mission to look at Atlanta's minor league teams. Turner put on uniform No. 27 and "managed" the Braves on May 11 in Pittsburgh. The string of losses reached 17 when the Pirates prevailed, 2-1.

National League president Chub Feeney, not amused, ruled that Turner had to return to the stands. The Braves ended their swoon the next day in Pittsburgh under coach Vern Benson, but, when the club returned to Atlanta, Turner suited up again for a game against the Cardinals. This time he got a quick call from commissioner Bowie Kuhn, who told Turner to desist in the best interests of baseball.

Coming out of the shower in the manager's office that afternoon, Turner toweled off his Rhett Butler mustache and said with exasperation: "Yeah, he said no dice—said I didn't have enough experience." Turner explained that he just wanted to find out what was going on "between the white lines" with his team.

"You know what General Patton did when the troops were having trouble—he went to the front in a jeep to find out why," Turner told a St. Louis reporter. "When they marched to Bastogne, he went right with 'em and carried his own pack. Right? He didn't sit back on a phone in the office and say, 'What's going on?' If I'm smart enough to lose a million and a half bucks a year on this team, I'm smart enough to come down on the field and manage. Right?"

Turner said he had relied on Benson for the game strategy decisions, anyway. "I just figured the guys needed a little jacking up and

I'm a guy who can jack people up," he said.

The next night, Bristol was summoned to resume the managerial duties. Turner went back to his box seat. His managerial term is duly recorded in the Braves' annual media guide under the 1977 results: Dave Bristol 61-100, Ted Turner 0-1.

◆　◆　◆

One summer morning in 1977, the St. Louis Cardinals were in Atlanta and relief pitcher Al Hrabosky was in the team hotel's busy dining room. Someone asked for his autograph, which piqued the interest of a young woman at a nearby table.

Sniffing celebrity, she asked Hrabosky: "What do you do?"

Hrabosky summoned up a scowl. "I hate people," he said.

Well, the Mad Hungarian's intimidation act might have been lost on his audience that morning. He did not look very menacing. He was baby-faced and clean shaven—but not by choice. Facial hair had been banned in the Cardinals' clubhouse by hard-nosed first-year manager Vern Rapp, who was following the suggestion of team owner Gussie Busch.

Finally, the struggling Hrabosky felt compelled to rebel. At the All-Star break, he ignored his razor and had a confrontation with Busch. The owner struck a Great Compromise: He verbally lashed out at Hrabosky, but he gave him the OK to let his whiskers flourish. Hrabosky suddenly looked and felt meaner on the mound. Several other players, including first baseman Keith Hernandez and shortstop Garry Templeton, showed support by growing mustaches.

Rapp had his authority undercut, but Busch propped him up with a contract extension.

After the ban was lifted, the more relaxed Cardinals went on an 18-6 tear and got to within five games of first-place Philadelphia.

"I think it's fair to say there was an air of tension on the ballclub—created by myself," Hrabosky admitted.

But the Samson syndrome didn't hold up. In the long run, Hrabosky did just about as poorly after he stopped shaving as he did before. And the Cardinals finished third, 18 games behind the Phillies.

The next year, Hrabosky could begin hating people in the American League. The Cardinals traded him to the Kansas City Royals for pitcher Mark Littell and catcher Buck Martinez.

After a tough loss at San Diego in that same 1977 season, Rapp stormed into his office and slammed the door. Hard.

The door jammed. He was locked in. And workmen couldn't budge it. Utility player Roger Freed offered to kick in the door to free his imprisoned boss, but the workmen pleaded for patience.

Rapp, a strict disciplinarian, was not the most loved of managers. The players restrained themselves from going into loud convulsions of laughter. But they were obviously delighted.

Finally, after 20 minutes, the workmen were able to wiggle open the door.

Rapp emerged, grim-faced but unfazed. Immediately, all grins vanished throughout the Cardinals' clubhouse. The skipper was on the prowl again.

◆ ◆ ◆

There was a dead spot during the 1980 winter meetings at Dallas, and Cincinnati manager John McNamara wanted to spice things up. So he pulled California manager Jim Fregosi into a corner of the Anatole Hotel lobby and they plotted out a juicy rumor, just to see how far it could spread.

The San Francisco Giants were searching for a manager and McNamara filtered out word that Giants owner Bob Lurie had decided to bring back Alvin Dark. The rumor quickly became the talk of the meetings.

It became such an issue, in fact, that Giants general manager Tom Haller became incensed. When he saw Lurie walking across the hotel lobby, he cornered him and announced he was resigning because he felt betrayed the owner would hire a manager without consulting him.

Lurie was stunned. He had no idea what Haller was talking about.

McNamara finally stepped in and explained the rumor gone bad. But that did not stop him from pulling the same prank again. In 1986, another rumor mysteriously circulated during the World Series.

This time it was Jack McKeon, general manager at San Diego, who was looking for a manager. On a flight carrying baseball executives and media, McNamara nudged a writer seated next to him and winked.

"I hear McKeon's going to take care of Harry Dunlop and make him manager of the Padres," McNamara said.

Milton Richman of *United Press International* was seated in front of McNamara. Within minutes after the plane landed, UPI was reporting Dunlop's hiring.

◆　◆　◆

It was evident at the 1986 All-Star Game that Dick Howser was not himself. As manager of the 1985 World Series-champion Kansas City Royals, Howser earned the right to guide the American League team that played in the midsummer classic at Houston's Astrodome.

On the workout day, Tracy Ringolsby, a reporter who had covered the Royals' championship season in Kansas City before moving on to Dallas, walked by the open door to Howser's office.

"Where are you going?" Howser asked.

"Out on the field," Ringolsby said.

"Come in and sit down," Howser said. "We haven't had a chance to chat."

Ringolsby and Howser had developed a strong relationship over the three previous seasons in Kansas City. Often, the reporter sat with Howser behind closed doors for 30 minutes and went over what had happened in the previous game. He was able to ask, in a relaxed atmosphere, any question that came to mind.

Ringolsby stepped into the visiting manager's office at the Astrodome and sat down, figuring this would be a chance to renew that relationship. Howser, instead, turned his attention to some papers on his desk. After a few minutes had passed, he looked up.

"What do you need?" he asked Ringolsby.

"Nothing," he said.

"Well," said Howser, "I've got a lot to do. Let me catch you later."

Ringolsby headed for the field where Texas trainer Bill Zeigler was standing. Zeigler, whose ties with Howser dated back to Florida State University, had been selected to work the All-Star Game.

"You see Dick?" Zeigler asked.

"Sort of," said Ringolsby, who told him about the strange encounter.

"Something's wrong," Zeigler said. "He came into the training room talking about this neck ache that won't go away. I called Mickey (Cobb, the Kansas City trainer) and told him to get Dick in for tests the day he gets home from here."

Howser underwent those tests. Doctors found a malignant brain tumor.

THE CLUBHOUSE: BEHIND CLOSED DOORS

Tigers outfielder/designated hitter Gates Brown is a legend in Detroit for two reasons: his pinch-hitting prowess and his Rubenesque figure. He hit a pinch home run in his first major league at-bat and he finished his career with 16 pinch homers and 107 pinch hits. Tigers broadcaster Jim Price, a former Brown teammate, remembered one in particular.

"Gator never was called upon to pinch hit before the eighth or ninth inning," Price said. "He'd always stay out in the bullpen. In old Tiger Stadium, you could walk into the locker room from our bullpen without going through the dugout. Every game, about the fifth or sixth inning, he'd go into the locker room to get a couple hot dogs.

"I happened to be walking with him this one time when he ordered hot dogs and, like always, he got them with mustard, ketchup, relish and all that stuff. While he was in the locker room, one of our coaches comes up through the tunnel and says, 'Gator! Get your bat! Mayo wants you to pinch hit.'

"Brown responds, 'It's only the fifth inning. It's too early for me.'

" 'No,' the coach says, 'he's serious and he wants you to pinch hit.'

"If a player gets caught eating during the game, he gets fined. Brown's back was to the coach, and he doesn't know what to do with the hot dogs. So he wraps them up and stuffs them in his shirt. Now, I should mention, we have a beautiful white uniform here at home. The coach never takes his eyes off Brown. I'm laughing my butt off as we walk underneath the tunnel out to the dugout. Everybody on the team knows what is going on because they know Brown was getting his hot dogs. He comes out and you can see it in his shirt.

"Mayo just says, 'Get your bat. You're hitting next.'

"Brown says, 'I don't believe you're doing this to me.'

"Then he goes up, hits a double and slides head-first into second. Mustard, ketchup and hot dogs splash on the umpires and the infielders. Then somebody hits a single to drive in Brown, who as he goes past Mayo says, 'I can't believe you ruined my hot dogs.' "

◆　　◆　　◆

Bob Gibson, the St. Louis Cardinals' Hall of Fame righthander, was a great pitcher and a man of his word. Gibson was midway through his final season in 1975 when he appeared on a pregame radio show with broadcaster Jack Buck and conceded that he might retire early if the Cardinals were out of the race in September and called up young pitchers from the minor leagues.

Dick Kaegel, a reporter for the *St. Louis Post-Dispatch*, asked Gibson about his comments and wrote a story that appeared in the paper. The next day, Gibson summoned Kaegel to the clubhouse.

"Everything you write stirs up a bunch of (bleep)," Gibson said. "I'm not talking to you anymore."

Gibson was steamed because the Mets were in town and the large contingent of New York beat writers had read the article. All of them, apparently, had badgered him about it.

True to his word, other than an occasional "Hi," Gibson did not talk to Kaegel the rest of the season.

And when Gibson, in fact, did announce he was retiring early, writers gathered around him to discuss his career as Kaegel approached to offer his hand and wish him luck. "Thanks," Gibson said.

Kaegel lingered, without a notebook, just curious to see what would follow. A reporter asked another question, but Gibson paused and glared.

"I'm not saying another word until that (bleeping) Kaegel leaves," he said.

Kaegel, given that knockdown pitch, departed. Gibson continued his conversation with the other reporters, hard-nosed to the end.

Intensity can be measured in different ways. But there was no way to gauge the inner fire that stoked the competitive instincts of Kirk Gibson.

In 1988 spring training, new Los Angeles outfielder Gibson was the victim of a practical joke only minutes before the start of the Dodgers' first exhibition game at Vero Beach, Fla. Gibson discovered a black stripe across his forehead, courtesy of the shoe polish relief pitcher Jesse Orosco had painted on the inside rim of his hat. Gibson stormed off the field and refused to play.

"I like to have a good time," he said the next day. "But a good time to me is winning. I'm not here for comedy. I didn't think it was too funny. I'm fully aware this is the last thing they need around this clubhouse, but I have to stand up for what I believe. If (teammates) don't understand that, maybe I don't fit in."

Will Clark had that same old-school intensity. When he played for the St. Louis Cardinals over the final 51 games of the 2000 season, he lit a fire in the clubhouse that was badly needed.

A story is told about the moments preceding Game 3 of the Division Series at Atlanta's Turner Field. Gatorade, the official drink of the postseason for major league baseball that year, had posters planted everywhere, including the tunnel that led from the Cardinals' clubhouse to the dugout. As Clark made his way from the locker room to the field, he began tearing down the posters, one by one, and throwing them to the ground with no attempt to hide his disgust.

When asked later why he had attacked the Gatorade signs, Clark provided a terse explanation.

"I couldn't let those posters stay on the wall," he said, "because they had Braves logos on them."

◆   ◆   ◆

Montreal manager Buck Rodgers was describing the extensive pitching repertoire of Expos veteran righthander Dennis "Oil Can" Boyd in 1990.

"I guess he throws the usual stuff," Rodgers said, "if you call 12 pitches the usual stuff. He throws a fastball, curve, slider, change-up, sidearm slider, sidearm curve. ..."

"And the Uecker pitch," interrupted coach Ken Macha.

The Uecker pitch?

"That's the pitch he threw Kent Hrbek in Minnesota," Macha explained. "He hit it up in the seats where Uecker sits."

◆   ◆   ◆

Before the first game of every series, pitchers customarily meet to go over opposing hitters. Given the divergent and odd mixture of personalities on most major league staffs, those get-togethers some-times produce interesting exchanges. Former Cardinals reliever Rick Horton remembers one crazy 1984 meeting in Chicago.

"We were going over the Cubs hitters and we came to Mel Hall," Horton said. "Hall had been extremely hot and (manager) Whitey Herzog wanted to break him down. 'So, how are we going to pitch Mel Hall?' he asked."

Joaquin Andujar, who was scheduled to start the series opener, quickly jumped to his feet.

"Don worry 'bout Mel Hall, Whitey," he said in his broken English. "I take care of him."

"That's fine, Joaquin," Herzog answered, "but we have to decide how to pitch him."

"No, no, no, don't worry 'bout Hall," Andujar repeated.

Herzog looked at his unpredictable righthander and said, "OK, Joaquin, how do you figure you're going to take care of him?"

"I kill him," Andujar said without a trace of a smile.

Amused by the exchange, the pitchers took the field later and were shocked to see Andujar standing next to the batting cage, laughing and talking with none other than Mel Hall.

◆ ◆ ◆

Relief ace Sparky Lyle, a feared jokester in the New York Yankees clubhouse from 1972-78, had a longstanding reputation for sitting on birthday cakes. So when teammate Bobby Murcer got a special-delivery present in 1973, extra pains were taken to protect it from the mad plopper.

"Murcer got a beautiful strawberry cake for his birthday and the Colonel (pitching coach Jim Turner) was protecting it," Lyle said. "I had always said I'd never sit on one after it was cut, so the Colonel carried (the cake) around and sent (Jerry) Moses for a knife. When Moses returned, I was across the room from where the cake was.

"Moses told the Colonel he had the knife, so Jim set the cake down and stepped back to let Moses cut it. ... Just then I ran between them and plopped all over it. It was one of my better moves. The Colonel was really funny trying to find a piece I hadn't hit."

Righthanded pitcher Joe Cowley was a later-era Yankees flake who once prompted this classic line from teammate Don Baylor: "Joe's off on his own planet. He just lets the rest of us visit once in a while." On a March afternoon in 1985, it was Cowley who was doing the visiting when fellow pitcher John Montefusco targeted him for a spring training practical joke.

Montefusco had observed Cowley on several occasions hot rod-ding in the team parking lot outside Fort Lauderdale Stadium. He talked three city policemen into entering the Yankees' clubhouse on the guise of arresting the pitcher for reckless driving—and they came armed with a phony warrant.

Cowley protested his innocence while players throughout the locker room watched in silence, straining not to laugh. "Put the handcuffs on him," one shouted as Cowley, apparently resigned to his fate, asked the policemen to let him change into street clothes because "I don't want to go to jail in my pinstripes."

Cowley changed and as he was being escorted from the room, one of the policemen told him he was the victim of a prank. Everybody roared their approval, imitating Cowley's distinctive laugh. The pitcher kept right on walking out the door, returning only after he had properly recovered from his embarrassment.

◆ ◆ ◆

Atlanta righthander Phil Niekro was getting his arm rubbed down by trainer Harvey Stone on a July day in 1967 after fluttering his knuckleball past frustrated Pittsburgh hitters in a 2-1 victory at Atlanta Stadium. Stone commented, only half in jest, that the soft-throwing righthander probably could pitch again in the Braves' next game.

"No he couldn't, either," shot back Braves vice president Paul Richards, who was standing nearby.

"Why not?" somebody asked. "Do you think he needs the rest, as easy as he throws?"

"Naw," Richards answered, "but (catcher Bob) Uecker does. Every time Phil pitches, Uecker is the one who needs four days' rest."

◆ ◆ ◆

Bo Jackson was not only a tremendous two-sport athlete, he also was an avid—and talented—hunter. During his prime years with the Kansas City Royals, Jackson kept a crossbow in the clubhouse.

Because Bo was Bo, he was allowed to do just about anything he wanted, which was not always good news for the other players. So nobody said much when he set up a target with straw backing at one end of the clubhouse hallway, just the other side of the shower entrance, and sent arrows streaking into the target while practicing before games.

Bo was an outstanding shot, but what if some unfortunate teammate, cooling down after batting practice, had emerged from the showers at just the wrong instant?

It never happened, of course, because Bo Knows Crossbows.

◆　◆　◆

The story reads like something straight out of a made-for-TV movie. The 27-year-old rookie, hoping to play a major league game in front of hometown fans, goes to his legendary manager and dares to ask for a rare start. Couldn't happen? Think again.

Wayne Graham was that rookie in 1964, a third baseman who got a late-season callup by the New York Mets. His new manager was Casey Stengel.

"Casey didn't know me from Adam," Graham recalled. "My first few times at-bat I didn't do well, and I remember playing third in one game and Stengel told me not to let (Dodgers shortstop) Maury Wills bunt. Well, Wills gets two strikes and I move back. Players don't bunt with two strikes in the minors. Wills bunts for a hit and I don't get to play much after that."

Late in the season, the Mets traveled to Houston, Graham's hometown. Stengel used him as a pinch hitter in the opener of the three-game series at Colt Stadium and he was 0-for-1. Graham appeared as a defensive replacement in the second game, without an at-bat. After taking batting practice before the series finale, he checked the starting lineup, saw he was not in it and worked up the courage to visit Stengel in his office.

"I told him I was from Houston and asked if there was any chance of getting into the lineup for that one game," Graham said. "He told me that I was young, I would have plenty of time to play here. I told him, 'I don't know, Casey. This is my eighth year of pro ball and I might never get another opportunity.' "

Graham got no response and returned to the field. When he

checked the lineup just before game time, it had changed—he was the starter at third. Although he went 0-for-3, he remembered hitting the ball hard and playing error-free. He also remembered a magic moment in a 30-game major league career that would end in 1965.

"I always appreciated that," Graham said. "I will always be grateful that Casey did that for me."

Graham, the baseball coach of defending NCAA champion Rice University, has become a pretty good judge of young talent. That was not always the case.

It was during that three-game series at Houston that the Mets got their first look at another late-season call-up, a young second baseman named Joe Morgan.

"We all thought that the Colt .45s must really be desperate, bringing up a little old guy like him," Graham said. "He really looked small. We were all amazed."

Then Morgan, who had made an eight-game debut in 1963 before spending most of 1964 at San Antonio of the Texas League, chased down a short outfield pop that looked like a sure base hit.

"All of a sudden, we knew why he was there," Graham said. "First perceptions can be wrong."

◆   ◆   ◆

The infamous Pine Tar Game of 1983 did one thing for George Brett.

Before his explosive reaction to having a home run taken away from him in New York, the Kansas City star often was remembered for something else. He kidded about his "improving" reputation after being elected to the Hall of Fame in 1999.

"Prior to 1983, I was always ridiculed at ballparks about an ailment I had during the 1980 World Series," Brett said. "Now, since 1983, I'm always known as the Pine Tar Guy. Now what would you rather be known as?"

No one could argue the point. Who would want to be remembered as the Hemorrhoids Guy?

Brett, of course, will be remembered for a lot more than that. One of his many career feats was consummated on May 13, 1993, in a game at Cleveland Municipal Stadium when he became the sixth player in history to combine 3,000 hits with 300 home runs.

Brett, however, remembers that occasion for another reason. The 300th homer he hit that day was picked up and returned to him by Ralph Gay, a blind Army veteran of World War II. Gay, who was wearing dark glasses and carrying a white cane, brought the ball to the Kansas City clubhouse where Brett exchanged it for an autographed ball, a bat and a Royals jersey.

"You're my good-luck charm," Brett told him. "You've got to come back."

Gay was on an outing with a group from the Veterans Administration Hospital, sitting in the right field seats at Cleveland Stadium. When other fans failed to grab the ball, he sensed something was at his feet and picked it up. As the frail Gay shuffled off, on his way back to the hospital, Brett was obviously moved.

"He's a vet, you know," Brett said. "For those guys, you always have a soft spot in your heart for what they've done for us."

◆   ◆   ◆

There was the New York Reggie Jackson and the Southern California Reggie Jackson. The following story might have taken a whole different tack three years earlier when Jackson was working for the Yankees and George Steinbrenner:

In a late-season 1983 game played at Seattle, California Angels slugger Jackson was ejected for arguing that Mariners pitcher Gaylord Perry was throwing spitballs. Jackson retreated to the dugout and returned with a bucket of ice, which he sprinkled on the ground in symbolic protest.

The game was being televised in Southern California and Angels owner Gene Autry watched with concern. Autry had not had any problems with his volatile star in two seasons and had not needed to engage him in serious conversation. But the time was right.

"I knew he'd be in the clubhouse," Autry said, "so I called him. I said, 'Reggie, I might have done the same thing. But from here on in, you ought to take it a little easier.' I said we only had about a month to go and that it looked like we'd have a chance to win it.

"I said, 'If you were to do something like that again, they might suspend you a week or 10 days and, gosh, I can't afford to lose you and neither can the team.' I told him no matter how hot he got, to cool it a little bit.

"He said, 'Mr. Autry, you're right. I know that. I'll watch it. I won't get suspended.'"

Gene Mauch, who experienced more than his share of postseason disappointments over a 26-year major league managerial career, told this story about Autry after watching his 1982 California Angels blow a two-games-to-none A.L. Championship Series lead and lose in five games to the Brewers:

"After the final game in Milwaukee, the whole organization gathered in the clubhouse and I told them, 'I can't do anything right. You guys got me a two-game lead and I blew it. I can't manage, can't handle a pitching staff and I'm too short.'

"And Gene Autry calls out from the back, 'I don't think you're too short.'"

◆　　◆　　◆

Former New York Yankees star Bobby Richardson, speaking at a 2003 banquet in Quincy, Mass., told an interesting story about the final day of the 1959 season.

Richardson began the day with a .298 average and the Yankees were locked into third place. The team did not have a .300 hitter, which didn't sit well with manager Casey Stengel, who pulled Richardson aside in the locker room.

"(Stengel) came over to me and said, 'If you can get a hit the first time up tomorrow, we'll take you out of the lineup and the Yankees will have at least one .300 hitter,'" Richardson said.

The little second baseman from South Carolina, a popular figure throughout the league, soon received notice that Stengel was not alone in his desire.

"Word got around that I needed a base hit," he said. "Billy O'Dell was pitching (for sixth-place Baltimore). He's from South Carolina and he sent word over, 'I'll be putting one right in there for you.' Brooks Robinson was playing third base and he sent word over, 'I'll be playing deep if you want to bunt.' The catcher was Joe Ginsberg and he said, 'I'll tell you what's coming.' The first base umpire, Ed Runge, said, 'Just make it close.' "

Richardson did just that.

"I hit a line drive to right field," he said, "and my best friend, Albie Pearson, made a diving catch. Somehow he didn't get in on it."

But there's a postscript to Richardson's tale: He stayed in the game, got hits in his next two at-bats and finished at .301.

◆　　◆　　◆

Los Angeles Dodgers manager Tom Lasorda opened his newspaper one morning in the spring of 1995 and read two items of interest. First, former Dodgers second baseman Steve Sax was planning to run for a seat in the California State Assembly. Second, former Dodgers outfielder Pedro Guerrero had been hired as a player-coach in the California Angels' system.

"Guerrero coaching and Saxy running for state legislature," Lasorda marveled. "What's happening to this country. Wow!"

Lasorda then shared his memory of a conversation in San Francisco, when Sax, still a player, was talking to a fan behind the dugout before a game against the Giants.

Lasorda: "Who was that?"

Sax: "I was talking to my brother-in-law."

Lasorda: "I didn't know that was your brother-in-law."

Sax: "Yeah, he married my cousin."

"That's the honest-to-god's truth," Lasorda said.

Sax never officially made it to the political arena, dropping out of the race well before the election. But he still finished fourth in the primary.

Sax was willing and able to fire good-natured jabs at his former manager. When the second baseman signed a free-agent contract with the New York Yankees in 1989 and Yankees second baseman Willie Randolph signed with the Dodgers—in effect changing places—Sax offered this advice to his Los Angeles replacement.

"I want to warn Willie to stay out of Tommy Lasorda's office," he said. "There's so much food in there, it's dangerous. Tommy doesn't stop eating when he's full; he stops when his arms are tired."

◆   ◆   ◆

Tommy Davis, the 1962 and '63 National League batting champion with the Los Angeles Dodgers, was among the group of aging veterans who helped define the designated hitter rule when it was adopted by the American League in 1973. Davis, in three seasons with the Baltimore Orioles, became a proponent of the clubhouse approach.

"I'd be known to sometimes come down from the clubhouse and take my at-bat with some mustard or ketchup on my uniform," he said. "For me, it was relaxing up there in the clubhouse. But it never took away from my concentration. I was always ready to hit."

Some might wonder about that level of concentration. During one game in 1974, a season in which Davis batted .289 and drove in 84 runs, the trainer came looking for him while he was talking to his wife on the phone.

"Tommy, you're up," he said in a panic.

"What do you mean, I'm up," Davis responded.

"You're holding up the game right now. You're due up at bat," the trainer said.

"I told him, 'OK, I'll be right down,'" Davis said. "And I told my wife, 'Honey, just hold the phone for a minute.' As I walked down the runway into the dugout, I walked right by (manager) Earl Weaver, who was giving me a real bad, funny look. I said, 'What's wrong, Earl, don't you feel good?'

"When I went up to the plate, there were men on second and third. The second pitch I saw, I hit a fastball and drove in both runs. They took me out for a pinch runner. I came back to the dugout and said, 'What's wrong, Earl? Did you think I'd miss something?' Before I went back upstairs into the clubhouse, I said, 'Earl, I've got to finish my phone call. I'll be back in a few minutes.' I went back upstairs and completed the conversation with my wife."

Davis might have won that little battle of minds with Weaver, but he soon discovered he never could win the war. The former outfielder told this story about another confrontation with his crafty manager:

"During one two-day period with Baltimore, I had gone 6-for-9. The next game, I look at the lineup card and I'm not on there. So I go into Weaver's office and say, 'Earl, baby, 6-for-9, what's happening?' And he looks up at me and goes, 'Tommy, baby, you're 0-for-2 years against (Boston's Luis) Tiant, who's pitching today.'

"See, Earl was way ahead of most managers. He was into numbers and computers even back then, keeping little cards with our averages against certain pitchers. He knew I hadn't had a hit off Tiant in two years. Instead, he put in a journeyman lefthanded hitter named Tom Shopay.

"I said, 'Earl, baby, Shopay's hitting .175.' And he said, 'Tommy, baby, let's just see what happens in the game.' Sure enough, Shopay (a .201 career hitter) got two hits off Tiant. From then on, I never doubted Earl or his methods."

The fiery win, win, win obsession of Weaver was not limited to the baseball field. Mac Barrett, a former assistant public relations director for the Baltimore Orioles, told this story about the team's always intense manager:

"He's relentless. We had a Christmas party at a friend's house a couple of years ago and Earl was there. He seemed bored with the party and started going through the closets for games to play. He found a checkers set and grabbed me.

"We sat down to play and Earl rubbed his hands together like he was going to start a fire. The rest of the party gathered around us, but Earl was totally absorbed by the checkers game. I soon made a dumb move and within two minutes, I'd been crushed. He was happy, though. He kept running around the rest of the party challenging everyone to play checkers."

In the case of Albert Belle, the game was table tennis. Cleveland teammates got a quick lesson on the consuming intensity of the controversial outfielder when a table was among the 1994 accessories in the new Jacobs Field clubhouse. Pitcher Eric Plunk made the mistake of beating Belle twice and quickly became the target of his reputation-restoring revenge.

Belle kept dragging Plunk to the table, and soon he had beaten him four straight times. Plunk marveled at his intensity. He was relentless, Plunk said, and his tunnel-vision focus on winning was almost frightening.

"I mean, I'm competitive, too," Plunk said. "But he's so serious about whatever he does. And he's smart. He could tell that I didn't have a great backhand, and he just started to attack my weakness."

Soon a clubhouse sign documented Belle's table tennis record: 32-2. "Eric Plunk beat me those two times," Belle bragged, "but I beat him four of six."

He said it without a trace of a smile.

Former Red Sox and White Sox catcher Carlton Fisk was a legitimate throwback who loved talking baseball and the camaraderie of the clubhouse. He also was an obsessive weightlifter and off-field worker whose attention to conditioning allowed him to catch a major league-record 2,226 games.

Fisk's dedication did not always translate with the modern player, but it was not lost on the coaches and managers who watched him with admiration. Jim Lefebvre recalled an evening in 1991 when he was managing the Seattle Mariners.

"We played a night game against the White Sox in Seattle and I remember Fisk coming by my office an hour after the game, carrying his weighted belt and heading for the (Kingdome) exercise room," Lefebvre said. "We talked for a while about baseball, then he went to the weight room for an hour and came back to my office to talk baseball some more.

"It was after 1 a.m. when we left—and we had a day game coming up in 12 hours."

◆　◆　◆

When you're talking rivalry, big-league style, you can't let minor distractions like a pennant race get in the way. Chicago pitcher Mark Prior made it perfectly clear how he felt about rival St. Louis, even though the Cardinals were in position to help the Cubs entering a series against first-place Houston in the second-to-last week of the 2003 season.

"I dislike the Cardinals so much that I will not even root for them," Prior said. "I hope that Houston beats their brains in and just sends them all the way back to whoever is in fourth place now.

"Hopefully, I'll leave it up to San Francisco (to beat Houston) next week, or Milwaukee. You know Milwaukee has a good offensive team. In talking with (first baseman) Richie Sexson, he would like to see us win. I think he might do us a little favor there."

Prior got part of his wish. The Giants won two of three games from the Astros and the Brewers split a four-game season-ending series as the Cubs rose up to win the N.L. Central Division title. But the hated Cardinals also won two of three from Houston.

◆　◆　◆

Jim Hannan was a righthanded pitcher with a knack for saying the wrong thing at the right time. His Washington Senators teammates liked to tell the story about Hannan's 1967 spring training introduction to a team vice president that left the clubhouse in stitches.

Hannan had read a newspaper account of former Washington outfielder Jim Lemon undergoing foot surgery. That same day, general manager George Selkirk was escorting new chairman of the board James Lemon through the Pompano Beach, Fla., clubhouse, introducing him to the players. When they stopped at Hannan's locker, Selkirk said, "Mr. Lemon, this is Jim Hannan."

Lemon extended his hand and said, "How do you do, Jim."

"Nice to see you Mr. Lemon," Hannan replied. "How are your feet?"

Lemon, taken aback momentarily, gave a tug at his slacks, looked down at his feet, apparently did not see anything out of order and answered, "Fine, Jim, how are yours?"

Ironically, the other Jim Lemon managed the Senators—and Hannan—the following season.

◆　◆　◆

Over his 12-year major league career, unpredictable Leon Wagner kept clubhouses loose in five major league cities. "Daddy Wags," never at a loss for words or quips, had a remarkable ability to keep teammates laughing through thick and thin.

Los Angeles Dodgers fans might remember Felix Torres, a Puerto Rican third baseman who arrived in 1962, unable to speak a word of English. Team officials asked Wagner, who could speak some Spanish, to take the newcomer under his wing.

Wagner obliged and quickly taught Torres to say "yes" instead of "si." Shortly thereafter, he demanded a raise for his work as an interpreter. His demand came with a good-natured warning.

"If I don't get (the raise)," he said, "I'll teach Torres four more words—'I want more money.' "

◆　◆　◆

Detroit Tigers second baseman Lou Whitaker was thrilled to be voted the American League's second baseman for the 1985 All-Star Game—his second straight starting berth. But Sweet Lou forgot something important en route to Minneapolis.

"Everybody was responsible for bringing his own jersey and equipment," Whitaker said. "I left everything in my Mercedes in the back seat. My cap, my jersey, my glove."

So Twins officials dispatched someone to purchase Whitaker a souvenir Tigers jersey. The No. 1 was removed from one of teammate Willie Hernandez's extra jerseys and stenciled to the back of Whitaker's $15 top with a Magic Marker. Whitaker had his own shoes and pants, but he had to borrow blue stirrup socks from the Twins (no black ones were available) and a spare glove owned by Baltimore's Cal Ripken.

For the record, Whitaker wore his new duds along with a collar—he was 0-for-2 in the A.L.'s 6-1 loss to the National League.

◆ ◆ ◆

The scars won't let Tony Muser forget February 27, 1986. The searing pain and the close brush with death came in the form of a fireball.

That's not the sort of thing you expect during spring training when you're reaching into your locker for a T-shirt. But that day in Chandler, Ariz., workmen were installing a ceiling furnace in the Milwaukee Brewers' new home. Natural gas leaked, a pilot light was ignited, and all hell broke loose.

Muser, bare-chested, was thrown 5 feet into a wall. He remembers a transparent orange fireball enveloping him, with snakes of blue swirling in the room. His left arm was seared and burns covered 55 percent of his body. He sank against the doorjamb of manager George Bamberger's office.

Harry Dalton, the Brewers' general manager, Bamberger and coach Larry Haney were in the office and rushed to the aid of Muser and a plumber who also was badly burned. Dalton comforted Muser, then left to get help.

Water poured onto the floor from broken pipes. The lights went out. The roof was blown off and Muser heard someone yelling to get out because the gas could not be turned off.

"So I panicked. I was the only one in there and it was dark," he recalled years later. "I started crawling on my hands and knees real slow. There was an AstroTurf floor and I was crawling through water from the broken pipes.

"I noticed as I was crawling, I couldn't feel my hands anymore. So I stopped and flipped my hands over. All the skin was coming off the palms of my hands and piling up on my wrists.

"I was like a boiled chicken. So I stopped and just rested my hands on my forehead. I thought three things: I'm going to be dead, my wife's going to be single, and who is she going to marry? Next thing, I thought some guy that I don't know is going to be raising my children. And the next thing, I thought this is probably it for my baseball career."

Nine men were injured but Muser got the worst of it. Surgeons took a 24-inch strip of flesh from his left thigh and hip and patched his left arm. There was a painful healing process that took months.

He did finally make it back, however. Muser returned to the Brewers, then coached for the Chicago Cubs, managed the Kansas City Royals and became bench coach for the San Diego Padres.

The scars won't let him forget.

"I don't look too good in a bathing suit," he said.

◆　　◆　　◆

Tall, quiet, mild-mannered Walter Alston ruled over the Brooklyn/Los Angeles Dodgers field fortunes from 1954-76. But those who saw the manager's laid-back personality as an invitation to take liberties were making a big mistake. Alston could melt miscreants with a well-timed glare or a subtle put-down. He also was known to take his anger to a higher level.

On one 1963 trip to Pittsburgh, Alston's Dodgers were trying to battle through a losing streak and stay in contention with the hot St. Louis Cardinals. After a miserable getaway game in the Steel City, there was much grousing about the slow midnight bus carrying the team to the airport. The grumbling only increased when the Pirates' team bus whizzed by.

Finally, as the Dodgers' bus chugged slowly up a hill, Alston told the driver to pull to the shoulder and stop. He stood near his front-of-the-bus seat and addressed his troops.

"Now," he said, "we'll discuss this bus, which is all you guys deserve the way you've been playing. I'm going outside. Now whatever you have to say, come out, one by one, and we'll settle it."

Alston stepped outside, but no one else moved. And the Dodgers traveled on to St. Louis where they won two of three games from the Cardinals.

◆　　◆　　◆

When the Baltimore Orioles' far-reaching kangaroo court decided to fine broadcasters Chuck Thompson and Bill O'Donnell in 1969, the indignant "men of the booth" decided to fight back. They hired a defense attorney to argue their appeal.

Thompson and O'Donnell had been convicted of invading Boog Powell's privacy when they announced on air that it was his birthday, generating so much mail that the burly first baseman became tired from just opening it all. They were fined $2 apiece.

But Thompson and O'Donnell brought in Baltimore resident Phil Burke to argue their case. Unknown to the players who gathered to hear the appeal in the clubhouse, Burke was a master of double talk—a mixture of real words and meaningless syllables that produce unintelligible speech. The players and coaches listened in disbelief.

"Slowly, the guys caught on," said manager Earl Weaver, "and there was more and more laughter."

Some, however, scratched their heads in total confusion. Pitching coach George Bamberger, who had a slight hearing problem, nudged Weaver three times and asked, "What did he say, Earl?"

Burke continued his spiel for 10 minutes, to the growing delight of the players. But when he finished, court members quickly denied the appeal and tripled the Thompson and O'Donnell fines to $6 apiece—"for taking up so much of everyone's time."

And Burke? He was fined $10.

◆　◆　◆

It's not unusual for ballplayers to have good-luck charms, but most of them stay hidden in pockets, beneath clothing or in lockers, providing a secret source of inspiration. Former San Francisco pitcher Ron "Bear" Bryant kept his in plain sight—right on the Giants' bench.

And inspirational it was. The 1973 Giants considered Bryant's 4-foot teddy bear—properly attired in San Francisco uniform—part of their dugout family.

Bryant had purchased the toy on a whim for $25 from two girls outside the Giants' hotel in Chicago a year earlier. The girls were Cubs fans and their bear was adorned with a Ron Santo button. After his purchase, Bryant began winning and assistant equipment manager Mike Murphy fashioned a small uniform for "Bear Jr.," who became a fixture in the clubhouse and on the bench.

The teddy bear even had its own seat on the team's charter flights. But one day, when the Giants took a commercial flight out of San Diego, airline inspectors decreed that Bear Jr. would have to fly in the baggage compartment—and he was not treated with respect.

"He fell off the baggage cart, got under a wheel and was dragged 50 feet," Bryant said. Bear Jr. lost his right eye in the incident, but he didn't lose his good-luck appeal for Bryant, who continued to win games. The 6-foot lefthander finished the 1973 season with a 24-12 record, a National League-high win total, and he claimed that, after getting his terrific teddy, he won 38 of 55 decisions over two years.

If Bear Jr. was still around in 1974, his luck ran out. Bryant was injured in a swimming pool accident in the spring and finished 3-15. One season later, he was out of baseball.

◆　◆　◆

Catching is a perilous business. Chad Kreuter discovered just how perilous—the hard way.

Kreuter was catching for the White Sox in a July 19, 1996, game at Chicago when Kansas City runner Johnny Damon, racing toward home, crashed into him as the throw bounced away. It was a jarring collision.

Damon was OK, but the damage report on Kreuter was not good: His left shoulder contained eight large pieces of shattered bone and countless fragments. Doctors told him he would never play again.

"It was like a shot to the heart," Kreuter recalled. But then things got even worse.

As Kreuter prepared for surgery in a Los Angeles hotel room, he began feeling lousy. There was undetected internal bleeding, caused by a cut from the collision, and "I looked like the Hunchback of Notre Dame." In his room, Kreuter took a shower, passed out and went into convulsions. It happened, fortunately, while his wife, Kelly, was talking to the hospital and paramedics arrived within minutes. At the hospital, no pulse could be found. His veins were virtually drained.

"It was very scary because I almost died right then and there from not having enough blood," Kreuter said. When laid flat, he went into convulsions again, which got the blood flowing back to his brain and the rest of his body. Eventually, surgery was performed and the shoulder bones were put back together with $40,000 worth of screws and plates.

After rigorous rehabilitation, he even resumed his career—and played with Damon in 1999 for the Royals.

Damon never did feel comfortable around Kreuter, who insisted the experience made him a tougher player and better person.

"He says it changed his life, but I'm still going to have a guilty conscience talking to him about it," Damon said.

◆　◆　◆

Over 17 major league seasons covering six cities, Jamie Moyer has played with a Hall of Fame-caliber lineup that includes such names as Greg Maddux, Nolan Ryan, Roger Clemens, Rafael

Palmeiro, Cal Ripken, Ken Griffey Jr., Randy Johnson and Alex Rodriguez. But when asked to choose his best teammate, Moyer hardly considers the stars.

He instead talks about players like Dan Wilson, his catcher for the last eight years in Seattle. Moyer looks for consistency in teammates, players who have the same professionalism, win or lose, day after day. Guys who know what to say at the right time.

He recalled how former catcher Jim Sundberg helped him when Moyer was a young Cubs pitcher preparing for a start against Houston's Ryan in 1987.

"I was lying on the training table and he walked up," Moyer said. "He must have seen how nervous I was because he told me, 'Kid, get out there and pitch. Let me call everything.' "

Someone called a good game. Moyer beat Ryan, 2-1.

◆　　◆　　◆

College baseball has evolved into a minor league-like feeder of talent into the major leagues, a trend not lost on those who play the game professionally. Likewise, the annual College World Series has become an anticipated event featuring backup sliders, breathtaking double plays and players who soon will be competing for the baseball dollar.

"The College World Series ended this week," said then-Colorado reliever Todd Jones in June 2003, "and let me tell you, every big-league clubhouse was watching it. The College World Series is big time now."

Not only are major league players watching it with interest, they are embracing it the way fans do basketball's NCAA Tournament.

"We have a lot of fun in (the Rockies') clubhouse when the College World Series is on," Jones said. "Guys pick their teams based on where they went to school, like Charles Johnson for Miami, or regionally, like California guys pulling for Stanford or Brent Butler, who's from North Carolina, cheering for South Carolina.

"We all watch the games and talk smack about whose home area has the best pool of talent to choose from. Or the guys from the

South talk smack about guys from the North. How good can you be if you can't get outside until May because of the snow? But then Larry Walker, who's from north of the North, sticks his head in the room and we say, 'Hmm. ... OK.'

"The CWS is the best thing for college baseball and we watched it all the way through. That ought to hold us over until the Little League World Series comes on in August. Then it starts all over again."

◆　◆　◆

It always pays to think before you speak. Texas outfielder Lee Mazzilli learned that lesson the hard way in the spring of 1982.

Mazzilli made a passing reference to left field as an "idiot's position" and immediately came under attack from many fronts. The first stones were flung by Boston left fielder Jim Rice, who visited the Rangers' dugout during a trip to Arlington to express his views.

"Tell him I know left fielders who are millionaires," Rice told two Texas sportswriters who were interviewing manager Don Zimmer. "I don't think I'd consider any of us idiots. ... Yaz, Willie Wilson, Dave Winfield, myself. Left fielders win batting titles and Most Valuable Player awards. I'd like to see him call me an idiot. If he doesn't like it, he can go carry a lunch pail."

Then Mazzilli got a call from an angry New Jersey father who said his son was refusing to go to Little League practice because he played left field. Mazzilli's quote had been twisted in the local paper to read, "Anybody who plays left field is an idiot." Mazzilli called the Little Leaguer to change his mind.

"This really hurts me," Mazzilli said later. "Kids look up to baseball players and I don't like the fact that something I said was turned around to this extent. I love kids and it hurts me for this to happen."

THOSE CRAZY BOYS
OF SUMMER

If baseball had a Superstition Hall of Fame, Kevin Rhomberg would be one of its most revered members. Few short-time major leaguers made a more lasting impression on teammates and opponents than the utilityman who played 41 games for the Cleveland Indians from 1982-84.

"The most superstitious guy I've ever seen in baseball? How about the kid from Cleveland?" asked then-New York Yankees outfielder Dave Winfield.

"That guy is superstitious," said former Texas pitcher Charlie Hough. "He has to be nuts."

Rhomberg's biggest obsession was touching. If someone touched him, he had to touch him back—immediately. And he would go to any length to fight off the evil that would surely befall him if he did not.

"Rhomberg came up in a game against us and I accidently brushed him with my glove when he stepped into the batter's box," former Baltimore catcher Rick Dempsey recalled. "He turned right around and tagged me on the arm. Then he got a single and was standing on first base when the ump came over and clapped him on the back and said, 'Nice hit!' And the kid reached over and slapped the ump on the arm and said, 'Thanks.'

"Next he took his lead off of first base, and Eddie Murray nicked him with the glove. So Rhomberg jumped back to the bag to tag Murray and then jumped out to his lead again."

Former Orioles pitcher Storm Davis took the Rhomberg tale a step further. He recalled a 1981 Class AA Southern League game when his Charlotte team was playing against Rhomberg and Chattanooga.

"This guy (Rhomberg) was taking the field between innings and our outfielder, who was coming off, brushed against him," Davis said. "Rhomberg chased our guy all the way into the dugout and halfway to the clubhouse to tag him back before he'd take his position in the field."

Any elite superstition club would also have to include former outfielder Lou Skizas, who played 239 games over four big-league seasons from 1956-59 with the Yankees, Athletics, Tigers and White Sox. He was known to teammates and opponents as the Nervous Greek.

"Lou felt he had to go between the catcher and the umpire when he stepped into the batter's box," said former catcher Les Moss, who played both against and with Skizas. "One day, I got (umpire) Hank Soar in on the gag and when Lou started toward home plate, Hank kind of leaned on my back. Lou actually begged us to let him get between us."

But that was not Skizas' only idiosyncrasy.

"Skizas always took his practice swings with only his left hand on the bat," said Chuck Tanner, who played against him. "He always kept his right hand in his back pocket until just the instant before the pitch. Everybody tried to quick-pitch him, but he always got that hand out of his back pocket in time. I don't know what was in there."

Whitey Herzog does.

"I know," Herzog said. "Lou was holding on to his lucky Greek medal. Oh, yeah, there was one other thing about him. He wore half a dozen pair of socks. And before every game, he had to rotate them—bottom pair to the outside and so forth."

Leo Durocher had more superstitions than anybody could count. But former infielder Joey Amalfitano recalled this story from 1954, when he played for the quirky New York Giants manager.

"During that pennant race," Amalfitano said, "Leo got it into his head that when we took a lead into the ninth inning, it would be good luck if he walked the length of the dugout to the water fountain to get a drink after every out by the opponent. Then, he got it into his head that it would be even better luck if all his coaches did the same thing.

"It was like a Chinese fire drill. Every time we got a ninth-inning putout in a game in which we were leading, five guys had to get up and march down to get a drink. It was like a parade."

Many players have their superstitions. Others simply have eccentricities. Cincinnati's Chris Sabo, the National League's 1988 Rookie of the Year, was a legitimate head case.

The young, flat-topped third baseman, according to Pete Rose, was very particular about his hair. During one trip to Atlanta, Sabo became so outraged in mid-haircut that he got up out of the barber's chair, stormed out of the shop and went looking for another option.

"Can't you just picture what people in Atlanta thought," Rose said, "seeing the Rookie of the Year stomping through a mall with half a haircut, then walking into another barber shop and asking, 'How much for half a haircut?' "

He was flaky, frizzy-haired and colorful, a young charismatic righthander Detroit teammate Rusty Staub called "the most exciting thing I've seen." When Mark Fidrych pitched for the Tigers during his magical 1976 rookie season, the baseball world stopped and electricity filled the air.

The skinny, happy-go-lucky "Bird" talked to the ball and pointed it toward the plate, as if telling it where to go. He got down on his knees before every inning and patted the dirt on the mound. He sprinted on and off the field. He strutted around like a mad stork after every out, applauding his teammates. He made faces. And he won—19 times.

The Cleveland Indians were so taken aback by Fidrych's unusual antics the first time they played against him, they forgot to swing their bats.

"My mind was more on what he was doing than concentrating on my hitting," said veteran Rico Carty, a former National League batting champion. "In the dugout, everyone kept saying, 'Let's get that guy; let's get him.' But we were too concerned about that and we didn't pay attention to our hitting.

"He had us psyched out with all that stuff he does on the mound. The more he does, the more you want to hit him. And the more you want to hit him, the worse you get. I've never seen anything like it. Sometimes I was almost laughing. How can you hit when you're laughing? It was like he was trying to hypnotize us. I said, 'Just throw the ball.' Then he did and I couldn't hit it."

Fidrych, who battled arm problems and never regained top form in limited appearances after his rookie season, never lost his connection with the fans. Everybody was attracted to the innocent sense of wonder he displayed, both on the field and off. Like when the Bird started for the American League in the 1976 All-Star Game at Philadelphia's Veterans Stadium.

"I remember at the All-Star Game doing a 360 on the mound," Fidrych said. "There are 70,000 (63,974) people there and I'm thinking, 'If I don't pitch, there's no game.' Finally, Thurman Munson comes out and I say, 'Thurman, check this out. This is awesome.'

"And he says, 'Yeah, great, but let's throw the ball.' "

Legendary Tigers broadcaster Ernie Harwell remembers Fidrych for his simple, no-frills honesty—and refreshing naivete.

"Mark Fidrych was such a sweet guy, whether he won or lost,"

Harwell said. "He sort of epitomized that poem by Rudyard Kipling: If Mark could meet both triumph and disaster, he'd treat them both the same. But he was my favorite to talk to because he led the league in malapropisms. He always had the wrong word at the wrong time."

Harwell recalled one interview with the Bird during his post-1976 struggles. Fidrych was coming off the disabled list for a start against the Kansas City Royals.

Harwell: "How's your arm, Mark?"

Fidrych: "Oh, it's pretty good."

Harwell: "What does Dr. Clarence Livingood (the Tigers' team physician) say about your arm?"

Fidrych: "Ernie, Dr. Livingood don't know nothing about arms and muscles. He's a skin doctor. He's one of them gynecologists."

Frenchy Bordagaray, a sometimes-volatile former major league outfielder, was handed a stiff 60-day suspension in 1947 when he was charged with spitting at a South Atlantic League umpire. Bordagaray, manager of the Dodgers' Class A Greenville team at the time, took the news stoically and said, "The suspension was more than I expectorated."

Carter Latimer, sports editor of the Greenville News, wrote a column defending the always-colorful Bordagaray.

"Bordagaray emphatically denies he mistook umpire Blackiston for a cuspidor," Latimer wrote. "When he gets excited, saliva wells up in his throat like a spring freshet, he claims, and his utterances are apt to be moistened and as dewy as morning glories in the meadow.

"I don't believe Frenchy would deliberately spit on an umpire or even spit on a sidewalk in a town where it's against the law. The Bounding Basque has what might be termed 'showery articulation.' He sprays when he speaks.

"Maybe it's an automatic sprinkler system that springs from a leaky esophagus."

◆   ◆   ◆

Cleveland fans still talk about Super Joe Charboneau, the American League's 1980 Rookie of the Year whose legendary talents ranged from opening beer bottles with his eye socket to chugging beer through his nose with a straw .

The colorful outfielder, who claimed to have once straightened his broken nose with pliers and cut out a tooth with a razor blade and vice grip, is also remembered for a pet alligator named Choppers.

"He was a great pet," Charboneau told Dan Coughlin of the Cleveland Plain Dealer. "I was really attached to him, but he hated my guts. He tried to bite me all the time. I was going to train him to wrestle me. He would have grown to about 6 feet long, so I would have had the height advantage. But my wife made me get rid of him when he tried to eat a kitten that belonged to another guy on the team. I was so attached to him I couldn't sell him. I gave him and the aquarium away."

◆   ◆   ◆

Utilityman Steve Lyons, who played nine seasons for four teams, never did anything conventionally. Hence his nickname, "Psycho."

Lyons is best remembered for a July 16, 1990, game while playing for the Chicago White Sox at Detroit. Trying to beat out an infield single, he slid headfirst into the first base bag and wound up with a serious load of dirt in his pants. Lyons simply did what any true baseball flake would have done. While Tigers pitcher Dan Petry argued the safe call with umpire Jim Evans, he calmly dropped his pants to his knees and dusted the dirt from his legs.

The crowd of 15,000 roared as Lyons, wearing only jockey shorts and athletic supporter, suddenly remembered where he was and quickly pulled up his pants.

"I could feel dirt running all down my legs," he explained. "After they started arguing, I just kind of forgot where I was."

When Lyons later returned to the Chicago dugout, several women waved money at him and a man offered him his belt.

"I wish I could make the highlight film for driving in the winning run instead of something off the wall," Lyons said.

When Lyons played first base during his five Chicago seasons, he sometimes drew tic-tac-toe grids in the dirt and challenged baserunners to a game.

"I never dig 'em too deep," he said. "I'd hate to say a ball went for a bad-hop single off my X."

According to Lyons, the only runners who did not take up his challenge were Toronto's Fred McGriff and Baltimore's Randy Milligan.

"I don't think they know how to play," he said.

◆　◆　◆

Former Boston lefthander Bill "Spaceman" Lee was known for his quirky behavior. The "Beautiful Downtown Burbank" native would hit fungo flies to himself in the outfield, smuggle watermelons into the bullpen, perform bullpen punting exhibitions with wads of rolled-up bubble gum and do animated, sometimes-hilarious imitations of opposing players.

"He's crazy," Red Sox catcher Carlton Fisk said on more than one occasion. But most of all, he was outspoken, a say-anything-at-any-time eccentric who often got himself in hot water with his lightning-quick tongue. It didn't take long for the reputation to take root.

After pitching in 20 games for the Red Sox in 1969, the young lefthander was called out of the bullpen to protect a 4-3 opening-day lead in 1970 for starter Gary Peters against the New York Yankees. Lee, working with the tying run on base, walked the first man he faced and went 2-0 on the next hitter. Red Sox pitching coach Charlie Wagner walked to the mound to calm his rookie.

"Just try to throw strikes," Wagner told Lee, who looked at him with a strange expression.

"Did you think I was trying to throw balls?" he asked.

Houston broadcaster Bill Brown, a play-by-play man for

Cincinnati during the Big Red Machine era, recalled this Lee moment in the 1975 Reds-Red Sox World Series.

"I remember after that exhausting Game 6, a television reporter asking Lee one of those great TV questions," Brown said. The Red Sox had just evened the Series on Carlton Fisk's dramatic 12th-inning home run and Lee was the scheduled starter for Game 7.

"So," Brown said, "the TV guy goes up to Lee with the camera rolling and says, 'Well, Bill, you're it.' Lee reaches out and touches the reporter as if to tag him and says, 'No, you're it.' "

◆   ◆   ◆

Another lefthander with a reputation for goofy behavior is veteran Brian Anderson, who talks freely about his misadventures. Like the time when his Arizona Diamondbacks were playing in Cincinnati and he went sleepwalking, stark naked, in the hallway of the team's hotel.

It was Anderson's routine to visit a Coke machine late at night. It was so much a habit, apparently, that he did not even have to be awake to do it.

"Well, that night I went to bed and, literally, the first thing I remember was the door slamming and I was out in the hallway," he said. "My first thought was, 'Well, I have my key on me. I wouldn't have left without my key.' But I had no key. I had nothing on. I didn't even have socks on—nothing."

Flashing down the deserted hallway, Anderson looked in vain for a house phone. So he decided to take the elevator to the fifth floor, where he knew there was a workout room.

"So I took the elevator down and got off, and there was a guy in there sweeping," Anderson said. "As I got off the elevator, there was a *USA Today* lying on the floor. I picked it up, threw it in front of me, waved the guy down, and he gave me a towel and escorted me back to my room."

Fortunately, Anderson didn't run into any of the other guests. Things could have gotten really embarrassing.

"There was a Southern Baptist convention at the hotel," he said.

◆　◆　◆

Coming back from a groin injury with the Kansas City Royals during the 2003 season, pitcher Jose Lima was scheduled to pitch a simulated game.

But he could not begin, he insisted, until he heard the national anthem.

So manager Tony Pena and pitching coach John Cumberland, willing to go to any lengths to get their unpredictable righthander back in the rotation, not only had the Star-Spangled Banner played at Kauffman Stadium—they joined Lima in singing it. Then Lima went through a successful workout.

◆　◆　◆

The flaky side of Oakland A's slugger Jose Canseco was on full display in the late 1980s, both on the field and off. One afternoon in the spring of 1989, longtime San Diego broadcaster Jerry Coleman experienced it first-hand.

Coleman, a former big-league player and manager well known for his broadcasting malaprops, approached Canseco and asked for a 30-second interview.

"Can't do it," the outfielder said. "I'm working hard."

"Hey, I'm working hard, too," said Coleman, taken aback by the brushoff.

"Not as hard as I am, buddy," Canseco said as he walked away.

Coleman ran after him for a few steps, then stopped and muttered, "See how demeaning this job can be when you find yourself running after 24-year-olds?"

Coleman later declared Canseco off his radar screen. "Well, I've thought it over," he said, "and there's no way I'm going to interview that damned Joe-say-co."

Canseco might have been working hard on the field, but he also was playing hard off it. He grabbed national headlines in 1989 and '90 when he was ticketed once for running a red light and five times for speeding, once at 120 mph and another at 104. The latter citation came on a Miami highway after the A's outfielder told Florida Highway Patrol trooper Rafael Lola he had just put special aviation fuel in his car and wanted to test it.

"I don't think it was a big deal to him," Lola said. "You could say he was kind of cocky. When I told him he clocked in at 104 mph, he said, 'Oh, you're so generous.'"

◆   ◆   ◆

One of the more harmless stunts pulled off by the always-controversial Jimmy Piersall came in the mid-1960s, when he was winding down his 17-year career as an outfielder with the California Angels. The Kansas City organist was sick during a series against the Athletics and the club kept playing Beatles records during stoppages in play.

When Piersall strolled to the plate in the first inning of the series finale, long, shaggy hair flowed out from under his batting helmet— a mocking tribute to John, Paul, George and Ringo. Not amused, the umpire in chief told Piersall, "Tell the photographers to get their pictures. Then you take that damn thing off your head and stop making a farce of the game."

Piersall listened, removed the wig, used it to dust off home plate and slapped it back on his head as the fans roared their approval. Then he struck out on three pitches and returned to the bench.

Piersall's most notorious stunt occurred in 1963, when he hit career home run No. 100 while playing for the New York Mets. He explained his actions with a sense of accomplishment.

"I was with the Mets then and they were the worst team in baseball," he said. "I stood up at home plate and watched the ball disappear into the seats. I decided that my No. 100 was going coast to coast, front-page pictures and national television. After all, I didn't figure to hit any more.

"So when the ball went out, I headed for third base. I went around clockwise instead of counter-clockwise. Naturally, the umpire wasn't amused."

◆　◆　◆

The sight of Cincinnati owner Marge Schott and her dog, a St. Bernard named Schottzie, had become a familiar sight in baseball circles by 1989. But the method to her madness in a complicated business world never ceased to amaze those who had to deal with her.

When negotiations between Reds general manager Murray Cook and outfielder Kal Daniels broke down over a $25,000 difference, Schott stepped in and offered Daniels a different kind of deal. She proposed a coin flip to determine whether Daniels would get his $325,000 asking price or a $300,000 offer from the team.

Daniels accepted and television cameras rolled when he met with Schott in the parking lot of the Reds' training complex in Plant City, Fla. Schott produced a 50-cent piece, Daniels flipped it in the air and Schott called "heads," as the coin clanked to the pavement. It was "tails" and Daniels got his desired raise.

"Unique? Quite," Cook said. "A rather humorous way to resolve the situation, frankly."

But the coin flip solution did not get rave reviews from other interested parties.

"If what I read is right," said National League president Bart Giamatti, "it is a ridiculous way to negotiate a contract and trivializes the whole process and demeans the participants. I'm sorry anyone thought it was a good idea. I look forward to talking with Mrs. Schott about it."

◆　◆　◆

Former Oakland Athletics owner Charlie Finley once offered this take on the oversized ego of his former star right fielder, Reggie Jackson:

"I never met an athlete in any sport who could talk as good and as fast as Reggie Jackson. He was loud, but good. I raised him. Reggie and I got along very good after we had an understanding. I called him in the office one day and said, 'Reggie, you know you're in a slump and you need help. I'm going to tell you what your problems are. Your big problem is—you're not going to like this, Reggie—but you think you're God. Reggie, you're all wrong. I'm God.'"

◆　◆　◆

Hans Lobert, known for his outstanding speed, prominent nose and quirky personality, was a solid major league third baseman for five National League teams from 1903-17. In 1913, he was a member of a John McGraw-led barnstorming team that toured the world playing exhibition games against another team led by White Sox owner Charles Comiskey.

As the tour began in the United States, McGraw also staged a series of match races between Lobert and former Olympic champion Jim Thorpe. Lobert won consistently. So, after a game at Oxnard, Calif., McGraw brought in a ringer for a race around the bases. Lobert would be paired against a quarter-horse—with plenty of racing experience.

Umpire Bill Klem, serving as the official judge, started the race and watched as Lobert rounded first base with a slight lead and increased his margin approaching second. But the horse suddenly cut inside, forcing Lobert to break stride midway between second and third, and the competitors rounded the base and headed home in a dead heat.

With the jockey delivering his whip and Lobert sprinting madly, horse and player crossed the plate in a photo finish.

"The horse wins by a nose," bellowed Klem to the shock of Lobert.

"Look at this horn of mine," he yelled at Klem, shaking his fist in the umpire's face. "No horse could beat me by a nose."

◆　◆　◆

Few players have ever matched former Chicago White Sox shortstop Ozzie Guillen's zest for baseball. That's why Tom Seaver's introduction to the fun-loving rookie came as something of a shock.

"I was standing on the field the first day of spring training in '85 in Sarasota, Fla.," Seaver recalled, "when this little guy I'd never seen before ran up and said, 'I'm going to make the last out of your 300th win, and I'm not going to give you the ball.' Then he ran away.

"I said, 'Who the heck is that?' and someone said, 'Oh, that's your shortstop. He probably will make your last out and he probably won't give you the ball.' "

When Seaver finally reached the 300-win milestone with a 4-1 victory at Yankee Stadium on August 4, Guillen scored the game-winning run. Seaver watched with some concern in the bottom of the ninth when pinch hitter Don Baylor lifted a short fly ball to left field—the potential game-ending out—and Guillen barely missed picking it off with a last-second leap.

Left fielder Reid Nichols did make the catch and Seaver got his keepsake ball.

Guillen's antics came fast and furious while playing for the White Sox from 1985-97. In games at Milwaukee and Toronto, he lurked behind members of the grounds crew as they smoothed the infield and replaced bases in the middle of the fifth inning. On both occasions, he sneaked up from behind, stole a new base and disappeared into the dugout, forcing the shocked groundskeepers to use a dirty base.

Guillen also was known for his unscheduled appearances at the mound when Chicago manager Jeff Torborg and catcher Carlton Fisk conferred with a struggling pitcher. "We were trying to figure out how to pitch to a certain hitter once when Oz appeared and said something so outrageous that we all forgot why we were out there," Torborg said.

◆　　◆　　◆

Mickey Hatcher stories have been circulating around baseball since his 1979 debut with the Los Angeles Dodgers. Always a supersub and clubhouse sparkplug, the unpredictable Hatcher also was a fan favorite wherever he played.

Hatcher was an outfielder for the Minnesota Twins in 1984 when Oakland slugger Dave Kingman launched a towering pop fly that became wedged in the seams of the Teflon roof at the Metrodome. The ball, which was ruled a ground-rule double, was located later and Hatcher was chosen to participate in a publicity stunt to be staged before the next game. According to best-laid plans, the ball would be pried free and drop to Hatcher, who would catch it for a symbolic "postmortem out."

But when the ball fell toward the turf, it fluttered like a knuckleball and Hatcher struggled to get in position. He missed it, the ball hit him in the groin and he fell to the ground in pain. An embarrassed Hatcher regained his wits and walked "crosslegged to the outfield" as the Minnesota fans booed in mock indignation.

Hatcher's reputation as a baseball flake developed early. He told this story about his first season in the professional game:

"My first minor league club was Clinton, Iowa (Midwest League), and I figured since I was a pro, I'd better chew tobacco," he said. "I put this wad in my cheek and, just as they were ready to start an inning, they found they had only two outfielders."

The third, Hatcher, was nowhere to be found.

"I swallowed some of that tobacco," he said. "I crawled beneath the outfield bleachers and got sick as a dog. I've stayed with Bazooka bubble gum ever since."

◆　◆　◆

Andy Van Slyke, a slick-fielding outfielder for St. Louis and Pittsburgh through most of his 13-year major league career, experimented briefly with playing third base for the Cardinals.

"They wanted me to play third base like Brooks," he said. "So I did play like Brooks—Mel Brooks."

◆　◆　◆

Hall of Fame righthander Gaylord Perry is best remembered for the spitballing tactics that both baffled and psyched out opposing hitters. But Perry also was respected in baseball circles for his pinpoint control and old-school philosophy.

Chicago Cubs broadcaster Steve Stone, Perry's San Francisco teammate in 1971, tells a story about a game in which the colorful righthander drilled Montreal pitcher Bill Stoneman in the back with a pitch.

"Stoneman didn't even flinch," Stone said. "He just ran down to first base. You have to remember one thing about Gaylord. He had pinpoint control. So everybody knew he was throwing at Stoneman.

"What people outside the game didn't know was that the year before, in our last series with the Expos, Stoneman had thrown a beanball at Bobby Bonds. This was just the first time that they could even things out."

Some pitchers took their revenge tactics even further. Stan Williams, a hard-nosed intimidator during his 14-year big-league career, kept a record of every pitcher who hit him with a pitch.

"Stan likes to tell people that every time he got hit, he would write into a book who he owed one to," Stone said. "Well, one season he had gotten even with everybody except one guy. Then, he was traded to the team where the guy played.

"During batting practice one day, that pitcher came up for his practice swings and Stan was pitching. Stan drilled the guy in the back with the very first pitch. The guy screamed, 'What the hell are you doing?'

" 'Hey,' Stan said. 'You were the last one in my book. Now we're even.' "

◆　　◆　　◆

Cubs outfielder Dave Kingman, known for home runs, strike-outs and his running feud with the media, was offered the chance to write a column for the *Chicago Tribune* in 1980. He said he agreed to write it only after realizing it would be his chance to show players "what it would be like getting quoted accurately for a change."

In one of his first efforts, Kingman wrote a critique of the press, quoting Cubs hitting coach Billy Williams. "Overall," he reported Williams as saying, "I think the careers of Ron Santo, Ernie Banks and myself could have been greatly enhanced if fair and encouraging reporting had taken place."

When approached by a Chicago writer a few days later, Williams said his comments had been taken out of context.

On the day that Kingman's first column appeared in the Tribune, Pulitzer Prize-winning columnist Mike Royko wrote this parody that appeared on the front page of the *Chicago Sun-Times.*

"Hi, I'm Dave Dingdong, and you're not. I really don't have to introduce someone as well-known as me. But for those who have been living in a cave, I'm the tall, dark, handsome left fielder who hits those towering homers. I'd be a standout anywhere, but especially in Wrigley Field, because most of my teammates are nothing. Not one of them is as tall, or as handsome or can hit the ball as far. ... You might wonder why I've broken my legendary silence. Well, I'm a frank and honest person. And to be frank and honest, I'll do anything for a buck, even break my legendary silence. And if you wonder why I've been silent so long, it's because basically I'm a shallow, self-centered person who has few ideas and nothing to say."

◆　　◆　　◆

In an unusual first-inning explosion against New York Mets ace Tom Seaver in a 1971 game at the Astrodome, Houston batters collected four straight hits and two runs, bringing the always colorful Doug Rader to the plate.

"What's going on?" Rader asked umpire Shag Crawford. "It looks like he's throwing pretty good from back there (in the on-deck circle)."

Crawford nodded in agreement. "He is," he said. "They're just hitting good pitches."

Three pitches later, Rader returned to the Houston dugout, a strikeout victim.

"The first two pitches he threw me sounded like fastballs," he said. "And then he threw me a curve that I had no chance on. I saw the spin and it was coming straight over the top. To throw me a pitch like that, the way I was going, was the same as kicking a dead dog."

◆ ◆ ◆

Wherever he played over his 22-year big-league career, Bert Blyleven was the clubhouse prankster—the man most likely to humble an unsuspecting victim. Some of his tricks were clever and subtle; others were perpetrated strictly for shock value.

Like the hit-and-run joke he played on Cleveland sportscaster Pete Franklin in 1982 at Tucson, Ariz., during spring training. Franklin was conducting a talk show in the hotel lobby when Blyleven arrived and, seeing an opportunity, dropped his pants and bent over. The moonshot literally froze the talkative Franklin and everybody nearby—before the momentary silence turned into raucous laughter.

"Bert will keep everybody loose," Indians pitching coach Don McMahon said a year later. "He is a great guy on the team. I don't know anyone who gets mad at him."

Teammate Dennis Lewallyn got a moonshot later at Hi Corbett Field, a "disgusting sight," and Indians public relations man Bob DiBiasio learned quickly that you should not walk, fully clothed, near a swimming pool if Blyleven is standing nearby.

McMahon also remembered an incident in 1977 when Blyleven was pitching for the Texas Rangers and defeated his former team.

"I was with Minnesota then," McMahon said, "and he beat us. After the game, Bert ordered six hot dogs and had them sent up to (Twins owner) Calvin Griffith's box. Since Bert used to pitch for the Twins, I guess he had a message for Calvin."

♦   ♦   ♦

John "Champ" Summers was a one-dimensional 11-year major leaguer who brought a folk-hero persona to the game he did not play seriously until age 22. He was a capable lefthanded batter, the prototypical designated hitter who toiled for six teams, primarily because of the defensive liabilities that kept him from playing regularly in the outfield.

But fans loved the enthusiastic all-around athlete, the former slow-pitch softball aficionado who turned down pro basketball and pro football contract offers and once beat 13-year-old Jimmy Connors in a tennis match.

He was colorful and earthy, a crowd favorite no matter where he played.

Summers' first big-league stop in 1974 was with Oakland, where he played 20 games and roomed briefly with Reggie Jackson. His first major league at-bat came as a pinch hitter for the ailing Jackson and Summers lined into a double play. Jackson once gave Summers some sage advice.

"I was autographing baseballs one day," Summers said, "and Reggie wanted to know why I was signing them 'John Summers.' He asked if I had a nickname. I told him I had one, but I was afraid of what the other players would think if I used it.

"Reggie said, 'This is show business. If there were two Summers with the same ability, one named John and the other named Champ, which do you think the fans would remember?' "

Summers heeded that advice and even received a World Series share that fall.

"The A's won their third straight World Series," he said. "I didn't get a ring, but Charlie Finley sent me a check for $93. That showed how good I was."

♦   ♦   ♦

Former Baltimore righthander Jim Palmer had his share of roommates over a 19-year major league career, but his favorite was an unpredictable righthanded pitcher named Dave Leonhard.

"Davey was the only guy I know who went to Johns Hopkins University and played in the major leagues," Palmer said. "When we won the World Series in 1970, he took a television at cost instead of a World Series ring. He said, 'I don't have a television.' We're in an era now where everyone talks about, 'The ring. The ring.' This was the only one he would have gotten. But he was just more practical.

"Of course, he's also the same guy who, one night in Boston, came in (the locker room), took off his jersey and had another jersey on underneath it. He wore two jerseys in the bullpen another night. He was absent-minded. One day, he's sitting on his stool in Detroit, looking around, kind of doing a 360. He says he's missing one of his outer socks, the orange ones that we used to wear. Well, they're both on his left leg.

"Davey was the ninth guy on a nine-man staff, happy to do whatever Earl (Weaver) asked. Nowadays the money is so excessive. Davey played the game because he loved to play. To me, that's what the game is all about."

The other side of Leonhard was that he was very bright, a quality that did not always translate in baseball conversations.

"He was smarter than most guys," Palmer said. "We were playing in Puerto Rico one winter. I can remember a day when it was raining, and we were sitting around in the dugout, watching it rain. It was Davey, Jim Hardin, Wally Bunker, myself, Juan Pizarro and Boomer—George Scott.

"We were talking about tough pitchers. We go through four or five. Well, Davey had been reading *Time* magazine. This was at a time when people were starving in Biafra. Davey goes, 'What about Biafra?' And Boomer says the same thing he was saying about all the other guys: 'That bleeping bleep, you can beat him in the late innings.' As if Biafra was a sidearming righthander.

"Jim Hardin fell on the dugout floor, he was laughing so hard. Boomer says to him, 'You're not like McAnally'—that's Dave McNally—'or Cuezzar'—that's Mike Cuellar. 'Your ass is a pleasure to hit off of.' We were all laughing. Boomer did not talk to us for the rest of that winter league."

◆　◆　◆

Mickey Lolich, a 217-game winner over 16 major league seasons with Detroit, the New York Mets and San Diego, was known for his off-center view of the world around him. And as a young lefthander in the Pacific Coast League, he did not follow instructions well.

One day in 1962, he was working on a blooper pitch that he threw to a surprised opponent, who took it for a strike. The batter glared at Lolich, who threw another blooper. This time the hitter caught the ball and fired it into the stands.

"OK, that'll be enough of that," said Portland manager and third baseman Leslie Peden. "No more blooper balls."

Lolich shrugged. But when the next batter stepped in, he threw yet another blooper, which was smashed down the third base line—and off the toe of Peden.

That WAS the last of the bloopers.

Peden was not Lolich's only "incidental victim" that season. The other came in a game at Hawaii, when the laid-back lefthander short-circuited with a rare temperamental outburst.

Lolich got two strikes on Hawaii hitter Stan Palys and fired the next pitch right down the middle—or so he thought.

"My folks told me that if I get mad, I make other people mad, and nothing is accomplished," Lolich said. "So I keep things inside me. But the umpire called it a ball and I began storming about. He told me if I made one more sound he'd run me out of the game."

The angry Lolich threw the next pitch as hard as he could. Palys swung through it for strike three and the catcher missed the ball, which struck the umpire—and broke his elbow.

◆　◆　◆

Jim Frey and Don Zimmer, who combined to deliver a National

League East title to Chicago in 1989 as general manager and manager of the Cubs, were buddies at Cincinnati's Western Hills High School in the late 1940s. It was not unusual for them to double date, usually in a green Dodge that belonged to Zimmer's dad.

"Zim had this habit," Frey remembered. "He'd leave the doors open when he pulled away from a parking spot. You know those poles where they hang street signs? Happened all the time.

"We'd take the girls to a movie, one of those fancy musicals with all that dancing and stuff. Zim and I would sleep through them. The girls woke us up when it was over. We'd take 'em for a milkshake. Zim would destroy his car on those poles, then we'd drive the girls home. Life in the big city."

"Then," Zimmer added, "I'd leave the car for my dad in 20-degree weather and he'd come out to go to work early in the morning and the doors would be frozen. Not frozen shut. Frozen open."

◆　◆　◆

Hall of Famer Juan Marichal was a shrewd observer of the game, a pitcher who kept a revolutionary book on opposing hitters. He noted the batter's stance, his position in the box, every telltale clue on where to deliver his pinpoint pitches. His book, some said, was more advanced than the San Francisco Giants managers and coaches he played for in the 1960s and '70s.

But a mystery always surrounded how the smiling Dominican righthander acquired his advanced baseball knowledge. Journalists who tried to discover his secret typically were flummoxed during interviews that followed this line:

Interviewer: "Where did you learn to pitch?"

Marichal: "In the army."

Interviewer: "Oh, what rank were you?"

Marichal: "No rank, just play baseball in army."

Interviewer: "You had a good coach then?"

Marichal: "No coach. I always knew how to pitch."

Interviewer: "Then, there must be ballplayers in your family—your father, perhaps?"

Marichal: "No father. Two brothers. They can't play."

Interviewer: "Then baseball must be a big game in your family."

Marichal: "Only me. I teach myself."

◆　　◆　　◆

Babe Herman was a productive .324 career hitter. He also was the centerpiece from 1926-31 of Brooklyn's infamous "Daffiness Boys," a colorful collection of baseball misfits who made life interesting for Wilbert Robinson's Dodgers.

Strange things just seemed to happen to the enigmatic outfielder, who was known for having fly balls bounce off his chest and shoulders in Brooklyn's difficult sun field. But nothing could top the 1926 game against the Boston Braves in which the incorrigible Babe doubled into a double play.

Herman stepped to the plate in the seventh inning with one out, the bases loaded and the score tied 2-2. Teammates Hank DeBerry (third), Dazzy Vance (second) and Chick Fewster (first) were the runners when Herman drove a George Mogridge pitch to right field.

"I hit a legitimate double against the right field fence, driving in DeBerry," Herman recalled years later. "After I slid into second, I hear somebody holler, 'Throw it home.' And the second baseman did. They had Vance trapped between third and home, it turns out. But I thought Vance had scored, so I figured it must be Fewster who was trapped. Naturally, I get up and streak for third base during the rundown.

"Actually, Fewster was standing off third base a couple of feet watching the play on Vance. I didn't see Chick until it was too late. Well, I was called out for passing Fewster. Vance got back to third safe. Fewster thought he had been called out, so he started walking out to take his position at second base to start the next inning.

"Doc Gautreau got the ball and tagged Chick for the third out. So help me, that's what happened."

Robinson, a 3-2 winner that day, was able to see the humor of having three of his players trying to occupy the same base.

"That's the first time those guys got together on anything all season," he said.

◆ ◆ ◆

Hall of Fame broadcaster Ernie Harwell is fond of telling this story, particularly on occasions when somebody is getting an award:

"When I worked for the Giants in New York during the 1950s, (Yankees outfielder) Hank Bauer was named the 'Good Guy of the Year' by the New York Sports Photographers. We're sitting around Toots Shor's. Somebody said, 'Hank, when you get that award, be sure to bring it over here to us and let us take a look at it so we can see what you got.'

"Bauer goes over to the Waldorf Astoria and gets his award. It's a grandfather clock. So he is struggling through the streets of Manhattan and he bumps into this guy who is sort of disheveled and had too much to drink and knocks the guy down in the gutter. And Bauer, who is carrying this big grandfather clock, is a little bit disturbed by this guy.

"Bauer says, 'Why the hell don't you look where you are going?'

"The guy looks up at Bauer from the gutter and says, 'Why can't you be like everybody else and wear a wristwatch.' "

◆ ◆ ◆

Nobody ever accused Rex Hudler of being dull. In fact, his humor, enthusiasm and unpredictable behavior brightened up clubhouses in six cities over his 13-year major league career.

So what was the accomplishment for which Hudler is best remembered by former teammates? "I ate a bug once in St. Louis," he said. "A lot of players on that bench remember that and they bring it up when I see them.

"I called it a rally bug, but it was really a June bug. We were down six runs to the Mets and we came back and won, 7-6. I chewed it up and swallowed it. I made 800 bucks."

◆　◆　◆

No one enjoyed life—and baseball—more than Dan Quisenberry, the submarine-throwing righthander who starred from 1979-88 for the Kansas City Royals. He was a delightful man. And Kansas Citians took it hard when, on September 30, 1998, a malignant brain tumor claimed his life at age 45.

Even after surgery in January of that year, he made reporters laugh by joking about his treatment.

"The radiation stuff has started, and we are zapping the bad cells," Quisenberry said. "They are getting whupped. Today we took our 15 minutes, and they were sizzling."

He also talked about his teen-aged children driving him around the city.

"My kids take me for rides, so I feel like a dog," he said. "I get to stick my head out the window and let the wind flap my ears. I love it; it's great. Little things really make me happy."

Quisenberry was an outstanding closer for Royals teams that reached the franchise's first two World Series in 1980 and '85. Along the way, he saved 238 games for the Royals and sprinkled a long list of clever quotes over adoring fans.

"I'm not a Mercedes at all. I'm more like a Volkswagen," he said after reaching the major leagues at age 26. "They get a lot of mileage out of me, but it's not going to look pretty."

After a bad night against the Chicago White Sox he said, "I had on my human suit tonight; there was no 'S' across my chest."

He called his sinker "Peggy Lee," in honor of one of the singer's big recordings—"Hitters see it and they say, 'Is that all there is?' "—but it became the "Titanic" when it didn't work so well— "I call it the Titanic because it's unsinkable. When I throw that one, it usually sails over the fence."

Although the Royals played on artificial turf, he had a fondness for the real thing. "Natural grass is a wonderful thing for little bugs and sinkerball pitchers," he said. "Home runs," he quipped, "are still ground balls. In this case, the first bounce is 360 feet away."

He could kid a teammate, like often-wild pitcher Renie Martin, with a gentle jab: "Some guys throw to spots. Some guys throw to zones. Renie throws to continents."

But one of his most noted observations was downright spooky. "I have seen the future," he said, "and it is much like the present, only longer."

For Quisenberry, though, not nearly long enough.

One of Quisenberry's most repeated lines comes with a story from longtime Royals broadcaster Denny Matthews.

"He really did have some of the great quotes of all time because of his wry sense of humor," Matthews said. "He had a stretch of 3-4 weeks where he was getting hit pretty hard. He looked at video-tape for a couple of days. He tried to compare tape of when he was going well with when he wasn't, so he put the video machines side by side.

"He finally figured out what was going on and after getting back on track, he summed it all up by saying, 'I finally found a delivery in my flaw.' "

BETWEEN THE WHITE LINES

The Throw. Those players and fans who witnessed a remarkable ninth inning play on June 5, 1989, at Seattle's Kingdome still shake their heads in disbelief. It was another Bo Jackson moment, delivered like a laser beam into the lore of two baseball franchises.

"It's crazy," said former Mariners second baseman Harold Reynolds as he watched on videotape as the Kansas City left fielder played a carom in the corner, turned and, standing flatfooted, fired a 300-foot strike to home plate that cut down the potential winning run. "I was there. I was the one thrown out. I've seen it on replay. And I still don't believe it."

The Mariners and Royals were tied, 3-3, and Reynolds was running on Steve Farr's first pitch to Scott Bradley, who lined a shot into the left field corner. Reynolds' first thought was "the game's over," and he already was rounding third base when Jackson grabbed the ball on the warning track.

"I saw Darnell (Coles, the on-deck hitter) put his hands up so I could come in standing up," Reynolds said, "but then he throws his hands down and I say, 'What?' So I'm about to throw a courtesy slide, and I see the ball in Bob Boone's mitt. I say, 'You've got to be kidding me.' "

Royals catcher Boone watched the play unfold from a different perspective. "When it was hit, I thought our only chance was to decoy Reynolds and hope he slowed up," Boone said. "Then I'm looking at the throw, and I say, 'This ball's carrying all the way. I can't believe it.'

"So I forget about the deke so I can catch the ball and tag him. It's still amazing to me. Not many people in the world can throw the ball that far, and I don't know anybody who can just grab it and throw as far and accurately as Bo did."

The play fooled home plate umpire Larry Young, who was standing well down the third base line. First base umpire Jim Joyce was still in his original position. Farr didn't bother backing up the plate because "I thought the game was over."

"It's the greatest throw I've ever seen in my life," said Royals manager John Wathan, who watched his team go on to record a 5-3 victory in 13 innings. "If I'm in the game another 30 years, I don't think I'll ever see another like it."

"This is not a normal guy," Royals star George Brett said.

Bo also could do home runs—the long, amazing kind that left everyone speechless, even in the less structured and less scientific world of spring training.

One year in the late 1980s, Jackson faced Boston righthander Dennis "Oil Can" Boyd in a game at Baseball City, Fla., and unleashed a shot that cleared the scoreboard. It went so high that even a keen-eyed scout such as former Negro League star Buck O'Neil lost sight of it for a moment. Longtime Royals scout Art Stewart was sitting next to O'Neil.

"The ball cleared the scoreboard by about 20 feet," Stewart said.

"Over the light standard," added Brett.

As Royals head groundskeeper George Toma manicured the field after the game, a reporter shouted down from the press box: "How far you think that ball went, George?"

Toma got out a tape measure. "I'll have the kids measure it," he said, dispatching several members of his crew to a parking lot beyond the left field fence. Soon they could be seen searching among the few remaining cars.

"They found the dent in the grille of the car it hit," Toma yelled to the press box.

"And how far was that?" the reporter inquired.

Toma took his rake and drew three figures into the dirt: 5 ... 5 ... 8.

"What! 558 feet?"

That's seven feet shy of the legendary home run New York Yankees great Mickey Mantle hit against Washington's Chuck Stobbs in a 1953 game at Griffith Stadium—the 565-foot moon-shot recognized by many as the longest homer in history.

Nodding, Toma smiled and went back to raking the field.

◆　◆　◆

Brett could not match Jackson in the power department, but he was never lacking for timing and flair. Those qualities were center stage in a September 30, 1992, game at Anaheim Stadium when he joined the 3,000-hit club with a four-hit game against the Angels.

Brett, then a 39-year-old designated hitter who had missed two games with a shoulder injury, collected his milestone hit in the seventh inning when his hard shot to the right side of the infield bounced over the head of California second baseman Ken Oberkfell. Brett hugged Kansas City first base coach Lynn Jones, shook hands with Angels first baseman Gary Gaetti and was mobbed by team-mates, several of whom were carrying camcorders to preserve the moment.

Brett walked toward the dugout and raised his hands to the cheering crowd. The ovation lasted five minutes and left the Royals veteran misty-eyed. When the game finally resumed, lefthander Tim Fortugno—the victim of hit No. 3,000—recorded a quick out and then fired a surprise throw to Gaetti.

Brett, at the crescendo of his career, was ingloriously caught sleeping.

"I was right in the middle of a conversation with Gaetti, and he picked me off," Brett said.

And he laughed about it, as he had every right to do.

Brett told this story about a play that occurred in a nondescript, rain-delayed game at Milwaukee in the late 1970s:

"(Marty) Pattin was pitching, and somebody hit a swinging bunt," recalled Brett, who in those days was known for his sometimes-erratic throws. "I grabbed it barehanded and fired away."

Pattin, for some astonishing reason, leaped off the mound and snagged the throw.

"He just did it without thinking," Brett said. "I was laughing so hard I had to keep my glove over my face for two innings. We were winning by something like 11-1 or 12-1. Good thing, or it wouldn't have been so funny."

◆ ◆ ◆

What happened to Cleveland left fielder Mel Hall in a 1986 Cactus League game against Oakland at Phoenix was bizarre and funny.

The A's Mike Davis was a baserunner at first when Carney Lansford hit a looping line drive over third that hit close to the line and skidded into foul territory near a wire restraining fence that separated the field from the bleachers. Hall gave chase, then stopped suddenly, his attention focused on the fence rather than the rolling ball.

Sensing something was wrong, shortstop Julio Franco raced to retrieve the ball but stopped suddenly, laughing hysterically as Davis and Lansford circled the bases. Hall's long-sleeve T-shirt was caught on the wire, and he could not free himself, allowing the slow-footed Lansford to record "the first inside-the-park homer I remember hitting."

Hall was still hung up on the fence as Indians manager Pat Corrales argued with umpire Don Denkinger. But Corrales claimed only that the ball should have been called foul. After the game, all parties shook their heads in amazement.

"That's a first," Corrales said. "In my whole career, I've never seen anything like that happen. Mel can really do it."

Oakland manager Jackie Moore looked at it from a different perspective. "This is the first time I can remember a discussion about whether a player, rather than the ball, was in play," he said.

Hall refused to discuss the play, but teammate Joe Carter offered some analysis. "He needs a tear-away jersey," Carter said. "That could only happen to Mel. Last year, he lost his glove over the fence, and now this."

◆　◆　◆

Gaylord Perry, a young San Francisco Giants righthander, was in the batting cage when he spotted manager Alvin Dark standing nearby.

"Hey Skip," he yelled at Dark, "you gotta pinch hit me today. I'll hit one out of the park."

Dark looked at the grinning Perry and sneered. "They'll put a man on the moon before you hit a home run," he replied.

Dark left the Giants after the 1964 season, managed the Kansas City Athletics for two years and was manager of the Cleveland Indians in 1969, when Perry finally did hit his first career home run for the Giants. Amazingly, the July 20 blow came on the same day that astronaut Neil Armstrong took "one giant leap for mankind" with his historic moonwalk.

"I had forgotten I'd made that statement," Dark said. "I saw that Gaylord had hit the home run, but I had forgotten what I had said. As soon as he saw me, he reminded me."

◆　◆　◆

Rusty Staub stole 47 bases over a 23-year career that stretched from 1963-85. But that didn't stop the stocky 6-foot-2, 215-pound redhead from bragging about his speed and baserunning acumen at a 1969 All-Star break function that also included Atlanta traveling secretary Donald Davidson.

"He was kidding around about how fast he was," said Davidson, who couldn't resist a little dig at the Montreal outfielder. "I'll tell you what, Rusty," he told Staub, "if you ever steal a base against us in Atlanta, I'll give you the bag. That's how fast I think you are."

In a June 7, 1970, game against the Braves, Staub did just that. He stole second base, jumped to his feet and looked toward the press-box with a big grin, pointing toward the bag.

"I knew what he meant," Davidson said, "so I called Bob Johnson, our head groundskeeper, and told him to give it to Rusty after the game."

Staub, who swiped a career-high 12 bases that season, kept his prize in the Expos' clubhouse with the inscription: "X, Stolen From Atlanta Stadium, June 7."

◆　◆　◆

Sure, outfielders can make putouts and assists on the same play. But how often does the assist come before the putout?

It happened to Colorado center fielder Preston Wilson on July 31, 2003. In the words of former major league pitcher and current Rockies television broadcaster George Frazier, "It was one of the neatest plays. I had never seen it happen before."

The Rockies and Reds were tied 4-4 with one out in the bottom of the third inning of a game at Cincinnati's Great American Ballpark. Reds catcher Jason LaRue was on first base when Russell Branyan hit a shot off the right-center field wall. Wilson corralled the ball and threw it home, where catcher Bobby Estalella tagged out LaRue after a brief rundown.

In the meantime, Frazier said, "Branyan rounds second base a little too far, and who do you think tagged him out at second? Preston Wilson. What are you doing there? What gave Preston the inclination to run that hard, that far to get to that position to make that play?

"I kept saying, 'You've got to be kidding me!' He was 398 feet from home, and then all of a sudden he was at second base to get the other end of the double play. I've never seen anything like that in my life."

◆　◆　◆

"Basebrawls" have been taking place since the game's humble beginnings in the 19th century. But few can match a 1956 fracas between Milwaukee first baseman Joe Adcock and New York Giants pitcher Ruben Gomez for sound judgment and spontaneous hilarity.

Gomez, a 175-pound righthander, hit the 6-4, 220-pound Adcock on the wrist with a pitch. The two players exchanged words before the angry Adcock began walking toward the mound. Gomez, who had already received a new ball from the umpire, took one look at his hulking adversary and fired at him again, hitting him this time on the thigh.

Then, obviously operating from the theory that discretion is the better part of valor, Gomez sprinted for the dugout and escaped to the safety of the Giants' clubhouse.

"I'd rather be smart and live," he explained later, "than die brave."

◆　◆　◆

Fans remember Steve Carlton as the silent warrior who posted 329 wins over his 24-year Hall of Fame career. But former teammates remember Lefty for different reasons. "He had that mystique about him, even among us," said former Philadelphia teammate and coach John Vukovich. "On days he pitched, about the only conversation you'd ever have with him was, 'Hi, Lefty.' We left him alone."

When Carlton pitched, he was in a zone that nobody was allowed to penetrate. His focus was incredible, his toughness the stuff of legend.

Former Phillies first baseman Tommy Hutton recalled a spring training game in West Palm Beach, Fla., when a Montreal hitter fouled off a Carlton pitch. Carlton, who made it a point never to watch a foul ball, turned immediately toward the plate, expecting to get a new ball from the umpire.

"Except the third baseman (Kiko Garcia) picked the ball up," Hutton said, "and fired it back to the mound. And Lefty wasn't looking, so it hit him right in the side of the head—and he never flinched. It was like a fly ticked him."

Larry Bowa, Philadelphia's shortstop for 10 seasons with Carlton, topped that story.

"I saw Billy Williams hit a line drive at Wrigley Field that hit him right in the neck," Bowa said. "And it was not a broken-bat job. This was a line drive. Most guys would have crumbled. I mean, you could see the laces from the ball on his neck.

"But Lefty just picked the ball up, threw it to first and got the out. Then everybody started running out, and he just waved his glove like, 'Get out of here.'"

Ted Sizemore, who became the Phillies starting second baseman in 1977, was introduced to the Carlton mystique the hard way—thanks to a little conspiracy between Bowa and third baseman Mike Schmidt. The Philadelphia veterans suggested to newcomer Sizemore that he should go to the mound and tell his pitcher to "calm down."

"Lefty was standing there, rubbing up the ball, and here comes Size," Bowa said. "And Lefty just says, 'Don't take another step. ... I'll handle this side of the diamond, you handle yours.' And poor Size—it was like he hit a brick wall. That's how fast he stopped."

◆　　◆　　◆

Tim McCarver was a 21-year-old prospect when he was handed the job as starting catcher for the 1963 St. Louis Cardinals. Lefthander Ray Sadecki recalled the problems McCarver faced in dealing with a veteran pitching staff that included Curt Simmons, Bob Gibson and Lew Burdette.

"Now you've just got to know that 21-year-old catchers aren't about to stop the game and go out and read off guys like that,"

Sadecki said. "When they pitched, they pitched their own games, or 90 percent of them. But like all of us, they could get sloppy and start pitching too fast or aiming the ball, and it's up to their catcher to go out there and straighten them out. Sometimes it takes a little screaming and threatening to get through to us.

"Well, poor Tim. He was only 21, and management wanted him to develop a take-charge attitude, and right now. Johnny Keane was the manager then, and I remember one game Tim was working and Simmons was pitching. Well, you should have seen it.

"Keane would yell from the bench for Tim to go out to the mound and slow Simmons down. Tim would nod OK and start out to the mound. He'd get about 10 feet from Curt, and Curt would growl and tell him to get back of the plate and leave him alone. So Tim would go back. Pretty soon, Keane would run McCarver out there again, and Curt would run him back. Out and back. Out and back.

"Poor Tim. He didn't know what to make of it. But he finally got the idea, took charge, ran out there and stayed out there as long as he believed necessary and, well, we won a pennant (in 1964)."

On July 4, 1976—the nation's 200th birthday—McCarver, then catching for the Phillies, touched off a few fireworks by driving a pitch from Pittsburgh's Larry Demery over the right field wall at Three Rivers Stadium. But McCarver's sixth career grand slam quickly changed to a single when he was called out for passing teammate Garry Maddox as he rounded first base.

Maddox was tagging up in case the ball was caught, and both players were watching its flight, not aware of the looming danger. McCarver returned to the Phillies' dugout with a sheepish smile, and his teammates responded with a few perfectly aimed needles.

"The dugout would have been like a tomb, but Tim, he's got such a terrific attitude and such a terrific sense of humor that we had to laugh," teammate Tommy Hutton said after the Phillies' 10-5 victory. "If it had been any other player on the team, nobody would have said a word."

One year and one day later, McCarver hit a "real" grand slam in a game against the New York Mets at Philadelphia's Veterans Stadium. He took the occasion to return the needle to a teammate.

"It was Garry's fault," he said, referring to the 1976 lost home run. "I never said that before, but there's a statute of limitations, and it runs out after a year."

To this day, McCarver has little use for players who put on a show when they homer and slowly make their way around the bases. In the 2003 American League Championship Series, a player known for such styling, Bret Boone, worked in the booth with McCarver as an analyst for the national telecast.

When the subject of showboating came up, Boone admitted he was not above flipping his bat and admiring his handiwork. McCarver, of course, shared his opinion that he does not think that's the way to play the game.

But Boone had quite a comeback. His father had played on the '76 Phillies, and Boone remembered watching the game when McCarver was called out for passing Maddox after the would-have-been grand slam. "Just think Tim," Boone said. "If you'd taken your time, you wouldn't have cost yourself a home run."

Though McCarver usually has plenty to say about everything, this was one time when he could say nothing more than, "You could be right about that."

◆　◆　◆

The 1967 All-Star Game at Anaheim Stadium was a memorable event in Hall of Fame righthander Tom Seaver's career—and a coming-of-age moment for the New York Mets rookie. He pitched the bottom of the 15th inning, after the National League had taken a 2-1 lead in the top of the inning on a Tony Perez home run, and retired three hitters without incident.

Seaver recalled his experience for *The Sporting News*:

"I'm nervous warming up, but I start in from the bullpen and I begin to lose some of it. As I walked by Clemente in right field, I said to him, 'Let's get three and go home.' Roberto smiled. 'That's right,' he answered. 'Go get 'em, keed.'

"As I passed Pete Rose at second, I made a remark to him. 'How about you pitching and me playing second?' I asked. Pete just laughed. 'No,' he grinned, 'I'll stay where I am. You can do it.' I guess it was like a guy whistling past the graveyard at midnight, but talking to those two guys on my way helped give me confidence.

"When I got to the mound, I wasn't nervous. ... Not until I picked up the resin bag and turned around to make sure everyone was in position and ready. That's when I got my greatest thrill of the day.

"Imagine turning around and seeing Clemente in right, Mays in center, Aaron in left and an infield of Cepeda, Rose, Alley and Perez! What a team of stars behind me and what a thrill! I'll never forget it."

◆　　◆　　◆

Jose Canseco will always be remembered for two things: his Bunyanesque power and flaky behavior. The power was on center stage in Game 4 of the 1989 American League Championship Series when the 6-4, 240-pound Oakland slugger set off baseball's Richter scale with a titanic third-inning blast that settled into the fifth tier of the left field stands at Toronto's SkyDome.

The blast, off Blue Jays lefthander Mike Flanagan, was estimated by an IBM computer to have traveled 480 feet, although most observers considered that a conservative projection. "IBM means Improper Baseball Measurements," Toronto pitcher John Cerutti cracked.

The home run drew these comments from other witnesses:

A's outfielder Billy Beane: "That wasn't just a home run. That was a home run of Biblical proportions."

A's outfielder Dave Parker: "As Jay Johnstone once said, 'Anything that goes that far should have some food aboard it.' "

A's pitcher Matt Young, comparing Canseco's blast to a moon-shot hit earlier in the season by teammate Mark McGwire: "That one looked at Mac's, spit on it and kept going."

Blue Jays catcher Ernie Whitt: "I've never called a pitch that went that far."

◆　◆　◆

Wally Joyner was a California Angels rookie in 1986 when he got a quick lesson about baseball in New York. Joyner and winning pitcher Mike Witt were walking off the field after a 2-0 victory at Yankee Stadium when he felt something brush his arm.

"It didn't cut me or anything, so I thought it was a big comb or something," Joyner said. "The side of it hit my arm and glanced off. Then I looked down, and it was this big Bowie knife. The next thing I saw was the back of the dugout wall. I was out of there!"

Angels center fielder Gary Pettis picked up the knife, which had a five-inch blade, and gave it to manager Gene Mauch.

"You wouldn't have too much trouble killing a bear with it," Mauch said. "There are places I'd rather play than Yankee Stadium. I've been hit with nuts and bolts there, but that's the first knife I've ever seen."

Yankees officials gave the knife to the New York City police, who determined that it must have been thrown by somebody in the upper deck.

◆　◆　◆

The 1977 All-Star Game at Yankee Stadium opened with the American League's Cy Young winner pitching to the National League's Most Valuable Player. Baltimore righthander Jim Palmer recalled his thought process after going to a 3-and-2 count in his first confrontation with Cincinnati second baseman Joe Morgan.

"I knew if I walked him and he felt good, he'd steal second," Palmer said. "And if he felt really good, he'd steal third. That would be like throwing a triple. So I gave him a low fastball, and he hit a home run."

Palmer made it through his 19-year major league career with an interesting distinction: He never surrendered a grand slam. But he does remember an oh-so-close call in Cleveland.

"I'm pitching against (Dennis) Eckersley in '77," Palmer said. "I had to win my last seven starts to win 20. This is my next-to-last start. I'm going for No. 19. For some reason, I had tennis elbow. I couldn't throw my slider, and Eckersley starts off punching out a bunch of guys, shooting his pistol, blowing on his finger.

"We get to the bottom of the eighth inning. Paul Dade hits a single. Somebody bunts, and (third baseman Doug) DeCinces falls down. The field was horrible in Cleveland. There's another bunt, and I fall down. I won four Gold Gloves. And now the bases are loaded with none out.

"Andre Thornton comes up. He's their big RBI guy. I don't know how to get him out. I throw him a first-pitch fastball, and he pops up. Then Bruce Bochte comes up. ... He fouls off a bunch of pitches. I throw him a high fastball on 3-and-2 and strike him out. Two outs. Now it's Rico Carty.

"He had hit .366 in 1970, led the National League. I had thrown him a low-and-away slider earlier in the season, and he hit it out, 430 feet to right-center field. He was a pretty aggressive guy. And he used to talk to you: 'C'mon Chico,' stuff like that. My first pitch is down the middle, a good high fastball. He takes it for ball one. Then I throw another fastball for ball two. I'm not going to throw him a low-and-away slider. And I don't want to get down 3-0.

"It's not only about the grand slam. It's about winning 20, too. What are you going to do? ... Well, I throw a 2-0 fastball, and he hits a lazy fly ball. ... I'm moving toward the third base line. It looks like it's playable. But the wind is blowing to left center. And the ball keeps going and going and going. I'm getting nervous. It looked routine off the bat. But it's not routine. Al Bumbry keeps going back and back. He catches it, just as it would have gone over the wall. It's not like Torii Hunter leaping over the wall to bring it back, but the inning is over.

"We go to the ninth. Eckersley is still shooting guys, blowing on his pistol. Our guys want to beat him badly. And then (Ken) Singleton and Eddie (Murray) hit two of the longest back-to-back home runs I've ever seen. We get three runs and win, 4-1.

"I win my 20th in my final start when Rick Dempsey hits a little blooper. We win, 3-2, in 11 innings. I pitched all 11. Hey, I was going for 20."

◆　　◆　　◆

During a 1986 game at Shea Stadium, New York Mets third baseman Ray Knight was getting an earful from an obnoxious fan. The man colorfully suggested that Knight might do better at the plate if he substituted his wife's putter for his bat.

"This fan was sitting two rows in front of me," said Nancy Lopez, a Hall of Fame golfer and Knight's wife. "So I asked the person in front of me to tap him on the shoulder. He turned around and just looked at me. I smiled and waved. He was very embarrassed.

"I said, 'Ray can't use my putter. I've got it right here.' He didn't say anything the rest of the game."

◆　　◆　　◆

Bang-bang plays at the plate, with runner and ball bearing down on the catcher in heart-pounding symmetry, are among the most exciting in baseball. It only stands to reason that the double-barreled assault the New York Yankees put on Chicago catcher Carlton Fisk on August 2, 1985, was twice as memorable.

The game was tied 3-3 as the Yankees batted in the bottom of the seventh with two runners on base at Yankee Stadium. Bobby Meacham, the runner at second, held up when Rickey Henderson drove a pitch deep into the left-center field alley, watching to see whether White Sox center fielder Luis Salazar could run it down. When the ball sailed over Salazar's glove, Meacham stumbled, allowing Dale Berra, the runner on first, to catch him between second and third.

Yankees third base coach Gene Michael waved home Meacham but tried to hold up Berra—to no avail. Fisk braced at the plate as both runners bore down and the relay from shortstop Ozzie Guillen arrived right on target. As Meacham lowered his shoulder, Fisk side-stepped and threw out his glove for the tag. Meacham's momentum spun Fisk around and he made a sweeping lunge at Berra, who was sent sprawling by the collision.

Double play!

"I thought Meacham was going to try to run interference for Berra," said Fisk, whose effort preserved the tie in a game eventually won by Chicago in 11 innings. "I could see them coming all the way. I figured Meacham would try to tie me up, but he spun me, and Berra was right behind. I anticipated more of a crush at the plate.

"If I had stayed in (Meacham's) way, he might have run me over and Berra could have walked over the plate."

How would Fisk have fared if that second runner had been the ever-intense Kirk Gibson? Boston catcher Rich Gedman found himself in precisely that predicament in a June 14, 1983, game at Tiger Stadium.

Detroit outfielder Gibson, who had already hit a mammoth home run over the Stadium's right field roof, later clobbered a pitch to deep left-center field that gave teammate Lou Whitaker a chance to score from first base. Boston center fielder Tony Armas picked up Gibson's drive and heaved the ball to cutoff man Glenn Hoffman, who fired home, where Gedman applied the tag to Whitaker—an instant before the speedy Gibson came barreling into the play.

But Gibson plowed into startled home plate umpire Larry Barnett and drove him into Gedman, who was knocked down. Barnett was knocked out in the collision and had to be carried from the field on a stretcher.

"First base umpire Ken Kaiser comes running down the line and sees a ball on the ground and calls Gibson safe," said Red Sox radio broadcaster Joe Castiglione. "Gedman can't believe it because he thinks he's got the ball in his glove. What Kaiser didn't realize is that the ball on the ground came from a pouch on Barnett's belt when the plate umpire was knocked out.

"Gedman was right. There should've been two outs on that one play at the plate."

◆ ◆ ◆

Glenn Adams did not have to run over anybody to score in a May 4, 1979, game at Minnesota's Metropolitan Stadium. He simply had to force himself to circle the bases.

In the seventh inning of a 7-6 Minnesota victory, the lefthanded-hitting Twins outfielder drove a pitch well over the right-center field fence, where it landed at the base of the scoreboard. Halfway to second base, Adams abruptly turned and headed back toward the Twins dugout.

"I thought the ball had been caught," he explained. "I didn't see the ball and (Detroit center fielder Ron) LeFlore was right at the fence. I thought maybe he caught it."

Twins first base coach Karl Kuehl intercepted Adams, and the embarrassed youngster completed his game-deciding home run trot.

◆ ◆ ◆

Through most of his 16-year major league career, Boston's Jim Rice was one of the most feared hitters in the game. But the 6-2, 205-pound outfielder with the beefy arms and natural scowl also was feared for reasons other than his bat.

In a 1977 game against Kansas City, Royals pitcher Jim Colborn breathed a sigh of relief when Rice hit a tremendous drive that barely curved foul. There was only panic, however, when his next pitch hit Rice on the arm, and he dropped his bat and walked toward the mound.

Both benches emptied, and a few comments were exchanged. But the tension quickly diffused, and Rice ambled slowly to first base without further incident.

"He just asked me if I meant to hit him," Colborn said. "For a while, I thought I was going to be 'Rice-a-roni.' "

◆ ◆ ◆

Facing Frank Tanana and his frustrating assortment of pitches was never a treat, but the crafty veteran made life even more difficult for hitters in 1990 as he approached his 200th career win. That's when the Detroit lefthander came up with a hesitation pitch.

"I've never seen anything like it," said Kansas City's Kevin Seitzer after striking out on the pitch in a spring exhibition game. "I thought he was stopping to reload."

Tanana threw the unusual pitch by stopping his motion momentarily with his right foot planted and his arm already cocked in mid-delivery. After the hesitation, he followed through and released the ball to the startled hitter. Tanana called it "my stop-slop pitch."

"I'll use it once in a while because it's one more pitch to keep the hitter off balance," he said. "Besides, it makes my 65 mph heater look like 90."

◆　◆　◆

Mike Sweeney, a husky Kansas City Royals first baseman, would never be confused with Lou Brock or Rickey Henderson on the basepaths. Yet, Sweeney executed a baserunning rarity in today's game—a straight steal of home in the sixth inning of an August 14, 2002, contest at Kauffman Stadium.

Most modern-era thefts of home come on the back end of a double steal. The runner on first base takes off for second and, when the catcher throws through, the runner at third bolts for the plate. But Sweeney would have none of that.

Playing against the New York Yankees, he hit an RBI double, moved to third on a bunt and waited there through a strikeout. When lefthander Andy Pettitte didn't pay him much attention with Aaron Guiel at the plate, Sweeney decided to pull his surprise on a 1-2 pitch.

"I got a good lead, and when Andy came set, I charged for home," Sweeney said.

Royals manager Tony Pena had given Sweeney a nod, but he never expected him to run. "Oh, my God," he muttered in the dugout. Pettitte reacted with a hurry-up pitch (ball two), but Sweeney scooted past catcher Jorge Posada's tag.

"That was the last person in the ballpark I expected to steal home," said Paul Byrd, the Royals' pitcher that day. "But he has a lot of heart."

Adding to the element of surprise was that Sweeney had only recently returned after missing 30 games with back and hip ailments. It was the Royals' first straight steal of home in a quarter century.

The story would be complete with a victory. But, alas, the Yankees prevailed in 14 innings, 3-2.

◆ ◆ ◆

A Detroit radio announcer referred to Cecil Fielder as "the eighth continent" because of his 250-plus-pound girth, and his running was usually limited to the 360 feet he covered on one of his home run trots. So, yes, it was something of a big deal on April 2, 1996, when the Tigers slugger swiped his first major league base after 1,096 games and 10 steal-free seasons.

The bolt of lightning occurred in the ninth inning of a game at Minnesota's Metrodome. Fielder, who had walked, surprised everybody by running on a full-count pitch from Dan Naulty to Melvin Nieves, who struck out swinging. Catcher Greg Myers' throw sailed right of the bag, and shortstop Pat Meares dropped the ball as Fielder slid in safely.

Minnesota fans gave the hefty Fielder a standing ovation and bowed to him in mock worship. "It was cool," he said. "The crowd got a kick out of it." So did umpire Tim Tschida, who gave Fielder the base as a keepsake.

The Tigers' 10-6 victory was the first under new manager Buddy Bell.

◆ ◆ ◆

San Diego manager Bruce Bochy, a former big-league catcher,

also had Fielder-like speed. So it's not surprising that he remembers, and even brags about, his two career triples.

One came at San Diego's Jack Murphy Stadium, a shot into the right field corner that bounced around under chairs and benches long enough for Bochy to reach third base. The other was hit down the left field line at St. Louis' Busch Stadium—a most unlikely spot for any triple.

"You hit one down the left field line and get a triple, you can brag on that one a little bit," Bochy said. "Andy Van Slyke was the left fielder. He got in the corner, and the ball was bouncing around the wall, hitting off him. He said, 'I was playing pinball out there and won a free game, so I played another one.'

"They gave me a triple," Bochy emphasized. "They didn't give him an error."

◆　◆　◆

Former catcher Joe Pignatano is best remembered for another kind of triple. His occurred as a fitting cap to the New York Mets' 120-loss 1962 expansion campaign.

In a season-ending game at Chicago's Wrigley Field, pinch hitter Sammy Drake singled for the Mets, and veteran leadoff man Richie Ashburn singled him to second. Cubs righthander Bob Buhl, his 5-1 lead suddenly in jeopardy, now faced the light-hitting Pignatano. "Piggy" hit a line drive to Chicago second baseman Ken Hubbs.

With typical Mets flair, the inning came to a quick conclusion when Hubbs flipped to Ernie Banks at first base to double up Ashburn, and Banks fired to shortstop Andre Rodgers, who tagged second base to triple up Drake. The game ended, 5-1, and Pignatano's six-year big-league career ended with him hitting into a triple play.

But there's more: Ashburn, after getting his 2,574th career hit, never played again. Neither did Drake, whose three-year career ended after 72 games and 11 hits. Hubbs, the National League's 1962 Rookie of the Year, played one more season before he was killed in a plane crash.

◆　◆　◆

What's it like to face Nolan Ryan and suddenly have to dodge a 95-mph fastball hurtling madly toward your head? That mind-numbing prospect sometimes is shared by big-league pitchers, who have to dodge vicious line drives as a natural hazard to their occupation. Former Milwaukee lefthander Scott Karl will never forget his experience with a career-threatening liner hit by Montreal's Shane Andrews in 1998.

"I didn't even really see the ball," Karl said. "My initial reaction was to cover my face because that's the most open area. I threw my hands up. I heard the crack, and I lost it. I knew it was coming back at me. I sensed it.

"That was it. The ball hit me so hard it bounced to our second baseman, who threw him out by five steps. My catcher came running out, thinking I had got hit in the face. I was actually more scared and a little sick to my stomach afterward, just thinking about what could have happened.

"I saw it the next morning. I watched my reaction time. I didn't even flinch until the ball was halfway there."

◆　◆　◆

Through rain or snow or chill of night, baseball plugs heartily through its long schedule. But there's nothing in anybody's job description about bugs.

In a game played August 27, 1990, at Toronto's SkyDome, umpire crew chief Don Denkinger called a temporary halt to a game between the Blue Jays and Milwaukee Brewers in the bottom of the fifth inning when the stadium was inundated with swarms of flying ants, gnats, mosquitoes, midges and moths. Fans and players were driven to cover while baffled officials scrambled to find relief.

"I've never seen anything like it," Denkinger said. "I've seen games called by rain, wind and snow, but never by bugs. I've seen bugs before, but I've never seen them this heavy and this thick. They were just flying around, but there were so many, it was impossible for not only the players, but the umpires as well."

Stadium engineers drove them away by closing the SkyDome's retractable roof and turning up the air conditioning. The game was delayed for 35 minutes. Frank Feneck, the grounds crew chief at Detroit's Tiger Stadium, recalled a game some 30 years earlier when the Tigers and Cleveland Indians halted play temporarily because of bugs.

"Those bugs were really a pain," said Jimmy Piersall, an Indians outfielder that day. "But the ones (in Toronto) were bombers. I think they were Canadian bugs."

Former Tigers reliever Todd Jones remembers another bug incident during the 2000 season at Detroit's new Comerica Park.

"A tremendous cloud of bugs just descended on us," said Jones, who was watching the game from the Tigers' bullpen. "Mosquitoes, gnats, all kinds of bugs. There were millions of them. They were in your hair, on your hat ... everywhere."

Jones first noticed that something was up when he looked into the stands and saw fans waving their hands in front of their faces, swatting at the air with programs and moving toward the concourse. "It was a mass exodus," he said.

Batters stepped out of the box to swat away bugs from their face, and pitchers paced and swiped to clear their vision. But the game went on. Things got so bad in the bullpen that coach Lance Parrish, an avid outdoorsman, was forced to take action.

"Parrish built a fire in the bullpen," Jones said. "He built it between the mound and the plate. It wasn't a big fire, mostly kindling, but the smoke helped keep the bugs out of the bullpen. But the thing I remember most is all the people walking out."

◆　　◆　　◆

Nobody evacuated the stands during a May 3, 1986, game between Pittsburgh and San Diego at Jack Murphy Stadium, but all activity ceased in the seventh inning when an intruder strolled casually onto the playing field.

"The longer you play, the more you see," said Padres first baseman

Steve Garvey. "I've seen streakers, cats, dogs. ... but it was the first time I'd ever been skunk-delayed."

The animal emerged from beneath the tarpaulin along the stadium's right field wall and sauntered toward Garvey. The game skidded to a sudden halt.

"I saw the crowd standing up and looking past me," Garvey said. "I thought maybe Morganna was coming out again. Then I saw it. I thought, 'OK, what should I do?' Then I thought, 'I'm not going to do anything.' I didn't want to be sprayed with '*eau de skunk.*' "

Umpire Dave Pallone called time, and everybody watched silently as the skunk slowly made its way around the perimeter of the infield. Finally, escorted gingerly by groundskeepers, it ducked under the left field tarp and departed—with no lingering aftereffects.

Padre Le Pew made an unscheduled return to San Diego about a decade later when the Cincinnati Reds were playing the Padres. Whether the black and white-striped varmint was the same one that had visited Garvey in 1986 or maybe a close relative, nobody could say for sure. But his presence was equally distressing.

"For some reason, San Diego always had a lot of wildlife that found its way into the stadium," said Reds broadcaster Chris Welsh, who pitched three of his five major league seasons for the Padres. "When I played there, there were incidents of owls coming down and almost dive-bombing outfielders. They had squirrels, raccoons and, on this particular night, a skunk."

This one ambled along the base of the outfield fence. It disappeared under the stands, then re-emerged in the seats at the loge level. Welsh and broadcast partner George Grande had a great view of the action.

"Even without spewing its odor, it cleared out the whole section," Welsh said. "People saw it coming, and they just scattered. You'd think there was a bomb ready to go off; in fact, there may have been a bomb ready to go off for all they knew. The groundskeepers and ushers weren't really sure what to do. All people could do was part the human sea everywhere the skunk went.

"We could always tell where the skunk was because of the parting of the people. When it was on the field, they delayed the game. When it was in the stands, they didn't. But all the eyes in the stadium were not on the field; they were on the stands.

"In fact, a couple of foul balls went into the stands, and people weren't ready to catch them because they were more worried about the skunk. Finally, I told my broadcast partner, 'Listen, George, I'll keep an eye on the skunk and you keep an eye on the game.' "

◆　◆　◆

The Baltimore Orioles, A.L. East Division champions in three of the last four seasons, were struggling along at 17-17. And fans were having trouble getting emotionally involved with their team in the young season.

So the sight of a male, overweight streaker running wild during a rain delay in the opening game of a May 19, 1974, doubleheader against Boston came as welcome relief. There he was, circling the Memorial Stadium infield and slipping down on the slick tarp near second and third base. The 24,839 fans roared their approval. And when the jolly exhibitionist tried to make his escape, veering toward the first base stands and into the arms of waiting police, the crowd groaned.

After the game, in which the Orioles committed six errors and lost 11-2, a Boston writer asked Baltimore general manager Frank Cashen what would happen to the streaker. In Boston, he said, they are fined $500. Cashen had a better idea.

"I think the police should give him $50 and tell him to come back Wednesday," he said.

Jack Dunn, the Orioles' vice president of business affairs, called it "the best one-game streak I've ever seen."

But Red Sox manager Darrell Johnson was not amused.

"What gets me," he said, "is that we get fined by the league when we cuss within earshot of the fans, yet the very people whose ears we aren't supposed to singe applaud when some nut runs around the field with his clothes off."

◆　　◆　　◆

If it was not the longest single in baseball history, it was at least the most dramatic. Everybody who witnessed Mike Schmidt's first-inning hit off lefthander Claude Osteen in a June 10, 1974, game at Houston's Astrodome described the blow with a sense of reverence.

"It was awesome," said Astros manager Preston Gomez.

"That's what you call a real power shot," said Astros second baseman Tommy Helms.

"I knew the ball was going out," said Houston center fielder Cesar Cedeno. "I gave up on it, but kept running back because I wanted to see how far it would go."

There's the rub. The towering drive by the Phillies third baseman didn't go all that far, thanks to a speaker suspended from the Astrodome roof, 117 feet over center field and 329 feet from home plate. Schmidt's drive hit the bottom left side of the object and dropped straight down to the AstroTurf field. According to ground rules, the ball was in play.

"I took one look and knew it was gone," said Phillies second baseman Dave Cash, who was on base. "Then I took another look and there it was coming down in front of Cedeno."

Schmidt ended up with a single, and 9,487 fans and many players tried to figure out what had happened. It was the first time a fair-territory speaker had been hit in the Astrodome's nine-plus seasons. What should have been a tape-measure home run became a moment locked in everyone's memory.

"When it was all over," Schmidt said, "I realized the ball hit the speaker and cost me a home run, and it's a shame. I may never hit another ball like that one."

Cedeno, whose team benefited temporarily in an eventual 12-0 Phillies win, sounded disappointed.

"It could have been over everything," he marveled. "It could have hit the flag above the message board. I never saw a ball hit so high and so far."

Hall of Fame catcher Johnny Bench hit 389 home runs. One he will never forget occurred May 30, 1972, in a game at the Astrodome.

Bench drove a second-inning pitch into the left-center field gap and Houston outfielders Bob Watson and Jimmy Wynn went for the catch and missed connections as the ball bounced off the wall behind them. "I haven't hit one like that since I was playing Little League ball," Bench said after circling the bases for an inside-the-park homer. "Of course, in Little League the distance to the bases was shorter, and there weren't too many fences to hit a ball over."

Bench did not complete his gut-wrenching dash economically, making wide turns around each base before chugging home ahead of a late throw. "I didn't set any records," conceded Bench, whose arrival at the plate was noted with some amusement by Reds players and coaches.

"I don't think Johnny slid when he got to home plate," manager Sparky Anderson said. "I think he just fell down."

After getting back to the dugout, Bench sat gasping for air as pitcher Gary Nolan fanned him with a towel. "I figured if I didn't, he wouldn't get through the inning," Nolan said.

Anderson gave Bench a straw and some much-appreciated Gatorade, saying Bench's hands "were too weak to hold the cup."

Gene Mauch was always looking for an edge. Sometimes, he did not find it.

On July 11, 1977, Mauch's Minnesota Twins were locked in a 5-5 tie with the California Angels in the bottom of the 10th inning at Anaheim Stadium. Mauch brought in sidearming righthander Dave Johnson, who opened the inning by hitting Dave Chalk with a pitch. After Rance Mulliniks sacrificed Chalk to second, Ron Jackson was intentionally walked and Willie Aikens drew a walk to load the bases.

One out, bottom of the 10th, score tied, bases loaded.

Mauch needed that edge.

So he pulled left fielder Bob Gorinski from the game and inserted infielder Mike Cubbage, giving the Twins five infielders and two outfielders—Larry Hisle and Danny Ford. A medium fly ball would score the winning run, anyway, so Mauch wanted to limit the chances of a ground ball getting through an infield that was now aligned, right to left, with Rod Carew, Jerry Terrell, Luis Gomez, Roy Smalley and Cubbage.

Johnson, working to Rusty Torres, went into his delivery for the first pitch and caught his cleat on the mound. The pitch sailed to the backstop—in the air—allowing Chalk to score the game-ending run.

"I put in five infielders," Mauch said. "I never thought I would need two catchers."

◆　◆　◆

From 1984 through '89, New York Yankees first baseman Don Mattingly was one of the best players in baseball. The five Gold Gloves he won over that period were sometimes overshadowed by his six-year averages of .327, 203 hits, 114 RBIs and 27 home runs.

But Mattingly, the 1984 American League batting champion, played for mediocre Yankee teams that never qualified for the playoffs over his first 13 major league seasons. When the 1995 Yanks qualified for a wild-card spot, Mattingly was only a shell of his former self, tormented by a bad back and ready to end his career. It was a bittersweet closing scene for manager Buck Showalter.

"I remember in the 1995 playoffs, his back was hurting so bad, he couldn't sit down all the way back on the flight from Seattle," Showalter said. "He walked into my office and said, 'The hell with it. I've got two weeks left in my career.' He couldn't torque with his back. He knew he'd blow it out. He would hit singles, doubles, an occasional home run. But he said, 'I'm going for it.'

"For those two weeks in the playoffs, he was the player everyone remembered, the player he was before. The guy couldn't even sit down. He would come in at 11 or 12 o'clock, just to get his back to the point where he could get on the field that night. The media wanted to know why he was in the lineup; he was hitting maybe .260 or something. But people didn't realize what he meant to the club. He knew he was going to shut it down."

Mattingly justified Showalter's faith. After basking in the emotional embrace of 57,178 adoring fans at Yankee Stadium in the Division Series opener against Seattle, he stroked a sixth-inning single that snapped a 2-2 tie in an eventual New York win. Then he crashed a tie-breaking home run in a Game 2 victory, triggering another emotional outburst from 57,126 fans.

"I'll never forget the crowd when Bob Sheppard introduced him (in Game 1)," Showalter said. "He had finally made the playoffs after all these years. Then when he hit that home run (in Game 2), the dugout, old as the stadium was, was actually shaking.

"To this day, all the guys who played on that Yankee team will tell you that was the loudest they had ever heard Yankee Stadium—when Donnie was introduced, and when he hit that home run."

◆　　◆　　◆

Another beautiful summer evening in Los Angeles turned ugly for a pair of Phillies when a Dodgers hitter popped a fly into shallow left field. Philadelphia's 160-pound shortstop, Larry Bowa, went racing in pursuit while a freight train of a man came chugging in from left: Greg "The Bull" Luzinski.

The combination of early evening twilight and crowd noise kept the converging fielders from hearing each other. The collision was violent and mostly one-sided, like when a bug buzzes into the windshield of a 18-wheeler. Luzinski caught the ball while Bowa played the role of poor insect.

"I remember going for the ball and hearing the sound of somebody puffing and grunting," Bowa said later. "The next thing I remember was waking up and looking up at the sky and Bull saying, 'Are you OK, man?' "

Bowa had to leave the game, but when he returned to the lineup he offered to get Luzinski "a bleepin' cowbell to put around his neck" so Bowa could know where the Bull was at all times.

♦ ♦ ♦

In a game played in the late 1970s, San Diego lefthander Bob Shirley was getting belted around in the first inning, prompting a visit from catcher Gene Tenace and manager Roger Craig. As Craig conferred with his battery at the mound, he looked at Tenace and asked, "How's he throwing?"

"I don't know," said Tenace, "because I haven't caught one yet."

Tenace's response gave the situation a lighthearted air, and Shirley went on to throw six straight shutout innings in an eventual Padres' victory.

♦ ♦ ♦

Former Atlanta broadcaster Milo Hamilton told about a memorable play in an August 29, 1969, game at Wrigley Field when the Braves were on their way to the N.L. West championship. The Cubs, serious contenders in the East, tried to go for the early kill.

"Both races were tight. It was a big series," Hamilton recalled. "In the first inning of the first game, the Cubs had runners at second and third with nobody out, and they didn't score because the Braves pulled off a triple play. Seven people handled the ball! And, the final out was made on a tag play by the left fielder, Rico Carty, at second base. He had come in to back up the play and tagged out the runner at second!"

The unusual "triple" started when Billy Williams grounded to first baseman Orlando Cepeda with Don Kessinger running at third and Glenn Beckert at second. Cepeda stepped on first for one out with Kessinger holding, but Beckert broke for third and the Braves caught him in a rundown. Kessinger, seeing that Beckert was hung up, broke for home and was thrown out. Catcher Bob Didier fired to Carty covering second to nail Beckert and complete the triple play.

That got the Braves out of a jam, but the Cubs still won, 2-1.

◆ ◆ ◆

The game at Kauffman Stadium was hyped as a showdown between two great pitchers—Texas' Nolan Ryan and Kansas City's Bret Saberhagen. Fans lined up for tickets at 8:30 in the morning. By the time it was over, hardly anyone remembered they had pitched.

"I kept thinking that everybody came to see Ryan and Saberhagen, and it turned into a complete fiasco," Royals catcher Brent Mayne said.

A fiasco, maybe, for the several thousand of 38,523 fans who left when both Ryan and Saberhagen were pulled after seven innings. But Mayne had another thought: "I kept thinking that people got their money's worth."

Did they ever—two games for the price of one.

The game started at 1:36 on a Thursday afternoon and ended at 8:04 that night—18 innings, 6 hours and 28 minutes of baseball fun. The Royals won, 4-3, when Kevin Seitzer scored on pitcher Kenny Rogers' throwing error.

Mayne caught all 18 innings and called for 354 pitches. Plate umpire Jim Evans looked at 634 pitches. After departing, Saberhagen went into the crowd to give his wife the car keys so son Drew could make his 6:30 baseball practice, watched a while longer and then got back into uniform for the 14th inning. There was plenty of baseball still to play.

Afterward, Saberhagen was asked how he liked his first-ever matchup against Ryan.

"I don't know," he mused. "I think I enjoyed it. Was that today or yesterday?"

An oddity: The longest day (by time) in Royals history came on the anniversary of "The Longest Day"—the World War II invasion of Normandy on June 6, 1944. The game was played June 6, 1991.

OH, WHAT A RELIEF IT IS

Ron Davis, coming off a 29-save season, was proud of his 1984 numbers, even though he had let two leads slip away in the final week as his Minnesota Twins slipped out of pennant contention. Still, the 6-4, 210-pound righthander was comfortable enough to go on a winter goodwill tour through South Dakota with former Twins great Tony Oliva, broadcaster Herb Carneal, catcher Tim Laudner and team publicist Remzi Kiratli.

Patrick Reusse of the *St. Paul Dispatch-Pioneer Press* recounted a story from that caravan for *The Sporting News*, focusing on a side-trip to tiny Redfield, S.D., to visit 90-year-old Cora Goodell, who was described by Oliva as the world's greatest Twins fan. "She is Tony's wife's great aunt, or something like that," Davis said.

Davis took the story from there:

"We pull up in front of this little old house, and there's a dog (a black Labrador) out in front, sitting in the back of a pickup. The other guys—Tony, Herb and Tim—go by the dog, scratch him behind the ears, and the dog loves it. I reach over to touch it, and all of a sudden that dog is snarling and barking—like to tore me apart. Right off, I thought that was strange, because I usually get along with dogs.

"Now we walk into the house, with Tony leading the way. He gives this lady a hug, and Laudner gives her a hug, and Carneal gives her a hug, and Remzi, the kid from the P.R. department, gives her a hug. Everyone is smiling and laughing, and she is thrilled to death. I'm last in line. Remzi says, 'And Cora, this is Ron Davis.' She sees me standing there and gets this look on her face. I couldn't figure it out; she was angry. If looks killed, I would've been dead right there.

"She says to me, 'I don't like you. I don't like it when the manager brings you in to pitch.' Then she starts reaching for her cane. I thought she was going to start strapping me with it. I sat way across the room, out of cane's length. I started thinking: She must have shown that dog my picture and said, 'If this guy ever comes around here, get him.'

"Then we start talking about the Twins and she knows everything about our club. She knows Tony is coming back to the big leagues as a (first base) coach, and she says to him, 'If there's one thing you can do with the Twins, I hope it's get rid of Davis.' I'm sitting right there, and she is telling Tony to get rid of me.

"After a while, Remzi is going to take a picture. So I get over there with the rest of the guys, and she didn't want me in it. She told me to trade places with Remzi; she wanted me to take the picture. Remzi finally talked her out of that. We left there, and those guys horse-laughed at me for the next two hours."

Laudner found the experience uplifting. "It was awesome to be there,' he said. "We got back on the road and I said, 'Tony, you don't have any more relatives for R.D. to visit and brighten their day, do you?"

But Oliva added an addendum to the story.

"What Davis did not tell you is that he won her over," he said. "When we left, they were friends. Cora said, 'Now that I've met you, I know you're a nice man. I'm going to pray for you. I won't be mad the next time the manager brings you into a game.'"

Davis admitted he had left on good terms. But he planned to cement the relationship during the 1985 season—just in case.

"I'm going to try to get a ticket for the All-Star Game (at the Metrodome) and send it to her," he said. "I hope she feels well enough to make the trip to Minnesota for the game. As long as she doesn't bring that dog with her, we'll get along fine."

◆　　◆　　◆

Life can be interesting for relief pitchers warming up at Wrigley Field, especially those not wearing a Cubs uniform. The bullpens at Wrigley are located in foul territory down the left and right field lines, putting pitchers and catchers in close proximity to the always rowdy Chicago fans.

"I was warming up in Chicago one day, right next to the stands," former St. Louis lefthander Rick Horton recalled. "I was getting ready to come into a game against the Cubs, warming up about three feet from the fans."

Horton noticed one fan lining items along the top of the wall that separates the fans from the bullpen and playing field. The items, he quickly discovered, were mustard and ketchup packets that the man pounded, one after another, spraying the contents with a fair degree of accuracy at the unsuspecting pitcher.

"When I went into the game," Horton said, "I had yellow and red splotches on my uniform. (Manager) Whitey Herzog looked at me like I was crazy. He never said anything, but I'm sure he must have thought I was eating in the bullpen. And not doing a very good job of it."

Food was allowed in the Cardinals bullpen during Horton's six years in St. Louis (1984-87, 1989-90), "but it wasn't normally a good idea." St. Louis relievers found other ways to pass the time until their services were needed.

"I remember certain guys would sleep during the game," Horton said. "Lee Smith would nap until about the seventh inning. He would sack out in the pickup truck (parked along an inner access ramp that circled St. Louis' Busch Stadium).

"It was really a case of doing whatever made you relax. We always played a lot of games, kind of a loosening-up thing. Of course, you had to pay attention to what was happening on the field, but we'd play *Password*, *Family Feud*, those types of games. Bill Dawley was a great Richard Dawson."

◆ ◆ ◆

Atlanta backup catcher Bill Nahorodny thought it was business as usual when he delivered a pinch-hit single off Philadelphia left-hander Steve Carlton with two out in the eighth inning of a game played May 5, 1980. But he quickly realized something was different when he stood on first base as fans gave the Phillies star a standing ovation.

"I didn't know he had a no-hitter going," Nahorodny admitted to Phillies first baseman Pete Rose. "I was down in the bullpen the first half of the game and wasn't paying that much attention."

◆ ◆ ◆

With bullpens located in close proximity to seats in most major league ballparks, there's always a fair amount of give and take between players and fans. Sometimes the exchanges can be clever.

"I remember we were playing in New York one day," said then-Detroit reliever Todd Jones. "The bullpens in Yankee Stadium are beyond the left field fence and there was one fan who kept yelling at me, 'Can I get a ball? Can I get a ball? Can I get a ball?' Finally I told him, 'No, I can't do it now while the game's going on.

"He said, 'That's OK, I'll get one when you pitch.' "

◆ ◆ ◆

On April 8, 1974, slugger Hank Aaron rewrote baseball history when he hit record home run No. 715 off Los Angeles Dodgers left-hander Al Downing in the Braves' home opener at packed Atlanta Stadium. Relief pitcher Tom House played a non-scripted role in the event when he caught the historic drive in the Braves bullpen and returned the souvenir to his teammate.

"Everybody in the bullpen was assigned a designated area," House recalled. "It was maybe 10 yards for each player. We all had agreed not to fight for the ball, to let the player catch it in the area he was assigned. Assignments were made by seniority, with the more experienced players getting spots closer to the left field line on out. Buzz Capra and I were the last two, out more toward left-center field.

"If I would have stood perfectly still, the ball would have hit me in the forehead. It was not a great catch or anything. It all happened like it was in slow motion. I remember (left fielder) Bill Buckner climbing the fence. He got high enough, but his timing was off a little bit. I remember catching the ball, then running toward home plate as fast as my little legs would carry me. I had to fight my way through the crowd.

"When I got to Henry, he was hugging his mother. I remember there was a tear coming down his cheek. That's when the scope of the moment really hit me. It was just incredible emotion. I handed him the ball and he took it and said, 'Thanks kid.'"

◆ ◆ ◆

Rollie Fingers, the hard-throwing reliever with the handlebar mustache and nerves of steel, helped set the bar for major league closers. He was an American League MVP, a Cy Young winner and a World Series MVP over a 17-year career that produced 114 wins and 341 saves. Fingers also raised the bar in another bullpen prerequisite.

"Rollie's just a daydreamer," said former wife Jill in 1973. "When he does daydream, though, it's about baseball. Everybody teases Rollie about being a giant flake, but he knows baseball as well or better than the other players."

Fingers preferred to describe himself as occasionally absent-minded. His Oakland teammates liked to tease him about the time he went to the plate without a bat.

"I never got to the plate," Fingers said. "I just stepped out of the dugout during an exhibition in Salt Lake City. In all our other exhibition games, the bat racks were outside the dugout. There, they were inside. As soon as I got on the field, I realized what was happening, but you know those guys. They said there goes Rollie doing something dumb again."

His Athletics teammates also would not let him forget the time he stood on the left field line, hat over heart, well after the game-opening national anthem had concluded.

"For crying out loud," Fingers said. "Those guys make such a big thing out of that. They say I was standing out there alone for two minutes. It was only for five or six seconds.

"I realized it when I heard everybody clapping. I asked myself, 'Why is everyone clapping?' Then I figured out that the national anthem had been ended. I was just thinking about the ballgame."

The easy-going, always-cool Fingers was the perfect pitcher to pull off one of the "flakiest" plays in World Series history. The 6-4 righthander was working in relief of Catfish Hunter in Game 5 of the 1972 Fall Classic when A's manager Dick Williams decided to take drastic action to thwart a Cincinnati rally.

Joe Morgan was on third base and Bobby Tolan at second with two out in the eighth inning as Fingers faced Reds cleanup hitter Johnny Bench. Fingers ran the count to 3-and-2, prompting a visit from Williams. The manager pointed to Bench, then the on-deck circle, then first base, indicating that he wanted to intentionally walk Bench. As he went through all the motions, he told Fingers to throw a slider over the middle of the plate.

"Williams started pointing everywhere and all the while he's telling (A's catcher) Gene Tenace and me how Geno is going to stick his arm out and then hop back behind the plate," Fingers said. "I came up nonchalant and I looked over to third base and I heard Joe Morgan yelling, 'Be alive! They're going to pitch to you.'

"As soon as I heard that, I got rid of the ball quick. I don't know whether Bench heard him or not—he looked about half ready. Bench looked like he couldn't tell whether it was going to be a ball or strike and as if he thought he would be better off taking it. The pitch was right there over the outside corner. It couldn't have been in a better place."

Bench started to throw his bat away and run to first, before realizing he had been duped. But the play became only a footnote in Cincinnati's 5-4 victory. The A's, however, won the Series in seven games.

◆　◆　◆

In baseball circles, seeing is not always believing. And spying is a matter of interpretation.

Whitey Herzog was managing the American League West-leading Kansas City Royals late in the 1976 season and the hard-charging Oakland Athletics were in town. In the sixth inning of the September 21 series opener, a groundskeeper stationed near the A's bullpen quietly called the Royals bullpen to report a blatant case of baseball subterfuge.

"They were looking at our catcher (through binoculars), getting the sign, and they had a walkie-talkie relaying it over to the bench," Herzog said. "Now isn't that something?"

According to Herzog, A's reliever Jim Todd was standing on a ladder, idly watching the game, while Rollie Fingers hunched behind him with binoculars, peering in at catcher Buck Martinez's signs.

Herzog informed plate umpire Nestor Chylak and demanded a search. Umpire Joe Brinkman was dispatched to the bullpen but found nothing. Then Chylak and Greg Kosc went out. Nothing.

So Herzog, taking matters into his own hands, charged into the bullpen, yanked up a towel and snatched up a pair of binoculars in triumph. The A's relievers expressed shock over Herzog's accusations, explaining they were simply scanning the pass section of Royals Stadium to make sure family and friends got their tickets. And what of the walkie-talkie?

"We had a CB radio down there, too," cracked Fingers.

Even Chylak joked about the matter.

"Next, they're going to have radar out there," said the grizzled umpire.

Although his Royals won, 3-1, Herzog was not amused.

"If they were just watching beavers, I wouldn't say a thing about it," he said.

◆   ◆   ◆

Closers, always on call to get a late-game summons in a pressure-filled situation, approach their craft in different ways. Some do everything within their power to relax; others prefer to work themselves into a frenzy. Former San Francisco Giants closer Rod Beck began preparing for every game in the sixth inning with a tried-and-true routine that gave him his mental edge.

"I'll go into the clubhouse, I'll start stretching, I'll watch the umpires on TV, trying to get a feel for how their strike zone is that day," Beck said. "Then when I go to the bullpen, you start playing the game in your head, situation by situation. Either you're up by three or two or one, your emotions are running wild at that point. When the phone rings, it's total concentration.

"The second that manager gives you the call, it's just like tunnel vision. You go out there, and you don't hear the fans, you don't even see your teammates behind you—I mean, you know they're there, but it's just you and the catcher, that's all there is."

◆   ◆   ◆

Roberto Hernandez will be remembered as one of the game's elite closers, a fireballing righthander who posted more than 300 saves in the 1990s and early 2000s. But the 6-4, 250-pound Puerto Rican's biggest save might have come off the field, when he battled through a courage-testing ordeal that might have cost him his strong right arm—or even his life.

In 1991, Chicago White Sox prospect Hernandez was throwing on a chilly spring training day in Florida when his right hand went numb. The problem was blamed on the cold weather, and Hernandez gave it no more thought—until, that is, he was assigned to Class AAA Vancouver and the numbness persisted. His right hand seemed to be frozen. And this time it wasn't blamed on the cold Canadian weather. A specialist diagnosed a dangerous situation: Hernandez had a blood clot in his right forearm, and surgery was necessary—right away. He listened to the potential results:

"A: I could die on the operating table; B: I could come out alive but lose my right arm; C: I'd have a slim chance of being a major league player," Hernandez recalled. "At the time, I was just hoping to be alive."

On June 4, 1991, Hernandez underwent 11 hours of surgery. But the vein did not fuse properly, and five more hours of surgery were required the next day. Amazingly, Hernandez was pitching again by August, and he was called up by the White Sox in September. He made his major league debut—as a starting pitcher—against Kansas City in a September 2 game at Comiskey Park.

The stadium was jammed by 37,187 fans and the press box was filled with reporters from around the country. But they had not come to see the hard-throwing rookie. They were drawn by the major league return of Bo Jackson, who was making his comeback with the White Sox after undergoing hip replacement surgery because of a football injury.

Hernandez stole the show. While Jackson was going hitless in three official at-bats, Hernandez sailed through seven scoreless innings, losing his no-hit bid when the Royals' Bill Pecota doubled to start his final inning of work. It was the only hit Hernandez allowed in a 5-1 victory.

"It sounds like a fairy tale, but it happened," Hernandez said. "And after the game, instead of going to Bo Jackson, all the reporters were going to me."

◆　◆　◆

All closers experience the horror of a ninth-inning home run, the nightmare of a horrible outing that results in a blown save for a deserving teammate. The trick is to minimize those moments—and forget.

Dennis Eckersley, whose 390 career saves rank third on baseball's all-time list, knows that's easier said than done. The former Oakland bullpen ace couldn't sleep the night after surrendering the stunning ninth-inning, Game 1-deciding home run to Los Angeles slugger Kirk Gibson in the 1988 World Series, and the pain didn't end there.

"How did I get past it?" Eckersley said almost seven years later. "I honestly don't know, other than to say that over time, I got some distance. Looking back, it doesn't seem all that difficult. You know, that was like 250 saves ago. Now the Alomar thing ... that hurt far more."

Eckersley was referring to another two-run, ninth-inning homer, this one delivered by Toronto second baseman Roberto Alomar in Game 4 of the 1992 A.L. Championship Series. Alomar's homer tied the score and the Blue Jays went on to win the game in 11 innings—and the series in six games.

"I was like a little kid after that game," Eckersley said. "I remember I walked to the car with my wife. I got behind the wheel and then I just broke down, that was it. It was just something I had to release. How could I hold it in?"

◆　◆　◆

Kent Tekulve, the submarining righthander who was a premier closer over a long major league career that stretched from 1974-89, also recalled one day he did not get credit for a save—at least not officially. The Pirates' closer was called in to protect a one-run, ninth-inning lead in a 1979 game at San Francisco's windy Candlestick Park.

"We were leading by one run with two out in the ninth inning when Jack Clark, of all things, beat out a bunt," Tekulve said. "Darrell Evans, a lefthander, was the next batter, and Mike Ivie, a righthander, after him. (Righthander Enrique) Romo had already pitched, and (manager Chuck) Tanner wanted to keep me in the game in case Evans got on, so I could pitch to Ivie.

"Managers must sit in their room and dream up zany things to do in a game."

Tanner made an unusual double switch as he brought lefthander Grant Jackson in to face Evans.

"He got the brilliant idea of hiding me in left field, figuring that Evans, a pull hitter, would never hit a ball in that direction," Tekulve said. "You know what happened. Evans hit a fly ball to left field and for one of the rare times during the year (at Candlestick) the wind was not blowing. I came in a few steps and made a routine catch."

◆　　◆　　◆

Terry Forster was a solid lefthanded reliever who had to deal with some weighty issues toward the end of his 16-year major league career. Pitching for the Atlanta Braves from 1983-85, and the California Angels in 1986, Forster's 6-foot-3 body carried as much as 260 pounds, a constant source of concern for team officials and fodder for late-night TV host David Letterman, who labeled the pitcher "that fat tub of goo."

Trying to combat the problem, the free-wheeling Forster spent three weeks of the 1985 offseason in the La Costa Lifestyle Center in California with his wife and three daughters. He exercised, cut his calorie intake to 800 per day and learned about such things as behavior patterns and stress management.

"When I got here," Forster said, "I ordered room service—a diet dinner for me, naturally, and two pizzas for my daughter Whitney. Only she didn't like them, so I ate 'em."

Whitney was 15 months old at the time.

Off the field, Rich Gossage was mild-mannered, friendly and easy to like, a welcome presence at a family reunion or in a major league clubhouse. But, oh, was he nasty when he stepped on the mound, transforming instantly into the intimidating, hard-throwing, mean-spirited Goose.

"My wife wouldn't know me out there," said the New York Yankees' 6-3, 220-pound closer in 1981. "If she ever came out to the mound and talked to me, she'd divorce me. I'm an S.O.B. out there. I don't like anybody with a bat in his hands because he's trying to hurt me with that thing.

"Hate is an ugly word, but I hate hitters. When I come into a game, I've got that adrenaline pumping. I look at that batter and, yeah, I hate him. I want to knock the bat right out of his hands."

Gossage, who recorded 310 saves over a 22-year career, did not seem to like teammates, either. When catcher Barry Foote, who had joined the Yankees in mid-1981, worked with him for the first time, he made the mistake of walking to the mound to warn the big righthander not to get careless.

"What the (bleep) are you coming out here for?" Gossage screamed. "Get the (bleep) back there and catch."

Former Yankees pitching coach Stan Williams also got an earful when he trotted to the mound to impart words of advice.

"What the (bleep) are you doing out here?" his pitcher demanded.

"I went out there a lot after that," joked Williams, "but always to shake his hand after he got the last out."

◆　　◆　　◆

Rob Dibble, a key member of Cincinnati's "Nasty Boys" relief corps in the late 1980s and early '90s, was almost as flaky as he was intimidating. After pitching the eighth inning of an early-season 1989 game at Houston, manager Pete Rose's 6-4 righthanded setup man retired to the clubhouse, undressed and threw his uniform in a washing machine.

As Dibble was heading for the shower, he was intercepted by pitching coach Scott Breeden, who told him in a panic, "You're pitching the ninth."

"Quickest I've ever dressed in my life," Dibble said. "Hey, we had a two-run lead. I figured (closer) John Franco would pitch the ninth."

◆　◆　◆

Major league debuts can be traumatic as well as memorable. It would have been understandable if Jeff Reardon had contemplated another profession after appearing in his first game for the New York Mets in 1979.

Reardon worked a scoreless eighth inning against the Cincinnati Reds in his Shea Stadium debut and stood to be a winner as he warmed up for the ninth. Left fielder Joel Youngblood's two-out, two-run homer in the bottom of the eighth had given the Mets a 4-3 lead. Reardon faced George Foster to lead off the ninth, and the slugging left fielder fouled a pitch straight back and into the throat of home plate umpire Ed Montague.

As team trainers attended Montague, Reardon stood silently on the mound. After more than 10 minutes, a stretcher was brought out and Montague was wheeled away, replaced by second base umpire Dutch Rennert. The game resumed without the nervous rookie having thrown a ball for almost 20 minutes.

The next pitch was a doozie. Foster, hitless in his last 10 at-bats, drove it 400 feet over the left-center field wall to tie the game. Catcher Johnny Bench followed with a double to end Reardon's workday. When Bench came around to score during the Reds' five-run uprising, Reardon was credited with his first loss.

To say the bulldog righthander persevered through that difficult debut is something of an understatement. Over the rest of his 16-year career, he posted 367 saves, fourth on the all-time list.

◆　◆　◆

So how long does it take to spot a major league closer? Mike Krukow, a righthander who pitched 14 seasons with the Cubs, Phillies and Giants, knew something special was brewing the first time he saw Bruce Sutter—a hard-nosed youngster with that devilish split-finger pitch.

Krukow was pitching in a 1974 game at St. Petersburg, Fla., for Key West of the Class A Florida State League, "probably the worst team (37-94-1) in professional baseball that year.

"I'll never forget Bruce that night," Krukow said. "I was losing, 2-1, in the ninth inning and had the bases loaded with no outs. Bruce came in and struck out the next three guys on 10 pitches.

"We all knew, even then, that Bruce would be in the big leagues."

Gregg Olson considered himself part of the "now generation." That's why he was well beyond "miffed" when the 1991 Baltimore Orioles staged a "Turn Back the Clock" promotion at Memorial Stadium that set him back about 25 years.

Olson, the curveballing closer who had posted 64 saves over the previous two seasons, was called on to protect a 4-3 ninth-inning lead in a game against Minnesota on a day commemorating the Orioles' first World Series championship in 1966. But the 6-4 righthander, decked out in his 1966-era uniform, threw three wild pitches and committed an error as the Twins rallied for an 8-4 victory.

"I will never again wear anything associated with 'Turn Back the Clock Day,' " fumed the 1989 Rookie of the Year as he peeled off his vintage uniform and fired it, piece by piece, into a trash can. "I wasn't supposed to be here. I wasn't even born in 1966."

Actually, he was. Olson was born two days after the Orioles completed their 1966 four-game Series sweep of the Los Angeles Dodgers. But, alas, none of that championship magic seemed to rub off.

He gave up four hits and two walks. Two runs scored on curveballs that bounced away from catcher Bob Melvin. Another came home when Olson retrieved one of his errant pitches and threw wildly past Melvin. It wasn't pretty for one of the game's top closers.

"I know this much," he said. "You know you're in trouble when you're fielding your own wild pitches. If the Orioles ever have another 'Turn Back the Clock Day,' I don't want to be here."

Workhorse reliever Greg Minton compiled 125 saves for the San

Francisco Giants from 1975-87. But the fun-loving righthander also was a force off the field. The man teammates called "Moonie" could be downright ornery at times.

Like in September 1982 when Minton departed from the Atlanta hotel early, and boarded a bus waiting to transport the team to the ballpark. "Everyone else has left for the park," he told the unsuspecting driver, who accepted the information and promptly started for Atlanta Stadium. When the bus arrived at the ballpark, Minton remained on board to gloat as miffed teammates arrived by cab.

"Between seasons," Minton joked, "I'm going to get a pilot's license. Then I can steal the team plane."

The Seattle Mariners' 1982 bullpen was not lacking for comic relief. The ringleader of the M's "fun brigade" was righthander Bill Caudill, who wrapped his sometimes clever hijinks around a 12-9, 26-save performance.

Caudill was known for his hit-and-run handcuff pranks, courtesy of the manacles presented him by teammate Richie Zisk because he "handcuffed" hitters. "One day, (rookie pitcher) Mike Moore was signing autographs," Caudill said, "so I handcuffed him to the railing of the stands and left him there for half an hour."

But Caudill's best moment came during a rainout at Tiger Stadium in Detroit—a game that was supposed to mark the Mariners' debut on NBC's *Game of the Week*. Losing that national-television exposure did not sit well with the imaginative closer.

The teams were awaiting word on the postponement when Caudill suddenly appeared on the field, wearing a conehead mask and a Gaylord Perry jersey stuffed with a pillow. He entertained fans with a humorous pitching pantomime that bore a striking resemblance to the typical routine of his veteran teammate—complete with fidgets, twitches and other Perry mound antics.

"I've got to make the *Game of the Week* highlights any way I can," said Caudill.

The performance ended when the real Perry ran out and tackled the impostor. Perry held Caudill to the ground and banged the conehead playfully up and down.

◆ ◆ ◆

Some of the lessons learned in the bullpen are best left there. Righthander Dave Sells found that out the hard way when he was working for the California Angels in the early 1970s.

"When I was with California, we had a kid pitcher named Dave Sells who had a major league fastball and slider," said former Angels catcher Art Kusnyer. "But he'd be hanging around the bullpen and he'd see Jim Maloney throwing the spitball. So Sells decided he had to try it.

"He learned the spitter and went nuts over it. He carried K-Y and Vaseline and Slippery Elm and all kinds of junk around in his jacket. But he became too dependent on it. The spitter is a predicament pitch. You use it just once in a while to get out of a predicament. It isn't effective if you try to use it all of the time. In fact, a spitball that doesn't work becomes a nothing fastball.

"At any rate, when Sells fell in love with the spitter, he gave up his slider. And then he couldn't get it back. And it ruined his career."

Sells worked in 90 games and posted an 11-7 record for the Angels and Los Angeles Dodgers from 1972-75 in his much-too-brief big-league career.

◆ ◆ ◆

Seattle lefthander Rick Honeycutt gave new meaning to the term "cut fastball" when he pitched against the A.L. West-leading Kansas City Royals on September 30, 1980.

Honeycutt, the Mariners' starter in a game at Royals Stadium, was unaware the Kansas City players were watching his every move, suspicious that he had been doctoring balls when he pitched against them a week earlier at Seattle.

"We knew exactly what he was doing," said Royals reserve catcher Jamie Quirk. "We just didn't know how he was doing it."

Willie Wilson tripled in the third inning, and watched closely from his side angle as Honeycutt worked to U.L. Washington. When George Brett singled Wilson home, the Royals center fielder asked umpire Bill Kunkel to check the ball and Honeycutt's gloved hand. The examination was revealing.

Kunkel found tape on the tip of Honeycutt's index finger with a tack sticking through. Royals manager Jim Frey said he also found sandpaper attached to the tape. For his transgression, Honeycutt was ejected from the game and received an automatic 10-day suspension—five for the remainder of the 1980 season, five at the beginning of 1981.

"I'm just taking my penalty and trying to get it over," said a contrite Honeycutt, who apparently learned his lesson. He went on to pitch 17 more major league seasons in a good career that ended in 1997 with St. Louis.

◆　◆　◆

It looked like a chapter straight out of baseball's version of the Keystone Kops. The September 22, 1974, game featured those bitter rivals—the Chicago Cubs and St. Louis Cardinals—and was tied 5-5 in the top of the ninth inning at Busch Stadium.

Lefthander Al Hrabosky, who had relieved starter Bob Gibson, was facing Cubs third baseman Bill Madlock. Hrabosky was well known for his "self-psyching" routine, during which he turned his back to the batter, dipped his head in meditation and then slammed the ball in his glove as he stalked angrily to the rubber.

Madlock kept stepping out of the box. Finally, when he strolled toward the on-deck circle to get a resin bag from next batter Jose Cardenal, plate umpire Shag Crawford lost his patience. He ordered Madlock back to the plate.

Madlock ignored Crawford. So the ump instructed Hrabosky to start throwing pitches for automatic strikes. Hrabosky threw one pitch and Crawford called "strike" as Madlock rushed back to the box. Then things really got crazy. Cardinals catcher Ted Simmons remembers Cardenal rushing onto the field and taking a swing at a pitch "at about 42 feet" from the mound, and enraged Cubs manager Jim Marshall at the plate trying to snag a pitch with his bare hand.

Soon, Cardenal, Madlock and Marshall all were in the batter's box screaming at Crawford. The umpire told Hrabosky to throw again, which he did—barely missing Marshall's head. It was a knockdown pitch that sent all three Cubs reeling away.

After order had seemingly been restored, mayhem returned to Busch Stadium.

"Madlock got back in the box and turned to me and asked me what I was looking at," Simmons recalled. "I was at the point in all this where I wasn't much for conversation and all hell broke out."

Simmons clocked Madlock in the jaw. "I must have hit him pretty good," Simmons said at the time. "I cut my knuckles."

That, of course, triggered a brawl that was quelled in minutes. No one was ejected because Crawford decided there were too many guilty parties. A revved-up Hrabosky struck out Madlock and pitched a perfect ninth inning before the Cardinals punched home a run in the bottom of the inning to win, 6-5.

Before the game, the Cardinals had retired the uniform number of the wacky and wonderful Dizzy Dean.

"They must have done this for Diz," said Pat Dean, his widow. "It looked like the old Gas House Gang."

◆　◆　◆

Curtis Leskanic has that loopy personality that helps closers survive in their often-stressful occupation. He has a special affinity for the practical joke.

One day at Dodger Stadium, when Leskanic was pitching for the Milwaukee Brewers, first baseman Richie Sexson aggravated the righthander by throwing baby powder all over him.

Leskanic retaliated quickly. He swiped Sexson's jersey from his cubicle and put it on a clubhouse table with a sign, "Please sign for Richie." Since it's common for players to have jerseys autographed by their teammates as mementos, the Brewers happily complied. Leskanic also conspired with the equipment manager to tell

Sexson that was his only gray traveling jersey available on the trip.

Sexson was in a panic. He couldn't take the field with a jersey bearing autographs. Or could he?

"Richie called the umpires' room and asked them if he could wear a jersey that was accidentally signed by the team," Leskanic recalled. Whether Sexson got an answer between the clubhouse guffaws is uncertain.

Leskanic finally offered a solution. "Sign mine, dude," he told Sexson. "I'll wear it. I don't care. Sign it."

That sounded OK to Sexson, who decided to go ahead and wear his jersey.

Just before game time, a pristine, unmarked jersey materialized, and Sexson was saved from the embarrassment.

◆ ◆ ◆

Baltimore hitters were pounding Detroit pitcher Denny McLain one day in the late 1960s when Tigers manager Mayo Smith told pitching coach Johnny Sain to get a reliever ready to go.

After another hit scored another run, Smith looked down to the bullpen, where nobody was warming up. He said to his pitching coach, 'Johnny, I told you to call and get somebody warmed up.' Another Orioles hit produced another run and Smith looked again toward the bullpen. Still, nobody was warming, so he screamed, "Johnny! I thought I told you to warm somebody up!"

Sain said, "I can't, the line is busy."

As it turned out, Tigers outfielder and pinch hitter Gates Brown was talking to a friend in California—on the bullpen phone.

◆ ◆ ◆

Further proof that bullpen phones are not always used for business was provided in 1980 at San Diego Stadium, where Chicago Cubs coach Joe Amalfitano was treated rudely by a mysterious Padres trickster.

Amalfitano, seated in the Cubs dugout just prior to the start of a game against San Diego, heard a ring. There were three phones on a nearby wall, and first one would ring, then another and another. Amalfitano, unable to determine which one was ringing, answered the first, then the second, then the third—with no response.

Then they started ringing again, one by one. Again he answered and again nobody responded as the frustration grew. Reserve third baseman Steve Ontiveros only poured gas on the fire when he shouted, "Tell them I'm available." Amalfitano finally caught on that somebody in the Padres' right field bullpen was playing games.

When the phone rang again, he grabbed a receiver and engaged in a one-sided conversation. "Hello, Finley?" he shouted. "Hell, no, I don't want that job." Then he slammed down the receiver and moved to the other side of the dugout.

◆ ◆ ◆

Call it fate or simply look at it as a life-changing revelation. But Mike MacDougal might still be languishing in the minor leagues if not for a painful crack to the head that forced him to change his career path from wannabe starter to up-and-coming closer for the Kansas City Royals.

The skinny 6-4 MacDougal, a late-season callup in a 2001 campaign extended by the September 11 terrorist tragedy, was a promising starter who could pop fastballs at close to 100 mph. During an October 4 game against Cleveland at Kauffman Stadium, he had just jumped up to the dugout rail and was talking to pitcher Kris Wilson when Royals hitter Carlos Beltran lost his grip on the bat. It sailed at MacDougal like a whirlybird and hit him on the head. He sprawled on the dugout floor, the victim of a skull fracture, and the right side of his body went numb—including his pitching arm.

"It was scary," MacDougal said later. "When you can't feel your body, it's scary. Probably not necessarily for life, but for baseball."

At first, MacDougal wondered if he would be able to play again. But he slowly improved. There was still some numbness in his right hand the next season, but he kept it secret. Working at Class AAA Omaha, he couldn't find the strike zone. He walked 55 batters and threw 15 wild pitches in only 53 innings.

MacDougal was put on the disabled list, then began working his way back through the low minors. He usually pitched an inning or two per outing, and his fastball was touching 99 mph—sizzling and sinking. The Royals had a brainstorm: Why not make Doogie a closer?

They did and he won the big-league closer job in 2003 spring training. He responded with 27 saves in 35 chances as a colorful rookie.

"I don't know for sure," he said, "but I think (the bat incident) made me into a closer."

◆　◆　◆

World Series Game 1. It's the ultimate stage, the showcase every prospective major league pitcher dreams about. Bases loaded in the sixth inning, two out and ... Dave Parker steps to the plate.

"I was so nervous I couldn't even spit," former San Francisco reliever Jeff Brantley recalled. Brantley, a second-year righthander, was making his first Fall Classic appearance for the Giants against the A's in the opener of the 1989 Bay Area Series at the Oakland Coliseum. The A's already led 5-0 behind Dave Stewart, but that did not diminish the overwhelming fear of failure.

"I think probably the biggest memory that I have is pitching in Oakland, in Game 1, coming into the ballgame with the bases loaded and two outs, and facing Dave Parker," Brantley said. "And at the time, Dave Parker, even though he was at the end of his career, could still hit the ball about a hundred miles; and being a guy who grew up as a Cincinnati Reds fan and seeing all the home runs he hit (there), here I am in the ballgame and I've got to face this guy with the bases loaded.

"It was nerve-racking. (Catcher) Terry Kennedy wanted to throw a fastball in and I shook him off. All I'm thinking is, 'He's going to hit that pitch in the seats.' And Kennedy comes out and says, 'J.B., he's not going to hit your fastball inside.' He goes, 'Let's just jam him.'

"So I'm thinking, 'All right, if you've ever believed in what you have, you better believe in it now.' I threw a fastball in, broke his bat, he hit a ground ball to second base and we got out of the inning."

Brantley pitched a scoreless seventh to complete his memorable day.

Byron McLaughlin was different. The Seattle Mariners suspected as much when the 6-1 righthander had to be scratched from an early career start at Minnesota because of lacerations on his pitching hand. McLaughlin was practicing his delivery in a hotel room, the story went, and shattered a mirror on his follow through when he got too close while admiring his form.

There were other incidents of unusual behavior that made him feel right at home in the Mariners' bullpen. But nothing could top the team's August 1980 visit to Anaheim for a weekend series with the California Angels. During the opener, Mariners manager Darrell Johnson called the bullpen and told coach Don Bryant to get McLaughlin up.

"I can't," Bryant said.

"Why can't you?" asked Johnson.

"Didn't he tell you?" asked Bryant.

"Tell me what?" asked Johnson.

McLaughlin, it turned out, wasn't in Anaheim. With the team playing in Southern California, he had gone to Mexico to marry a woman he met while pitching there the previous winter. But that's only half of this strange story.

Trainer Gary Nicholson was trying to do McLaughlin a favor by toting a bag he left behind back to Seattle. He decided to carry it on the plane rather than try to locate the rest of the team's luggage and check it through. That was a big mistake.

While passing through security at Los Angeles International Airport, Nicholson set off the alarms. There was a loaded pistol in McLaughlin's bag. Nicholson was detained while the team flew home, left to explain why he was carrying a loaded weapon. He did, and caught a later flight that delivered him home 3½ hours behind the team.

THE MEN IN BLUE

There was a foul wind blowing when the Kansas City Royals played at Seattle on May 27, 1981, and former American League umpire Dave Phillips remembers it well.

"It was crazy," he said. "(Amos) Otis hit a slow roller down the third base line. The Mariners let the ball roll, hoping it would go foul, and it began rolling slower and slower, hugging the line, on that Kingdome carpet. Suddenly, as I was standing near second base, I saw third baseman Lenny Randle on his hands and knees, crawling along with the ball, and Otis already standing on first base."

Phillips knew there was going to be trouble the instant home plate umpire Larry McCoy threw his arms up to signal foul. Kansas City manager Jim Frey came shooting out of the dugout. All of the Royals were shouting, "He blew the ball foul! He blew it foul!" Phillips, the crew chief, conferred with McCoy.

"McCoy said, 'Dave, it was the damnedest thing I've ever seen,' " Phillips said. "He told me that Randle crawled along and blew the ball foul. He said he couldn't think of anything in the rule book to cover that and so he ruled it foul."

Phillips, however, decided otherwise. He overruled McCoy, saying Randle had changed the course of the ball without physically touching it. Mariners manager Rene Lachemann put up a spirited argument before going directly to the source.

"Did you blow the ball foul?" he asked Randle.

"Skipper, I swear I never blew on that ball. I never did it," Randle said with great conviction. "All I did was yell at the ball, 'Go foul! Go foul!'"

Phillips and everybody within earshot of the demonstrative Randle suddenly broke into laughter. Lachemann shook his head and returned to the dugout, Otis remained at first and the game resumed without further incident.

Phillips, who worked American League games from 1971-2000, was on friendly terms with many catchers over his career. One, however, took the term "friendly" to an extreme.

"Thurman Munson was forever talking," Phillips said. "He never stopped. He'd talk to the batter, the pitcher, the ballboy or anybody else within earshot. 'Hey, how's your family doing?' he might greet one batter. 'Are the walleye biting this year?' he might ask somebody from Minnesota. 'Did you ever eat at such and such restaurant?' he might ask somebody else."

The Yankees catcher would carry on a constant monologue, probably to distract the hitter. But his gamesmanship also distracted Phillips, who sometimes found it hard to maintain his concentration.

"One day George Brett came up to the plate," Phillips said. "Munson started off by asking him about his golf game, but before he could take it any farther, Brett cut him off.

" 'Listen,' he said, 'my golf game is good, I have not been fishing lately, I can't recommend any good restaurants and I am not dating anybody. Now, would you let me hit?' "

◆　◆　◆

Another catcher who liked to yap it up behind the plate was Joe

Tipton, who played from 1948-54 for Cleveland, Chicago, Philadelphia and Washington in the American League. Tipton, said longtime A.L. umpire Larry Napp, could be very annoying.

"Tipton was always singing or kidding the batter," Napp said. "One day, Ted Williams stepped out of the box, complaining that it wasn't the pitchers, but Tipton who bothered him most.

" 'This pitch is coming right down the middle,' Joe informed Williams. 'Nice and fat. Bet you a hat you don't hit a homer.'

"Sure enough—right down the middle. Ted blasted it out of the park, then turned to Tipton and said, 'You owe me a hat.' For once, Joe was silenced."

◆　◆　◆

Talk about pressure! Umpiring at third base in the intense 1978 A.L. East Division playoff game between heated rivals New York and Boston was bad enough. But then Steve Palermo had to ride home with his inconsolable father.

The senior Palermo, an elementary school principal in Oxford, Mass., played hooky on that memorable Monday afternoon to watch his beloved Red Sox battle the Yankees in their one-game, winner-take-all showdown at Fenway Park. "He was really excited," Palermo said, and the game was everything a serious baseball fan could possibly want.

It was ultimately decided, of course, by light-hitting Yankee shortstop Bucky Dent's three-run, seventh-inning home run over Boston's Green Monster—a high fly ball that barely cleared the wall as Palermo watched in his official capacity.

"After the game, my father comes to the locker room," Palermo said. "He didn't say a word for the first 20 or 25 minutes. Finally we were ready to go and everybody said their goodbyes and we walked to the car to drive home.

"My dad was driving, my mom was in the back and I was in the passenger seat. We're driving along quietly for 15 or 20 minutes and finally I say, 'Dad, that was a hell of a game, wasn't it?' He glanced over at me and said, 'You could have called it foul.'

"I said, 'What?' He said, 'You could have called Dent's home run foul.' I said, 'I couldn't call that foul; it was about 25 feet fair.'

"My dad said, 'You are in Boston. Nobody would have said a word.' "

Palermo was the home plate umpire in another famous game—Dave Righetti's no-hitter on July 4, 1983, at Yankee Stadium. "I remember it was the day before the All-Star break," Palermo said, "because that All-Star Game was scheduled at Comiskey Park, 50 years to the day (July 6) from the first one in Chicago."

The amazing thing about the Righetti game is that not everybody in the ballpark knew what was unfolding as the big lefthander worked into the late innings.

"I remember it was festive that day," Palermo said. "There were giveaways and all kinds of goings-on at Yankee Stadium. Then, when Righetti came out in the top of the ninth, the crowd gave him a standing ovation.

"I thought, 'That's really nice giving the kid an ovation like that. He didn't make the All-Star Game and he maybe should have. He's a good guy and they're showing their appreciation.' "

Then Palermo looked up at the scoreboard. Something, he thought, wasn't right. The Red Sox's line score showed no runs or hits.

"I wondered if the scoreboard was broken," he said. "When we got ready to start the inning, I tapped (catcher) Butch (Wynegar) on the shoulder and said, 'I want to talk to you about something after the game.' He looked back at me and said, 'You better talk now because I'm going to be jumping up and down after the game.'

"I said, 'That's kind of what I wanted to discuss. I didn't realize Righetti had a no-no going.' He said, 'I don't believe you. But maybe that's why you're as great (of an umpire) as you are.' "

◆　◆　◆

Ron Luciano, an American League umpire from 1969-80, was well known for his showmanship, controversial comments and legendary run-ins with managers. The colorful arbiter was particularly obstinate and sensitive when dealing with Baltimore manager Earl Weaver.

Luciano could settle most arguments with the fiery Orioles boss by sending him to an early shower. But occasionally the solution was not that simple. In a May 17, 1975, game at Baltimore, Luciano's dramatic style got him into an embarrassing situation that triggered the wrath of 48,042 fans and the players and managers from both dugouts.

The California Angels and Orioles were tied 2-2 when Tommy Harper, batting with two Angels teammates on base, lofted a fly ball into the left field corner. Luciano, running down the third base line, gave one of his typically flamboyant signals that the ball was a home run. Weaver and shortstop Mark Belanger raced to the umpire and protested violently that the ball was foul as fans rocked Memorial Stadium with boos.

Luciano, struck by the intensity of the protest, decided to consult with his fellow umpires. He listened, considered and changed his call, triggering an equally volatile reaction from Angels manager Dick Williams, who eventually was ejected.

"I never saw the ball," Luciano admitted later, "so I pointed fair. I knew something was wrong when 28 guys came after me. ... But I had a 50-50 chance of calling it right and I had to take it."

Weaver might have come out ahead in that battle with Luciano, but he was a two-time loser on September 30, 1985, when his Orioles played a doubleheader at Yankee Stadium.

The Weaver histrionics—ranting and raving, kicking dirt, cap turned backward—started early and were directed at home plate umpire Nick Bremigan. Weaver, upset over an uncalled dropped ball by Yankees catcher Butch Wynegar on a checked-swing third strike, argued with the umpire in each of the first three innings and finally was ejected. But he refused to leave the field.

"As crew chief, I had to get the game back on track," Jim Evans recalled. "I went to Weaver and tried to reason with him. 'Earl, you're giving me no option,' I told him. 'I might have to call a forfeit.' "

" 'You wouldn't do that,' " Weaver replied.

"One of my partners had a stopwatch and I took it, clicked it and told Weaver, 'You have one minute to leave the field.'

" 'You can't do that,' " Weaver insisted.

"I was walking toward the Baltimore dugout and Weaver was walking right alongside me. We get just about to the on-deck circle and he says, 'How much time do I have now?' I lift up the stopwatch to look at it and Weaver grabs it, like a pickpocket. He jerks it right out of my hand and flings the watch into the Baltimore dugout. Frank Robinson, his bench coach, is sitting there and it lands right under his dangling legs.

"Well, Earl is smirking and I'm seething. But I keep my cool, walk right into the dugout, reach between Robinson's legs and pick up the watch. 'Takes a licking, keeps on ticking—you've got eight seconds,' I said. I was amazed the watch was still working. Weaver smirked again, waved his hand at me and left."

But the story didn't end there. Weaver also was ejected before the second game even started—during the exchange of lineups.

"If my arm was still good," Weaver said later, referring to the stopwatch incident, "I would've thrown it into the stands."

◆ ◆ ◆

The Philadelphia Phillies were playing the Cardinals on one of those brutally hot St. Louis afternoons when a lot of guys would rather have the day off. Lenny Dykstra led off the game for the Phillies with a walk. He quickly attempted to steal second and was out by quite a bit—as second base umpire Eric Gregg ruled.

But Dykstra popped up and really got into Gregg's face. Dykstra called the umpire a few choice names, including one that usually gets a player ejected instantly. But Gregg just kept smiling and shaking his head. He finally said something to the fuming center fielder that really made him blow a gasket.

Phillies manager Jim Fregosi watched the theatrics before slowly making his way toward second base, obviously not in any hurry to leave the comfort of his dugout. After Dykstra finally stormed off the field, Fregosi asked Gregg about the play.

The umpire said, "I called him out. He was out. Then he started calling me every name in the book and I told him, 'Lenny, you can say anything you want, but if I have to stay out here for nine innings today, then so do you.'"

Fregosi told Gregg that was fine with him and headed back to the shade of the dugout.

Gregg recalled a conversation between his son, Jose, and Mike Schmidt's daughter, Jessica, who were classmates at a private school they both attended in Philadelphia:

Jessica: "Jose, my dad told me that your dad called him out on a bad pitch."

Jose: "My dad said, with all the money your dad makes, he should hit that pitch."

◆　　◆　　◆

Umpires go through rookie jitters, just like young baseball players. For future National League umpire Harry Wendelstedt, his first 1962 game at Brunswick, Ga., in the Class D Georgia-Florida League was something to remember—or forget, depending on your point of view.

"When I put the pants on, they fit me like leotards," Wendelstedt recalled, referring to his first mail-order professional uniform. "Well, the third pitch of the game did it. The leotards couldn't stand the pressure. They ripped right up the butt.

"There I was, with only my long johns between me and the crowd. They howled and the ballplayers let me have it, too. It wasn't bad enough I was excited, working my first game on opening day. I was ready to call it a career right there.

"In the local paper the next day, on the front page, was a photograph of my rear end with a little arrow pointing to the seam. The headline read: 'Official Opening.'"

In an April 13, 1980, game at Seattle's Kingdome, umpire Ted

Hendry also had to make some "split decisions"—and he kept the Mariners crowd in stitches. Literally.

Hendry, wearing a new uniform while working home plate during a Mariners-Toronto Blue Jays game, bent over in the first inning and heard a ripping noise. Not only had the seat of his pants split, so had the shorts he was wearing under them, providing a full moonshot to fans behind and around the backstop. Hecklers were quick to pounce on Hendry's embarrassing plight.

At the end of the first inning, the red-faced ump retired to the dressing room for repairs. When he returned, a safety pin had closed the gap and ended, temporarily at least, the rude comments. But the pin didn't hold when Hendry bent over, and the pointed result was another trip to the dressing room in the third inning. The adjusted pin was repositioned, but again it failed to hold and Hendry was the butt of even more jokes by the sixth.

Hendry finally found relief when Mariners general manager Lou Gorman provided a pair of blue cutoffs that camouflaged the split in the pants.

Bottom line: Full attention, from both umpire and fans, was returned to the game.

◆　◆　◆

Umpire embarrassment is not limited to missed calls and split pants. Marty Springstead invented, to his chagrin, a new way to break up an argument.

Blue Jays manager Bobby Cox and umpire Durwood Merrill were going nose to nose near home plate during a game in the mid-1980s at Toronto's Exhibition Stadium. Springstead, the crew chief stationed at third base, watched for a minute, then decided to move things along. As he was trotting in, his foot snagged on the grass, he stumbled and fell into the combatants—like a linebacker going into the pile.

Merrill was jostled by the impact and Cox jumped back in surprise. Both looked at him with shocked expressions, wondering what in the world was going on. Merrill quickly went to

Springstead's aid, helped him up and brushed him off. Cox retreated back to the dugout, shaking his head, and the game quickly resumed.

Without saying a word, Springstead had negotiated a peace treaty.

◆　　◆　　◆

Longtime National League umpire Doug Harvey was working games in the era when peace treaties were best negotiated by hardnosed pitchers with intimidating fastballs. He told this story about former Dodgers great Don Drysdale:

"There was a kid, I can't remember his name, who was doing pretty well his first time through the league. He got in against Drysdale and he's digging and digging and digging. I'm watching and pretty soon I hear this loud voice, 'Hey, hey, you SOB,' and I look up and Drysdale is halfway to home plate, hollering at this kid. 'Yeah, you better dig it deep, 'cause you're gonna need a deep hole.'

"The next pitch is about three inches under this kid's chin. He gets up and looks at me, like, 'What are you going to do?' I just said, 'Son, I think you better get in the box and quit digging.'"

Harvey was considered one of the game's outstanding arbiters over a 31-year career that ended in 1992. When asked if the quality of umpiring had improved during his three-plus decades, he offered an emphatic yes.

"Absolutely, it's better now," he said. "People talk a lot now about umpires having short tempers. I go back to Al Barlick, Jocko Conlan, Shag Crawford. If somebody hollered once, they'd stare into the dugout. If you hollered again, they'd walk over to the dugout and say, 'If I need anything outta you, I'll get it outta you.'

"He'd tell the manager, 'If I hear anything else from these meatheads, I'll throw 'em out. And if I don't know who said it, I'll throw you out.' Conlin ejected 22 people in his first season. That's unheard of. People who say umpires are more hotheaded now either weren't there then or have just forgotten what it was like."

◆　◆　◆

Game 6 of the 1986 World Series will always be remembered for the New York Mets' stunning, stay-alive comeback and the game-deciding error by Boston first baseman Bill Buckner. But umpire Jim Evans recalls a moment that has been lost in the glare of that amazing finish.

The Red Sox were batting in the first inning with Mets left-hander Bob Ojeda pitching to Marty Barrett when Evans, stationed at second base, noticed something odd.

"You could hear the crescendo of the crowd building," he said. "I always thought that Shea Stadium was deafening anyway, but something was happening and the noise was building. It wasn't just enthusiasm. When I looked toward the stands I could see people looking into the sky."

Many fans had spotted Michael Sergio, a 37-year-old self-described musician who was descending on the field in a parachute. A "Let's Go Mets" banner was hanging from his chute and 55,078 fans let out a collective gasp, followed by a rousing cheer as he landed near the mound.

"When I looked up and saw him coming, my first thought was that there must have been a plane crash and bodies were falling from the sky," Evans said. "He landed, calmly folded up his parachute and then was escorted off the field by security."

Security was more of an issue for Evans in 1969, when he was a young umpire trying to draw notice while working in the Class AA Texas League. The kind of notice he received one day in a game at El Paso was not exactly what he had in mind.

Evans ejected El Paso manager Del Rice, triggering a storm among fans that seemed to build with every inning. As the game was nearing its conclusion, Evans decided discretion might be in order and approached a local sheriff who apparently was assigned to keep order.

"The sheriff was a big, heavyset guy—he kind of looked like the sheriff from *Smokey and the Bandit*," Evans said. "I told him my partner and I might need his protection leaving the field because the way to the clubhouse was right through the stands. He said, 'Don't worry, I'll be there.'

"When the game ended, we lined up behind him and walked right through the handicap section. One woman hit me with an umbrella. Other fans threw chunks of ice—they were like bricks. Everybody was yelling obscenities, but he led us right through and we finally got to the clubhouse.

"I shook the sheriff's hand and told him, 'I don't think we'd have made it if it wasn't for you.' He looked at me and replied, 'If I didn't have this uniform on, I'd kick your ass, too.'"

◆   ◆   ◆

During the 1994-95 lockout that introduced baseball to replacement umpires, veteran arbiters kept a close eye on a long-existing law in the Canadian province of Ontario that prohibits the use of replacement employees. What would happen, everyone wondered, if the government refused to give the Toronto Blue Jays an exemption when the regular season opened?

"They're going to have to use the honor system," said Richie Phillips, general counsel for the umpires union.

"I saw it happen once," said veteran umpire Doug Harvey, referring to players being allowed to make their own ball, strike, safe and out calls. "In 1990, in Tucson. It was a spring training game, San Diego against Cleveland. At the end of nine innings, they told us they wanted to play four or five more innings. We told them we were finished for the day.

"They said, 'No problem, we'll use our players.' The catchers on each side called the balls and strikes. I stayed around and watched. The second inning ended up in a fight.

"I've always contended I'd pay $500 for a box seat to watch a game played under the honor system because I've never seen anybody murdered."

♦ ♦ ♦

Hall of Fame umpire Jocko Conlan, never known for his patience with whining batters, conducted his own little experiment with the honor system one day when Philadelphia leadoff man Richie Ashburn made one too many protests.

"OK," Conlan said, "you umpire. You call the next pitch."

"Do you mean it?" the startled Ashburn replied.

The next pitch came in belt high, a little inside. Ashburn watched it closely and said, "Strike."

Here's Conlan's version of the rest of the story:

"I put my right arm up and said, 'Strike.' And then I called time and walked out to dust off the plate. As I did, I said, 'Richie, you have just had the only chance a hitter ever had in the history of baseball to bat and umpire at the same time. And you blew it.

"That's the last pitch you call. I'm not going to have you louse up my profession."

Conlan's patience with managers was also short. One day in the mid-1940s, when Leo Durocher was guiding the Brooklyn Dodgers and hobnobbing with theatrical stars, the umpire taught him a valuable lesson.

Durocher had invited comedian and actor Danny Kaye to suit up one day and work out with the club. When game time approached, The Lip told Kaye it would be perfectly all right if he wanted to remain in uniform and sit on the bench.

Not long after the first pitch, the sharp-eyed Conlan spotted the strange face in Brooklyn's dugout. He motioned Durocher toward him and said, "That guy next to you, is he a new ballplayer?"

"Don't you know who that is?" Durocher asked, obviously surprised by Conlan's unfamiliarity with an entertainment icon.

"I haven't the slightest idea," the umpire said.

"That," said Durocher, pausing for emphasis, "is Danny Kaye."

"Oh," said Conlan. "You mean Danny Kaye the movie star? Is that really Danny Kaye?"

"In the flesh," said a beaming Durocher.

"Well get him the (bleep) out of there!" Conlan screamed. "And if he isn't gone in 10 seconds, you can go with him."

◆ ◆ ◆

Lee Elia was managing the Phillies in 1988. The club wasn't playing well and Elia was getting heat from the press, the fans and the front office. Elia, a native Philadelphian, had a reputation for being tough, fiery and sometimes having a short fuse. But some were suggesting he had lost his edge in the midst of a poor season.

On a Sunday afternoon in front of a big crowd at Veterans Stadium, that perception changed. The Phillies had fallen behind early and the fans were already restless and riding the home team when a Phillies hitter ripped the ball down the third base line. It was close, but obviously foul.

As third base umpire Frank Pulli made the call, the crowd groaned. Suddenly, Elia came sprinting out of the dugout and engaged Pulli. The argument started slowly and gained steam as Elia really got into Pulli's face and Pulli returned the favor. Elia threw his gum at the umpire's feet. Pulli dramatically threw Elia out of the game. The Vet crowd went wild and got right back into the game, backing their Phillies.

"After the game," broadcaster Chris Wheeler recalled, "we found out what really happened. Elia runs down the line and says to his good friend Pulli, 'Frank, I know the ball was foul, but the fans and the front office are killing me about not being emotional. So I gotta get thrown out.' Pulli replies, 'OK, but let's make it a good one.'

"And it was all of that. One of the best agruments and ejections I've ever seen. Pulli never filed a report. Elia wasn't fined and everybody in Philly praised him for his emotional display."

◆ ◆ ◆

In 1993, when talk of a bigger strike zone was circulating through spring training camps, major league umpires vehemently denied they had been ordered to call the game any differently. But players watched closely during exhibition games, as did many fans—fanning the flames of yet another great debate.

Others, such as then-New York Mets manager Jeff Torborg, viewed the matter with a been-there-done-that detachment. Torborg recalled a spring training game a few years earlier, when as manager of the Chicago White Sox he was hearing the same discussion followed by the same complaints.

"I'll never forget it," Torborg said. "This guy yells out, 'Hey, Torborg, this game is timeless. Take off the watch.' And the guy is right. Baseball *is* timeless. That's the beauty of it. Is this something we should be tinkering with?"

◆   ◆   ◆

Baseball was indeed timeless for Emmett Ashford, the major leagues' first black umpire. Ashford, who broke the umpiring color barrier on opening day in 1966 at Washington's Griffith Stadium, performed with showmanship, flair and vision, making the game fun for both players and fans.

Boston Globe sportswriter Bob Holbrook filed this report in *The Sporting News* about Pacific Coast League umpire Ashford in 1962, when the aspiring major leaguer was working an exhibition game between the Boston Red Sox and their minor league affiliate in Seattle:

"Like we say, Ashford has flair. When the rains started falling in the game between the Red Sox and Seattle, Emmett called time and said there would be a 30-minute delay. After the allotted time, a shadowy figure emerged from the dugout.

"He was clad in oilskins and a fisherman's hat. It was Emmett. He made his way around the bases sloshing ankle deep in water. In pantomime, he acted out the part of *Old Man and the Sea*, bringing his catch shoreward. Once at home plate, Emmett removed his hat, placed it over his heart and delivered the following announcement in stentorian tones:

" 'Because of the authority vested in me as an umpire and chief of this ballgame, I have no alternative but to exercise my prerogative and declare the contest canceled!'

"Emmett strode from the field accompanied by an extended round of applause."

This story was told by umpire Billy Williams, who was working third base with Ashford behind the plate during an exhibition game involving the Yankees:

Ashford called a half swing by an opposing player a ball, Williams said, and New York manager Ralph Houk came charging out of the dugout.

"Ask Bill about it," Houk requested, asking Ashford to get help from Williams because he could not directly question a ball-strike call.

"No," Ashford replied.

"Ask him," Houk demanded again.

"Awright, awright. Did he swing, Bill?" Ashford inquired.

"No," Williams said.

"Well," Ashford gloated, "there you are, Ralph. Now you have it in black and white. What else do you want?"

During a 1985 roast of Sparky Anderson, umpire Rocky Roe took a lighthearted shot at the Detroit manager's sometimes out-of-sync language skills. The story begins with Anderson screaming at Roe about one of his ball-strike calls.

"Rock," Anderson griped, "where was that pitch at?"

Roe strolled to the Tigers dugout and answered his question with a question.

"Sparky," Roe said, "you're a great manager. You have the possibilities of a dynasty here. I really think I could like you personally, too. But don't you know you don't end a sentence with the preposition 'at?' "

"Well, then," Anderson shot back, "where was that pitch at, dipstick?"

Jose "Chico" Lind was a slick-fielding second baseman and something of a goofball. When he was playing for the Kansas City Royals from 1993-95, he took up the harmonica, a hobby that annoyed more than one teammate.

One day during a game at Boston's Fenway Park, a Red Sox batter doubled into the right field corner and Lind sneaked up behind him, pulled the harmonica out of his uniform pocket and began a squawking rendition of some unrecognizable tune. The umpires quickly put an end to the foolishness.

After the game, umpire Larry Young was asked if there was anything illegal about playing a harmonica on the field.

"Not unless he's playing 'Three Blind Mice,' " Young said.

◆　◆　◆

It was a well-planned, easy-to-execute practical joke on Milwaukee Brewers righthander Don Sutton. The future Hall of Famer, who was notorious for doctoring balls and baiting umpires, was working in a March 25, 1983, exhibition game against the Chicago Cubs at Mesa, Ariz.

The plan was simple: When Cubs shortstop Larry Bowa batted in the bottom of the first inning, he would call time and ask home plate umpire Bob Engel to examine the ball. Engel would throw it out and pull another out of his apron—only the substitute would not be a real ball. Engel would put an orange in play.

"We had it worked out," said umpire John Kibler. "All the Cubs knew about it. Bowa was going to ask to see the ball."

And then … Engel was charged with an error.

"Yeah," Engel said, "I screwed it up by throwing it over Sutton's head."

Brewers shortstop Ed Romero fetched the orange near second base and tossed it to the pitcher, who joined in the joke by pretending to scuff it on the snap of his uniform pants before rubbing it on the mound. He finally tossed it toward the dugout and the game resumed—with a real ball.

Despite Engel's misplay, the crowd loved the frivolity.

◆ ◆ ◆

One play, one missed call, one controversy can define an umpire's career. Terry Cooney, who spent most of his 18-year American League tenure flying under the radar screen, found that out the hard way on October 10, 1990, at the Oakland Coliseum.

Cooney was working the plate in the second inning of the fourth and final A.L. Championship Series game between the Athletics and Boston Red Sox when a storm hit. Boston ace Roger Clemens, already trailing 3-0 en route to a 3-1 loss that would end his team's postseason, began arguing with Cooney about ball-and-strike calls, a tantrum that grew in intensity, exploded into a string of obscenities and eventually earned him an ejection. Clemens, a two-time Cy Young winner and future Hall of Famer, was so aggressive that he later was suspended for five games and fined $5,000 by the league office.

"The magnitude soaked in, the reality, the feeling that it was some kind of big deal," said Cooney, referring to the impact his spontaneous decision could have on the Red Sox's championship hopes, not to mention the rest of his career. It provided food for thought during a nervous offseason.

"I remember once this February, I was in the midst of working on my house when, all of a sudden, my mind shifted," Cooney recalled. "I started thinking about what it would be like umpiring a game in Fenway Park and then going out onto the street—out onto Yawkey Way, alongside the stadium—and wondering how I'd have to handle going through the crowds.

"I never gave that any thought in the past. Oh, when I walked by, a few people might say, 'There goes an umpire.' But I always kept a low profile and most of them didn't know who I was. But I guess that won't be possible now."

◆ ◆ ◆

Joe Brinkman's defining career moment came in the infamous 1983 Pine Tar Game at Yankee Stadium. He was the crew chief when George Brett's ninth-inning home run was disallowed, a ruling that triggered Brett's emotional rampage and created a rift with the Kansas City team that carried into the next season.

Things really got out of hand after the Royals had posted a 3-2 victory over California in a June 24, 1984, game umpired by Brinkman and his crew. Media types hastily scribbled down notes as Royals manager Dick Howser and Brinkman threw some verbal haymakers from different clubhouses in the bowels of Anaheim Stadium.

"If somebody can tell me that's not some of the worst umpiring they've ever seen, I want to hear it," said an irate Howser, who had been ejected for the second straight day by the Brinkman crew—the fourth time in the season. "Something is wrong. I know a couple of those guys (Brinkman and Vic Voltaggio) aren't good umpires. I think they're gutless and they can be intimidated.

"Myself, the coaches and the players can take only so much. The last two games were classics. Twenty-three years, and that's the worst I ever saw."

Howser suggested things might go better with the crew if its members would get in position to make good calls. And he added he would appreciate a little less lip from Brinkman.

"Dick Howser just thinks I'm a crappy umpire," Brinkman told his audience. "He's teed off about the call we made in New York about that pine-tar thing."

When asked what he told Howser during a heated exchange that led to the manager's ejection, Brinkman said, "I told him he was a (bad) manager and he couldn't manage a whorehouse on an Army base. He said, 'Well how come I got such a good contract?'

"It's just a personality thing. I can't be hurt because he doesn't like me. I don't especially like looking at his little puss face, either. I'm not too fond of him, either, because he talks out of both sides of his mouth. ..."

Eddie Stanky was well known for his fire-and-brimstone approach to umpires, both as a player in the 1940s and '50s and his later years as a manager. But "The Brat" also was versatile enough to earn his ejections in a more gentlemanly manner.

One day in the mid-1950s, Stanky was managing the St. Louis Cardinals when star outfielder Wally Moon became enraged by a called strike from umpire Larry Goetz. Moon, ignoring the rule that forbids players and managers from disputing ball-and-strike calls, suggested that the previous "strike" had been inside by stepping back and drawing a line through the batter's box with his bat.

Goetz ripped off his mask and stuck his face inches away from Moon's. "Look, busher," Goetz said, "don't you draw any lines on me or you and that bat are both going to the clubhouse."

Stanky shot out of the dugout and grabbed Moon, wheeling him around for a lecture. "Wally," he said, "I told you you can't get on this fellow. Some umpires you can yell at, but not this guy. I've told you that time and again."

Goetz stood and listened to Stanky's speech. Then he watched suspiciously as the manager headed back for the dugout. Stanky had taken only a few steps when he turned and said, "The pitch *was* inside, Larry."

"Whoa," Goetz shot back as Stanky tried to make his retreat. "Manager, that was a great speech. The only trouble is that it ran one sentence too long. You're out of here!"

◆　◆　◆

Midway through his 20-year career, National League umpire Shag Crawford offered some thoughts about a pitcher whose first big-league season—1955—coincided with his debut.

"Man, what an erratic pitcher he was," Crawford said. "He was fast, very fast, but most of the time he didn't know where the ball was going. Neither did the batter or umpire. He led the National

League in wild pitches with 17 in 1958, the year the Brooklyn Dodgers became the Los Angeles Dodgers."

Yes, that young pitcher was Hall of Fame lefthander Sandy Koufax. And Crawford could not be blamed for his inaccurate assessment.

"Koufax then was wilder than a runaway locomotive," he said. "I never figured he would last in the majors. In those early years, the only time the Dodgers used him was when a game was hopelessly lost. Look at him now. He's one of the greatest in baseball."

◆　◆　◆

When Warren Giles became president of the National League in 1952, he attempted to add a new level of quality control to his umpiring staff.

He drew up a questionnaire that he distributed the following season to each of the N.L. managers, asking them to rate his arbiters. In short order, Giles had received a response from everybody except Pittsburgh manager Fred Haney. He waited and nothing arrived from Pittsburgh. Finally, he picked up the phone and called to check on the delay.

"I didn't send it back because I threw it in the waste basket," Haney said. "I'm in last place. I've got more to worry about than your umpires. If you want a real challenge, you try to rate my ballplayers."

◆　◆　◆

No discussion of umpiring is complete without mention of Bill Klem, the long-acknowledged king of his profession. The "Old Arbitrator" was working the plate one day in the mid-1930s when he became entangled in a verbal battle with Boston Braves pitcher Danny MacFayden.

MacFayden, an easy-going journeyman righthander who was not known for umpire baiting, took exception with a Klem call and stormed off the mound, calling him a variety of names. Then

MacFayden took the situation a step further by removing his glasses and offering them to Klem, an obvious commentary on his bad eyesight.

Just as the umpire was about to explode, Braves manager Bill McKechnie arrived at the scene and pushed MacFayden aside. McKechnie turned to Klem and made a plea for his pitcher. He pointed out that MacFayden was generally a calm and responsible guy. He argued the glasses gesture was a reflex thing and wasn't meant to embarrass anybody.

Klem seemed to calm down and told McKechnie, "I know he's not usually a troublesome fellow, and I just wish he hadn't been hollering so loud when he charged me."

MacFayden, who was standing close by and listening to the manager-umpire exchange, couldn't restrain himself any longer.

"I hollered that loud in case your ears were as bad as your eyes," he said, a remark that triggered an immediate ejection.

Beans Reardon, a colorful and respected National League umpire who crossed paths with Klem early in his 25-year career, was the recipient one offseason of the Bill Klem Award for umpiring excellence. Reardon started his acceptance speech with typical candor.

"It's nice to get the award," he told the audience, "but the truth is that (Klem) hated my guts and I hated his."

THE YOUNG AND
THE RESTLESS

He was an anonymous backup catcher who posted a .149 average for the Williamsport Bills of the Class AA Eastern League in 1987. But baseball fans in that northeast Pennsylvania community will never forget Dave Bresnahan. His talent was strictly minor league, but the "great potato caper" he pulled off in his final professional game will live in baseball lore.

Bresnahan had an idea: Why not shape a peeled potato to look like a baseball and then fire it over the third baseman's head as a ruse to trick a baserunner into an out at home plate? When he tested it on his Williamsport teammates, they dared him to give it a try and he spent several days peeling potatoes and preparing for his stunt.

Bresnahan got his opportunity in the nightcap of an August 31 doubleheader against the Reading Phillies. A runner advanced to third in the fifth inning and, feigning a problem with his mitt, he went to the dugout and returned with his ball-shaped potato. As the pitch came homeward, Bresnahan shifted the potato to his bare hand and heaved it high over the third baseman.

The fake pickoff worked like a charm. The runner headed home and Bresnahan was waiting with the ball to tag him out. But the prank quickly backfired. The umpire was not amused and called the runner safe. Manager Orlando Gomez told his young catcher, "I won't tolerate this stuff" and fined him $50. The parent Cleveland Indians took their disapproval a step further—they branded Bresnahan's act "unprofessional" and released him.

But it didn't take long for the story to draw national attention and Bresnahan to gain local prominence. Details of the caper appeared in wire service stories and newspapers throughout the country. Two nights after he was released, Williamsport promoted its final game of the season by lowering the ticket price to $1 for anybody carrying a potato and invited Bresnahan back to autograph the potatoes—"This spud's for you." He added to the publicity by "paying" his $50 fine with a sack of potatoes.

"I could run for governor of Idaho," joked Bresnahan, a greatgrand nephew of Hall of Fame catcher Roger Bresnahan. On May 30, 1988, the Arizona stockbroker returned to Williamsport for ceremonies retiring his No. 59 jersey, at which time he was presented with a golden potato and a painting commemorating the prank.

"He's probably the only .149 hitter in baseball ever to have his jersey retired," said Ken Weingartner, a team spokesman.

Twice. The Williamsport Cubs, on the 10-year anniversary of the potato ruse, retired Bresnahan's No. 59 again.

◆   ◆   ◆

Bresnahan earned his niche in baseball lore with a potato. Joe DePastino earned his with 11 years of hard labor. That's how long he spent in the minor leagues, five of them at the Class AAA level, before he made his first appearance in the major leagues.

"I always had hope," said the 29-year-old catcher, who persevered through four knee operations, two broken hands and the departure of friends and teammates who gave up on their dream. "I knew I could always get a shot defensively. Heck, I'm only 29 now so I can play another six or seven years."

DePastino was batting .269 in 2003 for the New York Mets'

International League team at Norfolk, Va., when he got the call. Norfolk manager Bobby Floyd delivered the news that DePastino would be meeting the Mets in Houston and the first-time major leaguer passed word on to family members, who gathered in force hoping to see him play his first game. On August 5, one day after his call-up, everybody's dream came true.

"I figured I might be going in," DePastino recalled. "We (the Mets) were way ahead, I got a sense this might be my chance and I really started getting nervous. I was walking up the ramp telling myself, 'It's the same game.' "

The record shows DePastino was sent to the plate as a pinch hitter in the ninth inning of the Mets' 10-1 victory over the Astros, but it does not reflect the joy and excitement that accompanied the moment. All of the Mets, even those who already had retired to the clubhouse, came out to wish him luck. Veterans such as Al Leiter, John Franco and Mike Piazza, as well as younger teammates and family members in the stands, were as excited as DePastino himself.

"These guys treated me like I was one of them," DePastino said. "They were all great. When I stepped up to the plate, Brad Ausmus was catching for the Astros and I told him I didn't know whether to go in my pants or throw up. He said, 'You'll be OK.' "

Dan Miceli got DePastino to swing and miss at a nasty slider, but the rookie completed his first at-bat with a ground ball to third base. When he returned to the dugout, the whole team was waiting to greet him with high fives and slaps on the back.

"It was awesome," said DePastino, who appeared in one more game as a pinch hitter and defensive replacement in his short-but-sweet 2003 big-league tour. "My first at-bat was exciting, but the best thing was the way they were all standing there waiting for me. That was the biggest thrill, the way they all were pulling for me. I'll never forget that."

And he'll never forget the words of Piazza, who captured the essence—and permanence—of what such a moment means to DePastino and every other career minor leaguer who finally gets his shot.

"Joe," Piazza said, "now you're in the Baseball Encyclopedia."

Matt Winters also was an 11-year minor leaguer when he finally "got into the Encyclopedia." In 1989, the 29-year-old outfielder got his call-up and played 42 games for the Kansas City Royals.

Winters managed to get 25 hits, belt two home runs and bat .234 during his brief big-league stay. But ask him about a highlight and he probably will recall a July 1 loss at Chicago, a game in which he was sent out to pinch hit for Bo Jackson.

The Royals' star left fielder was bothered by a strained thigh and had been used primarily as a designated hitter in recent games. But in the July 1 contest, Jackson started in left and his leg was bothering him as the game neared its conclusion.

"When I went up to home plate and said, 'Winters hitting for Jackson,' the umpire (Joe Brinkman) looked at me and said, 'I believe you, but I want to hear it from (manager John) Wathan first.' It's something I can tell my grandkids, that I pinch hit for Bo Jackson."

He grounded into a forceout.

◆　◆　◆

For a select few, minor league perseverance produces even bigger rewards. Just ask infielder Keith Lockhart.

The lefthanded-hitting Californian spent eight seasons in the minors before finally tasting life in the major leagues with the 1994 San Diego Padres. Then he spent parts of two more seasons in the minors before sticking with the 1996 Kansas City Royals.

Minor leaguers don't make a lot of money, so many of them take offseason jobs to make ends meet.

Lockhart worked for a video store and a pizza parlor.

"I delivered pizzas," he recalled. "That wasn't too bad. The tips were good."

He also sold stereo equipment, gave batting lessons to kids and played winter ball in Venezuela.

His worst job? A chimney sweep.

"It didn't take very long to figure out that wasn't my calling," he said. "You'd get covered with dirt and ash."

Lockhart kept hacking away in the minors, traversing the country from Billings, Mont., to Nashville, Tenn., to Las Vegas—with many stops in between. But after short stays with the Padres and Royals, his pizza-slinging, city-jumping days came to an end.

Lockhart found steady work in Atlanta, where he also tasted success with Braves teams that won N.L. East titles in each of his six seasons. As a playoff rookie in 1997, he tied an N.L. record by banging out four hits in a League Championship Series game.

Lockhart's dream, once a modest hope to play a few games in the major leagues, took on whole new meaning when he played against the New York Yankees in the 1999 World Series.

◆　　◆　　◆

Rollie Fingers played in 16 World Series games and 30 postseason contests over his 17-year major league career, but an early twist of fate almost kept that distinctive handlebar mustache from becoming a lasting image in baseball lore.

Fingers was 20 years old and newly married in 1967 when he started for Birmingham in the opening game of the Barons' Southern League season. Jill, his wife of nine days, sat in the stands at Rickford Field and proudly watched her husband cruise through the first three innings. Then disaster struck. Fingers threw a change-up to Evansville's Fred Kovner, who lined a shot up the middle.

"I saw it about three feet from me," Fingers said. "I threw up my hands in front of my face, but the ball came right through my arms and hit me in the jaw."

"I thought he was dead," said Birmingham manager John McNamara, who would go on to guide the parent Athletics and five other big-league teams over a long managerial career. "Blood was coming out of his right eye."

Fingers fell face down on the mound and teammates rushed out to roll him over. Jill sat watching in shocked silence.

"At first, I was frozen," she said. "I was waiting to see whether he was dead or alive, because he wasn't moving at all. I knew there were places in the head he could be hit and killed. Then he moved his leg, kind of brought it up, and I knew he was alive."

Jill rode in the ambulance to the hospital and then watched in agony for three days as Fingers vomited through his teeth—his broken jaw was wired together—because he was allergic to medicine he was getting. But the near-tragedy had a happy ending.

Oakland owner Charlie Finley called the Fingers at their apartment one day during Rollie's recuperation and told them to go anywhere they wanted in Florida, a delayed honeymoon—all expenses paid. And the following season, Fingers made his major league debut.

◆　　◆　　◆

Former Cincinnati and Detroit manager Sparky Anderson was known for his spring superlatives when assessing the merits of young players. In 1985, the Tigers boss went overboard with an aspiring third baseman named Chris Pittaro.

The 23-year-old switch hitter so impressed Anderson in spring training that the defending World Series champs traded Howard Johnson to the New York Mets, opening up third base. Pittaro batted .314 that spring and struck out only six times in 70 at-bats.

"He's the best young infielder I've had come through camp in 15 years," Anderson gushed. "I'm not comparing him to (Lou) Whitaker and (Alan) Trammell because they were already here when I arrived, but Pittaro is the best new kid I've ever seen."

Pittaro stroked three hits, including the game-tying single, in a 5-4 victory on opening day. But that was the highlight of his career. He was placed on the disabled list in late May, sent to Class AA Nashville a short time later and called back up in September. When his career ended in 1988 in the Minnesota organization, the "best rookie" Sparky had ever seen had managed only 21 hits in 53 big-league games.

◆　　◆　　◆

Gary Sheffield received no such buildup in 1988. In fact, his major league debut came near the end of the season, when the Milwaukee Brewers decided to take a good look at their hot-hitting young shortstop.

Sheffield will never forget his first big-league home run—and with good reason. It also was his first major league hit, it broke up a no-hitter and it set the stage for his first game-winning hit. The Brewers' 2-1 victory came at the expense of the Seattle Mariners and their star lefthander in a September 9 game at Milwaukee.

"It was Mark Langston at Milwaukee County Stadium," Sheffield recalled. "High fastball. It was funny. Everybody used to talk about me being a young kid hitting high fastballs, so guys would try to intimidate me, throwing at me and then coming back with high fastballs to show that I could not hit them.

"Just so happened, Langston was a top pitcher at the time and he threw this high fastball and I hit it, and it went. I think I got a little respect for that. I did not see so many high fastballs after that."

Sheffield's sixth-inning home run broke up Langston's no-hit bid and tied the game 1-1. His second big-league hit, an 11th-inning single off Langston, gave the Brewers a victory.

◆　　◆　　◆

The numbers just did not add up the way the Seattle scouting department wanted. While making final preparations for the June 1987 amateur draft, the Mariners had outfielder Ken Griffey Jr., an outfielder from Moeller High in Cincinnati, with the exact same ranking as righthanded pitcher Mike Harkey from Cal State Fullerton.

Bob Harrison, the Mariners' top scout, knew he had to make some sneaky adjustments. Mariners owner George Argyros lived near Fullerton, and a small-college coach who was a close friend of Argyros had been touting Harkey throughout the spring. And Argyros had always shown a preference for drafting college players.

The night before the final decision was to be made, Harrison decided to fudge on the reports. He brought Harkey's total down and raised Griffey's. He wanted to make sure there was no debate.

Both Harrison and scouting director Roger Jongewaard were sold on Griffey and, as it turned out, they were right.

Harkey struggled through an injury-plagued career. Griffey helped ensure the survival of baseball in Seattle, but not before forcing another tough decision for the Mariners' brass in the spring of 1989.

Griffey was invited to spring training that year so he could get his first taste of big-league life. But he was so dominating on the field, the Mariners decided to keep him on the roster.

"We were going around the room and it kept being mentioned that he had to be sent down," Harrison said. "He'd only played a couple weeks above the (Class) A level and that was at Double-A. Finally, I asked the question, 'Who's going to tell this kid he's not making the team?' "

◆　◆　◆

Mike Sweeney was understandably worried. During 1999 spring training, it appeared his opportunities with the Kansas City Royals were nearing an end.

Manager Tony Muser told Sweeney he would never catch for him again on a regular basis. So he drifted through spring training as a third-string catcher and part-time designated hitter. Almost every day, Sweeney asked reporters if they had picked up any trade rumors. At one point, he heard that he might be headed to Chicago for White Sox lefthander Jim Parque—a deal Sox owner Jerry Reinsdorf reportedly nixed with the admonition, "We're not giving him up for Sweeney."

Then fate intervened. First baseman Jeff King, who secretly had been considering retirement, was injured. Sweeney was rushed into the first base gap and, while his fielding was at first erratic, he blossomed into a run-producing hitter.

King did retire in May and went off to his ranch in Montana. Sweeney hit .322 with 22 homers and 102 RBIs while beginning his trek toward stardom.

Parque? He faded into journeyman obscurity.

◆　　◆　　◆

Roger Clemens, a 300-game winner and six-time Cy Young Award recipient, was asked about the first time he faced somebody in the major leagues and thought, "This is a Hall of Famer. I got this guy's baseball card." The Rocket came up with two nominations.

"One was at Fenway and the other was in Kansas City," he said. "The one at Fenway was Reggie (Jackson). He was with the Angels, and when (public address announcer) Sherm Feller announced Reggie—and he was hitting third or fourth—I had to step back and collect myself. ... My stomach was kind of churning a little bit and I said, 'Well, here we go.' I remember just whipping it in there.

"And the same thing happened when (George) Brett stepped in. They announced George, and you're like, 'Take a deep breath. This is the big leagues. You know you're here and this is where you're going to show it or shut it down.'"

Clemens also recalled his first meeting as a young Boston pitcher with former Red Sox great Ted Williams:

"Word traveled extremely fast that he was in town and might be making an appearance in the clubhouse," Clemens said. "It was 1987, the year after I had won (the Cy Young Award). I went into the back room, where the older players, the old-timers and the instructors were. I went back there to get a pair of sanitary socks.

"On my way there, I kind of glanced over and there were the DiMaggios, and I think Yogi (Berra) was there and, of course, Ted was there. He had a booming voice, and you could hear him. As I got my (socks), he stopped me in my tracks with a big loud voice, 'Hey kid, let me ask you something. I know you throw hard and everything, but if you had to face me, what would you throw me?'

"Of course, I am (saying) Mr. Williams, and Sir, and stumbling. He said, 'I would look for your slider. You know why, kid? Because I could hit your fastball.' I said, 'Yes sir, Mr. Williams.'

"I just kept moving on."

◆　◆　◆

The baseball passion exhibited by Hall of Fame first baseman Eddie Murray over a 21-year major league career had deep roots. Eddie was 8 years old and already enamored with the game in the early 1960s when this story took place:

The Murray children, five boys and seven girls, often played a game they called "Strikeouts" in the garage of the family's house in East Los Angeles. The batter would stand deep in the 20-foot-long garage and try to hit the tennis ball deliveries of a pitcher. The object was to hit line drives through the open front of the structure, with anything bouncing off a wall or the 10-foot ceiling counting only as a strike. The players, by necessity, developed level swings and great concentration.

One time, Eddie hit a ball that cleared the garage, sailing beyond the backyard boundary and into a 30-foot-deep concrete ditch. The kids did not have another ball, so Eddie volunteered to tie a rope around his waist and let brother Venice lower him into the pit. When Venice lost his grip, Eddie fell several feet and banged his head on the concrete.

Charles Murray was summoned and he used a garden hose to pull his son to safety. Everybody was in a panic—except for Eddie.

All he wanted was to resume the game.

◆　◆　◆

Hall of Fame lefthander Steve Carlton never gave much thought to a baseball career when he was growing up in North Miami. "My friends and I weren't the least bit concerned about big league baseball," he said. "The papers barely carried the scores. You thought of baseball as a game to play, not to make a living. ... But I always could throw."

Carlton's throwing ability was manifested in ways other than on a baseball field.

"We used to hunt with rocks," he said. "I used to knock doves off the telephone wires. I was about 12 or 13 then. I figured everybody could hit birds throwing stones. I didn't think my arm was anything unusual."

Carlton remembered walking down the street one day with an ax in his hand. He spotted a quail sitting on a tree branch.

"I was about 15 or 20 feet away," he said. "I threw the ax. It cut the quail's head off and stuck in the tree. We didn't do it to be mean or cruel. We were kids and it was our way of hunting game. There is no difference bringing down a game bird with a rock than a gun."

◆　◆　◆

The darting, fluttering knuckleball that carried Phil Niekro to the Hall of Fame was a gift from his father, a former semipro pitcher who made his living as a coal miner in Lansing, Ohio.

"He started throwing it to me when we had catches in the back yard," Phil recalled. "I was about 12 or 13 at the time. When I missed it, he would laugh. I asked him to teach me how to throw it. I worked on it and we had a lot of fun in the back yard, seeing who could throw the best knucklers.

"He'd come up from the mine, all covered with soot and dust. All you could see were his teeth and eyes. And we'd go right out to the back yard and play catch. Some nights, we wouldn't eat dinner until 9:30 or 10 o'clock."

And pretty soon, something clicked. Phil's knuckleball began doing nasty tricks that baffled even his father and tested his patience.

"Lots of times," Phil said, "he'd throw the glove down and quit. But we'd be right back at it the next day."

◆　◆　◆

Tom Tresh made his major league debut for the New York Yankees late in the 1961 season as Roger Maris was closing in on Babe Ruth's single-season home run record. It was quite an introduction to the big leagues.

"I was up the last month," he said. "I got there the first of September and they had a one-game lead over Detroit. They went on from there and I think won 13 in a row. I didn't know what it was like to be in the locker room after a loss for a long time because we won the whole homestand.

"It was a great thing for me. I was 22 at the time. The pennant race, the home run race. I was in a locker room with great players sitting around me. I looked around and said, 'Why me? Why do I get to do this?' "

◆　◆　◆

When 21-year-old Pete Rose reported to Macon of the South Atlantic League in 1962, manager Dave Bristol eyed the crew-cut second baseman with suspicion. He watched him dash madly to first base after walks, sprint back and forth from the dugout to his position, run the bases with abandon, challenge walls and pace the dugout between at-bats.

"I kind of sat back and watched him running all the time to everywhere," Bristol said. "I asked myself, 'Is he putting me on with all this razzmatazz, or is he real?' Well, he was. He never gave up all year—not once on anything."

◆　◆　◆

It took Bristol less time to decide that young catcher Johnny Bench was destined for big things in Cincinnati. The future Reds manager had Bench pegged for major league stardom "the first time I saw him play" in 1965 for Tampa of the Florida Instructional League.

The impression Bench made in 1966 at Peninsula of the Class A Carolina League was even more profound. After his superlative defensive play, .294 average and franchise-record 22 home runs in 98 games earned him a midseason promotion to Class AAA Buffalo, the team retired his No. 19 uniform. The 18-year-old prodigy also was ushered to the airport with a civic parade.

◆ ◆ ◆

Johnny Bench-type greatness can be spotted early. But some talented players take a little longer to develop. Jack Brett didn't spot baseball genius in son George until well after the future Kansas City Royals star had left home.

"I remember having a serious conversation with his mother (Ethel) one evening," he said. "I told her, 'He can't read, he can't write, he doesn't have good grades, he can't play baseball, he can't play football, he can't play basketball.' I said, 'What is this kid going to do?' Well, Mommy being Mommy, she said, 'But he's such a nice boy.' "

◆ ◆ ◆

It didn't take long for the world to take note of that classic Ted Williams swing—a swing that would produce a .344 career average and 521 home runs.

"I remember the first time I ever saw Ted Williams," recalled longtime teammate and friend Dominic DiMaggio. "It was 1937 and we were both in the Pacific Coast League, me with San Francisco and Ted with San Diego. I was sitting beside our manager, Lefty O'Doul, in the dugout watching Ted take batting practice. Lefty took one look at Ted and said, 'There's the next Babe Ruth.' And Lefty O'Doul was the greatest hitting teacher I've ever known."

◆ ◆ ◆

Kent Hrbek's professional career got off to a shaky start. The former Minnesota first baseman will never forget his 17th—and final—game for the Twins' Elizabethton farm team in the 1979 Appalachian League.

The young lefthanded power hitter, batting with a runner on first base, took a big swing, drove the ball into the outfield gap and crumpled to the ground near home plate with a serious knee injury.

"I remember I was still sitting there in the batter's box when the baserunner came around to score," Hrbek said. "I'll never forget him looking down at me and asking me, 'What in the hell are you doing here?' I never did get credit for a hit, of course, because I never did get to first base."

◆　　◆　　◆

With one game remaining in 1984 spring training, young reliever Rick Horton was called aside by St. Louis Cardinals coach Hal Lanier and told he would be pitching the next day for the final spot on the roster. So would fellow lefthander Dave Von Ohlen, who had pitched in 46 games for the Cardinals in 1983. "I know this is a lot of pressure," Lanier told Horton, "but we need to find out if you can handle it."

Horton remembers pitching five innings in that game against Cincinnati and Von Ohlen working the final four without giving up a run. The next day he returned to Al Lang Stadium in St. Petersburg, not knowing whether his big-league dream had become reality.

"Guys were packing and carrying their gear out of the locker room," he said. "There was a lot of activity, players coming and going, and I had no idea whether I had made the team. There were bags in front of my locker, but I didn't know what that meant. Andy Van Slyke was there and I told him I didn't know what to do."

Van Slyke took the direct approach. "Go ask Whitey (Herzog)," he advised.

"Really?" Horton asked. "Do you think I should do that?"

"Yeah," Van Slyke said, "go ask him if you're on the team."

Horton went to Herzog's office and stuck his head in the door just as the Cardinals manager was emerging from the shower. He was standing there without a stitch of clothing.

"I just wanted to find out whether I've made the team," Horton told him.

"Yeah, yeah, yeah, you're in," Herzog said. "I guess I forgot to tell you."

Horton remembers the moment like it was yesterday. "I was told I had made my first major league team by a naked manager. That's not the way I would have expected it to happen."

◆　　◆　　◆

Larry Bowa was a temperamental, skinny-legged shortstop in the winter of 1965 when the Philadelphia Phillies signed him for a meager $1,500. He was dispatched to the team's Class A Western Carolinas League affiliate in Spartanburg, S.C., where he got a rude welcome to professional baseball.

"You won't believe it," Bowa said. "But it was the first game I ever played, and who do you think was pitching for the other team? Some guy named Nolan Ryan. He struck me out four times. I didn't even get a foul tip. I wanted to go home. I felt like I was overmatched.

"But Bob Wellman, who was my manager, took me into his office and said: 'Hey, young fella, don't let that bother you so much. That guy who punched you out those four times in a row is someday going to be a superstar with that kind of fastball.' "

Wellman, of course, was right about Ryan. And 28 years later, the Texas Rangers righthander entered his final major league season as one of the most revered players in baseball history. A 1993 exhibition game at Houston—one of his four career stops—drew more than 50,000 fans to the Astrodome and made a lasting impression on another young player—Astros catcher Eddie Taubensee, who drove a Ryan pitch off the right field wall for a second-inning single.

"I tried not to think about it, but I'm glad I had the opportunity to face him because I probably never will again," Taubensee said. "When I got (the hit), I tried not to look at him. I was scared. I didn't want him to do anything to me the next time I went up there.

"But it was Nolan Ryan. I kind of peeked when he wasn't looking."

◆　　◆　　◆

Call it gamesmanship. Call it a travesty of justice. Call it anything you want, but suffice to say Wade Boggs' first professional batting championship did not come easily.

It appeared to be in hand on the final day of the 1980 International League season when his Pawtucket team entered the bottom of the ninth inning trailing Toledo, 6-1. Boggs, the scheduled fourth hitter, was toting a league-leading mark of .30695, barely ahead of the Mud Hens' Dave Engle, who appeared to be locked in at .30674.

Toledo pitcher Wally Sarmiento retired the first two PawSox hitters, and Boggs was on deck when light-hitting Ray Boyer stepped to the plate. But Sarmiento walked Boyer on four pitches, none even close to the strike zone and several of which sailed to the backstop. Boggs was forced to bat, needing a hit to stay ahead of Engle.

Pawtucket responded to the shady tactics. Boyer literally walked to second base. No throw. So he moved on to third and literally strolled home as Sarmiento sailed another pitch to the screen. Now, Boggs had to bat. And he grounded out, dropping his average to .30622 and giving the title to Engle.

"I should have pinch hit for him," Pawtucket manager Joe Morgan said later.

Boggs, disappointed over his near miss, bounced back and won the 1981 International League batting title—with a final-day hit.

◆　◆　◆

Major league debuts are moments to be savored by every player who makes it to "The Show." For Florida Marlins broadcaster Tommy Hutton, the memory of his first game with the Los Angeles Dodgers in 1966 was merely a prelude to the unexpected thrill that followed.

"I'll tell you a story," said Hutton, a 12-year major leaguer, when asked about his all-time favorite teammate. "This guy was a teammate for like six weeks, maybe not even that long. I never went out with him, nothing like that, we weren't close friends.

"I was 20 years old, got called up in September by the Dodgers and got put in a game, my first major league game, by Walter Alston, the Dodger's manager, to play one inning of defense behind this guy. It was 11-0, the Dodgers were leading, so they felt it was safe. After the game, it was his 25th win, he came over to my locker and congratulated me for getting into my first major league game."

"He" was Sandy Koufax, who would finish that 1966 campaign—his last—27-9.

◆ ◆ ◆

Bert Blyleven received a rude welcome to the major leagues. But, fortunately, his sense of feeling overwhelmed was only temporary.

The curveballing righthander, who was playing for Minnesota's Class AAA Evansville farm team in the American Association, was called to manager Ralph Rowe's hotel room one night in early June 1970.

"When Ralph told me I was going to the majors, I was shocked," Blyleven said. "The Twins were in Boston and I left right away. It was an all-night flight and I didn't sleep. I was so excited, I couldn't close my eyes."

Twins manager Bill Rigney didn't use his 19-year-old rookie at Fenway Park, but he penciled him in as a starter in the opener of the following series at Washington.

"And the first batter, Lee Maye, hit a home run," he said. "I didn't think much about that, because I knew someone would hit a home run against me sometime. But as Maye was rounding the bases, Frank Howard came out of the dugout swinging two bats. I couldn't believe my eyes. I had never seen anyone so big.

"I knew before the game that I wanted to do well against Howard because he was my father's hero, and I wanted to shine in my dad's eyes more than Howard. But I thought, 'If Maye can reach the seats against me, where is Howard going to hit it?' "

Howard grounded out and Blyleven went on to pitch seven innings en route to a 2-1 debut victory—his first of 287 big-league wins.

◆ ◆ ◆

Former outfielder Kevin Mitchell, who grew up on the mean streets of east San Diego, brought a tough-guy image to the major leagues when he made his debut with the New York Mets in 1984. Second-year Mets phenom Darryl Strawberry had first-hand knowledge of Mitchell's fiery temper, courtesy of a 1981 pickup basketball game in St. Petersburg, Fla.

"We were playing basketball one day," said Mitchell, who was Strawberry's teammate on a Mets instructional league team. "I didn't know anything about Darryl Strawberry. I even thought he was white before I met him. Well, I wouldn't pass him the ball, because where I come from it was run and gun. That was street basketball in San Diego. But he didn't like it and was calling me names.

"I said, 'Hey, you don't know me well enough to call me names. I didn't come here to fight, but I ain't backing down, either.' Well, we went at it. The other guys broke it up. I was mad. I was on top of him, and he was the rookie star. If he was on top of me, they wouldn't have broken it up.

"We laugh about it now, but he says he whupped me. But everybody who was there knows. He don't want to accept that."

◆ ◆ ◆

Anaheim Angels broadcaster Jose Mota, a former second baseman who played two seasons in the major leagues, tells a story about a particularly striking moment he experienced in 1993 while playing for the Omaha Royals in the Class AAA American Association:

"It was a day game and the sky was mostly clear," he said. "Yes, it was the Midwest, but it was (still) unexpected. There were storms in the area, but we were playing in sunshine. I am playing second base when lightning hits one of our light towers.

"The noise from the strike or the thunder was unreal. I see our third baseman, Craig Wilson, go down so fast. He was unbelievable. It was like he got shot or something. Kaboom and everybody thinks, 'Wilson's down! We got a man down!'

"Oh my, the way Wilson went down and stayed on the ground with his hands covering his head, it was hilarious. We talked about him for two weeks after that. Every time there was a storm in the area, we'd say, 'OK, everybody away from Craig, please.' "

♦ ♦ ♦

Righthanded pitcher Brad Voyles enjoyed an outstanding 2000 season for Class A Myrtle Beach of the Carolina League. He posted 19 saves, with a 5-2 record and 1.11 ERA.

The parent Atlanta Braves were so impressed that Voyles was given an outside chance of making the big club in spring training. What an opportunity for the 45th-round draft choice!

But just a few days before Voyles was scheduled to report to camp, he broke his leg in an accident at his Green Bay, Wis., apartment.

Working out? No. ...

"I was watching a movie and didn't want to miss any of it, and I had to use the restroom and I had to hurry back," Voyles explained. "I jumped down about five steps of stairs and I caught my foot on the bottom."

The 23-year-old prospect had to undergo surgery and missed his big chance.

The DVD movie Voyles was watching was "X-Men." So why didn't he just hit the pause button and take his time going down the steps?

"Next time, I will," he said.

♦ ♦ ♦

Anybody who doesn't believe fans can influence major league players should talk to Joe Morgan. The Hall of Fame second baseman was still a 23-year-old prospect in April 1967 when he stepped to the plate to face St. Louis veteran Bob Gibson in a game at the Astrodome.

Morgan was fighting a horrible slump, hitless in his last 24 at-bats, and struggling with his confidence. Gibson already had retired him twice in the game. As Morgan got set in the batter's box, he heard a woman's voice yell out, "This is gonna be the time, Joe. This is the time."

Morgan stopped, turned his head and spotted the woman in a front-row seat between home and first base. He nodded his head at her, stepped back into the box and drove a double into the right field corner.

"I don't know who that lady is," he said. "She's there for every game. I've never talked to her, but I could hear her yelling every night. And then, when she said, 'This is the time,' it just struck me that she was right, and so I turned around and looked.

"I've been trying to make up for my bad start every time I go to the plate, trying to make up for it with one at-bat. You can't do it; you just press then. I told myself this was the start of my season."

◆　◆　◆

There are certain lines you don't cross in baseball, whether you're playing at the major league or minor league level. Payback for sins of etiquette can be hard and swift.

Jayson Werth, a 21-year-old outfielder/catcher in the Baltimore organization, found that out the hard way while playing for Class AA Bowie (Eastern) in 2000. Werth hit a home run off 28-year-old righthander Joe Roa and made quite a production out of rounding the bases.

"It was like his first or second homer of the year," said teammate Joe DePastino. "He just stood and watched it. Then he did this slow trot around the bases and as soon as he touched third, he got hit right in the mouth. It was one of the funniest things I ever saw."

Roa apparently did not enjoy the show as much as DePastino. He sprinted at Werth and delivered a blow to his jaw as both benches emptied. Things got ugly before order finally was restored.

"I had never seen a pitcher charge a batter before," said Andy Frankel, director of communications for the Bowie team. "He was rounding third and the pitcher just came right after him."

That 2000 season also was eventful for DePastino, whose 19 games at Bowie were sandwiched by stints at Class AAA Rochester (International) and Class AA Round Rock (Texas). In his short stay with Bowie, the catcher gained All-Star acclaim—well, kind of.

"We hosted the 2000 Class AA All-Star Game in Bowie," Frankel said. "But one of the catchers selected to the team had played the night before in a 14- or 15-inning Texas League game. He didn't make it."

That left the American League-affiliated teams with only one catcher. So Bowie officials made an emergency search for DePastino, located him about two hours before game time at a local mall and asked him if he wanted to be a member of the All-Star team.

Who could resist?

◆　◆　◆

Former Pittsburgh general manager Joe Brown recalled his first impression of Richie Hebner, an outstanding 18-year-old hockey and baseball prospect, on a warm June 1966 day at Hebner's home in Norwood, Mass.

"When I first saw Hebner," Brown said, "I found it hard not to laugh. He greeted me at the door with Bermuda shorts and a big smile. It was a funny sort of a smile because Hebner's two front teeth were missing. The first thing I noticed after that smile was Hebner's heavy thighs. He must have weighed 205 or 210. I said to myself, 'This is a shortstop?' "

No, he wasn't. Hebner eventually signed with the Pirates and played mostly third and first base over an 18-year career with five teams. But former Boston Bruins general manager Milt Schmidt said the colorful youngster—Hebner was an offseason grave digger in his family's cemetery—could have made it in the National

Hockey League.

"I don't blame him for taking baseball because he probably got a bonus three times bigger," Schmidt said. "But I tell you one thing. Our scouts saw the kid play. They believe he could have made it with us."

◆　◆　◆

Phil Roof, starting catcher for the Milwaukee Brewers early in the 1971 season, was impressed by a young backup named Darrell Porter. Roof knew that it wouldn't be long before his job would be in jeopardy.

"I was talking about him with (Cleveland manager) Alvin Dark before a game one day," Roof said, "and I told him that this guy is going to be some kind of player some day.

"Dark took one look at the kid in warmups and yelled to me, 'I'm not impressed.'

"After the game, during which Porter got one hit and hit two line drives that should have been hits, I yelled to Dark, 'How do you like him now, Alvin?'

"He said to me, 'I'll take him. I'll take him right now.' I laughed because I knew he was going to say that."

◆　◆　◆

Further proof that first impressions can be deceiving comes from Felipe Alou, who spent more than two decades in the Montreal organization as a scout, coach, minor league manager and major league manager. Alou told about a 1978 visit to Venezuela.

"I was managing at Caracas," he said, "and the general manager, Francisco Rivero, asked me if I wanted to see a 'fat kid' who can hit hard.

"This fat kid showed up and he could hit all right. I liked what I saw of his power, but I couldn't recommend a fat kid like that to Montreal. I'm sure he was 250 pounds and he was just a boy. As a matter of fact, I was so sure this pudgy boy would never make the grade I showed him to another scout.

"That man said, 'No way,' because he didn't like the boy's body. The kid stayed around and continued to hit the ball out of the park. Finally, I recommended him to Montreal."

The Expos signed Andres Galarraga in 1979 and the "fat kid" grew into a 6-3, 235-pound slugging first baseman. The free-swinging Galarraga had hit 398 home runs in 18 big-league seasons through 2003.

◆   ◆   ◆

Umpire Dave Phillips was young, naive and still learning the ropes in 1964, his second professional season, when he worked a Class A Midwest League game between the Quad-Cities Angels and Fox Cities Foxes at Appleton, Wis. Phillips and partner Larry Barnett, both future American League arbiters, got a quick course in baseball subtleties from a Quad Cities manager named Chuck Tanner.

"We had two-man crews in those days and I was working the field," Phillips recalled. "There was a play at second, a steal maybe, and I called the runner out. I called the play right, there was no doubt about it. The player was arguing a little, but nothing serious.

"Suddenly Tanner comes flying out, pushes his player away and begins jumping up and down, screaming and yelling, going through all these gyrations like a madman. I couldn't believe he was that mad over that call. He's going crazy. Then it finally registers what he's saying. He's talking about this restaurant in Appleton, this place where you can get a great steak dinner.

"I'm befuddled. He's making it look like he was chewing my ass when he was really talking about this restaurant."

After the game, Phillips told Barnett the story and his partner wouldn't believe it. Phillips insisted it was true as Barnett gave him an understanding nod and skeptical look.

"We're meeting at home plate the next day," Phillips said, "and Tanner comes over and asks, 'Dave, did you go to the steak house last night?' I got Tanner to tell Barnett the story and he finished by saying, 'Dave, you were right on the call. But I had to show my players I would stand up for them and protect them.' "

◆ ◆ ◆

On April 30, 1982, young shortstop/third baseman Cal Ripken was struggling with his bat and wondering just how long Baltimore management was going to be patient with a rookie phenom. Two "meetings of the mind" took place that fateful day, setting Ripken's record-breaking career on a straight and level course.

Meeting No. 1 was a simple "back to the basics" speech from Cal Ripken Sr., the Orioles' third base coach. "When we talked," Ripken said, "my dad just told me to go back to doing things the way they felt best. He told me to just concentrate on seeing the ball and hitting it."

Later that day, after the game against the California Angels had started, Ripken found himself standing next to Reggie Jackson. The veteran slugger remembered watching Ripken play as a 15-year-old high school sophomore when Jackson played for Baltimore in 1976.

"Earl (Weaver) was on the field arguing (a balk call against Jim Palmer), and Reggie was on third base," Ripken said. "He said to me, 'Hey kid, I want to talk to you.' I remember thinking at the time, 'Uh, oh, here we go again—just what I need, somebody else to give me advice.'

"Reggie told me he knew what I was going through because he'd been through it, too. He told me to just be myself and everything would fall into place. It seemed like what he said to me was the same thing that was going through my mind at the time, the same thing my father and I had talked about that same day. And after that, everything seemed to click."

◆ ◆ ◆

For young players trying to claw their way to the major leagues, there are managers and there are mentors. Buck Showalter, who would go on to manage the Yankees, Diamondbacks and Rangers, learned the difference between the two in 1981, when he was nearing the end of a seven-year career as a minor league outfielder/first baseman.

"I was at Class AAA Columbus with the Yankees," Showalter recalled. "Johnny Oates was the manager. In those days, there were incentive clauses in a lot of minor league contracts; you would get a bonus if you spent, say, 30 days in Class AAA. It was getting toward the end of the season. Columbus already had made the playoffs. Nashville, the Yankees' Class AA team, was getting close.

"I was the type of player who wasn't going to get to the big leagues, but at Class AA and AAA I was a good player who could help a team get into the playoffs. I got called into Johnny's office. He said they feel like they need you. They wanted me to go down and play for Nashville for the rest of the season.

"I guess I had kind of a long face. He said, 'What's wrong?' I said, 'Nothing.' He asked a couple of times, 'What's wrong?' Finally, I told him that if I had stayed one more day at Class AAA, I would have gotten $1,000. That was a lot of money. But I told him I understood.

"He said, 'Why don't you go out for batting practice and let me make a call?' He called the farm director. He said he wanted to keep me one more day. There was a guy he wasn't sure could play that night. I got the one extra day. I got the $1,000. And I got sent out the next day.

"People ask all the time, 'Who are your mentors?' You don't want to say, because you're afraid you'll forget somebody. But Johnny was the best I ever played for. He just treated people with so much sincerity."

Most players can credit a special coach who helped them ascend to the major leagues. For outfielder Jon Nunnally, that coach was Pat Crawford. That's Pat, as in Patricia.

Nunnally was one of 11 children raised by Solomon and Marie Nunnally in Pelham, N.C. Crawford was coaching Little League in nearby Danville, Va. Crawford liked the little guy everybody called "BOO-key" and took quick notice of his potent lefthanded swing. She drafted Nunnally first for her team and thus began a strong pupil-coach relationship.

"She was like his godmama," Solomon Nunnally recalled.

Crawford, the mother of seven, had grown up watching the Boston Red Sox and jumped at the opportunity to coach her sons. The quiet Nunnally was a bonus. He looked like a natural and she soon had him swinging the bat a hundred times a day.

"He, of all the players, continued that," Crawford recalled after Nunnally reached the majors. "He continued listening. He worked hard. Never complained. He was just outstanding."

She sent Nunnally to baseball camps, helped him get a scholarship to Hargrave Military Academy in Chatham, Va., where she sent her triplet sons, and encouraged him to attend Miami-Dade South Community College.

In 1992, the Cleveland Indians made him a third-round draft choice, and three years later, the Kansas City Royals picked him off in the Rule 5 draft. Nunnally made his debut in 1995, hitting a home run in his first big-league at-bat against New York righthander Melido Perez.

Nunnally didn't gain star status, but he played six major league seasons for the Royals, Cincinnati Reds, Boston Red Sox and New York Mets. It was during his rookie year that he singled out Crawford as his mentor.

"She pushed me," Nunnally said. "It gave me somebody who wanted to see me do something with my talent. It was a great feeling to have somebody look over you and look out for you."

"I love that kid," Crawford said, "like he's my own."

◆　◆　◆

There are double plays and then there are *double plays*. The one turned by the Stockton Ports in an April 12, 1983, game against Redwood is a fixture in California League lore.

The play started innocently enough in the top of the fifth inning with Redwood's Greg Key stationed on first base and Luis Zambrana at the plate. Zambrana hit Rich Embser's first pitch to shortstop Mike Samuel, who fielded the grounder and tossed to second baseman Matt Sferrazza for an apparent forceout. But this is where things got complicated.

The throw pulled Sferrazza off the bag, and he then threw wildly past first baseman Ty Van Burkleo. But Key, thinking he had been called out, trotted back toward the Redwood dugout on the first base side of the field. Key was passed by Zambrana, who was called out between first and second base.

Key, realizing his mistake, turned around, headed for second and didn't stop there. He was gunned down on a close play at third by catcher Garrett Nago, who had backed up the play at first and fired a strike to third baseman Dale Sveum.

When everything was sorted out, the unorthodox double play went into the books with Sferrazza getting credit for a putout (he was closest to Key when Zambrana passed him), an assist and an error (the throw to first).

Another minor league double play, this one recorded in 1985 during a Class A South Atlantic League game between Asheville and Florence, almost defied explanation.

Asheville entered the ninth inning of that home contest trailing, 8-4. But the Tourists scored two runs before making an out and had Anthony Hampton running at third base and Norman Brock at first when Pete Mueller lofted a long fly ball to the warning track near the dimly lit left-center field wall. Florence center fielder Silvestre Campusano appeared to make the catch, but the ball popped free.

Both runners tagged up and Hampton scored, cutting Florence's lead to 8-7. But Brock and Mueller, thinking Campusano had dropped the ball, kept running and wound up at third and second. Umpires Steve Spano and James Trusiani conferred and decided that Campusano had indeed caught the ball and Mueller was out. When Florence appealed that Brock had failed to touch second base, the umpires agreed and ruled that he was the second out.

But instead of leaving the field, Brock remained at third base. The umpires mistakenly thought that Hampton had retreated to third on the play and did not send Brock back to the dugout. Complicating matters, the scoreboard showed only one out and Asheville manager Fred Hatfield thought his team had tied the game when the next batter grounded out and Brock scored.

Not so, said the umpires, who ruled the game was over.

"I've never seen a game end like that, with two out and a tie score," said an irate Hatfield. "We've got to go back and play sudden death. It's a tie game. Who's the second out on Mueller's fly ball? How can they get two out on that play and still leave Brock on third base? Surely this isn't a two-out, one-hop-is-out league."

Rounding out the strange-but-true double play collection is this one from a 1986 Class AAA International League game between Pawtucket and Toledo. The PawSox's Mike Stenhouse literally walked into an inning-ending twin killing—with a little help from his friends.

Dana Williams was running at third and John Christensen at first with one out in the bottom of the first inning when Stenhouse drew a walk on a 3-and-2 pitch from Toledo pitcher Ramon Romero. Christensen had broken with the pitch, triggering a confusing scenario.

Mud Hens catcher Pat Dempsey came up ready to throw to second when Christensen broke, but held the ball when he realized the pitch had been called a ball. Williams, apparently thinking Dempsey was going to throw to second, charged toward the plate and was caught in a rundown.

Christensen advanced to third and Stenhouse to second during the rundown, but Williams somehow scrambled back to third safely. Dempsey tagged both runners, who were standing on the bag, and the umpire called Christensen out. But Williams thought he was out and headed back to the Pawtucket dugout. He was called out for abandoning his base.

"Technically, the call was correct. I have no problem with that," said Pawtucket manager Ed Nottle, who was coaching at third. "My argument is over vocal chords. He (the umpire) didn't call out loud enough to say which one was out."

The double play did not really matter. Pawtucket won, 8-1.

VOICES FROM ABOVE

Hall of Famer Ernie Harwell is a broadcasting icon whose work has touched seven different decades. He has been a fixture in Detroit since 1960, the beloved Voice of the Tigers and one of the most influential voices in the game over the last half century. So what's the most cherished moment of his long and distinguished professional career?

"The Bobby Thomson home run," Harwell said, referring to the classic dagger that pierced the heart of Brooklyn fans and delivered a 1951 pennant to the New York Giants. "I was on the TV that day. Russ Hodges and I were the announcers for the Giants. We alternated; I'd do TV one day and radio the next and Russ would do the opposite. It just turned out to be my turn on that October the 3rd of 1951 to be on NBC-TV.

"I felt that I had much the better assignment. Poor Russ was just going to get lost on the radio because there were five different radio broadcasts that afternoon. And there was only one TV broadcast, and it was the first sports series ever telecast from coast to coast. Before that, everything had always been recorded for later airing. So it was sort of an historic moment. I really felt sorry for Russ, but I couldn't do anything about it because that was the luck of the draw. That was the way it had come up; it was my turn on TV.

"As it turned out, somebody recorded his famous call and Chesterfield, who sponsored the games, put it out on a record and it became the most famous sports broadcast of all time. We've heard it a million times as Russ says, 'The Giants win the pennant!' and so forth.

"I was on TV and we didn't have any replays in those days. They didn't have any real economical recording device, so nobody recorded it. And only my wife Lulu and I know that I was on that afternoon. Outside of going into the Hall of Fame, I think it was the biggest moment of my career."

Harwell has observed some wacky things on the field over his storied career. The strangest?

"Probably Norman Cash coming to bat at Tiger Stadium against Nolan Ryan, who was going for his second no-hitter of the 1973 season," he said. "He was pitching the best game I've ever seen. He struck out something like 16 or 17 guys. We were really more concerned about the strikeout record—because he'd racked them up in the early part of the game—even more so than the no-hitter. He was just untouchable. The Tigers literally were lucky to get a foul ball off him.

"Cash came to bat (with two out) in the ninth inning. But then he was sent back to the dugout by the umpire to get a new bat. After the game, I asked Cash, 'What happened? Why was the bat illegal?'

"He says, 'Well, Ernie, nobody was hitting that guy. And I wasn't going to hit him. So I went into the clubhouse and got a leg off the table and took it up to home plate.'"

Ryan got Cash to pop out and completed the July 15 no-hitter with 17 strikeouts, becoming the fourth pitcher to throw two no-hitters in a season.

Harwell said he could always tell early when he was going to have a rough day on the job. How early?

"The pregame show," he said. "Everything bad just starts with a bad pregame show."

Harwell recalled once in the late 1960s, when he was doing Tigers games on radio with Ray Lane, that just such a day unfolded.

"We were doing a doubleheader in Chicago against the White Sox," he said. "Everything started to go wrong. Our guest was going to be the home run leader of the White Sox. He got interested in a couple of babes up in the third row and forgot to show up. Then we lost our line back to Detroit. We blew a couple of commercials. The White Sox beat the Tigers in a miserable Sunday afternoon doubleheader.

"Ray and I missed the team bus going back to the hotel and hated that we had to get the expensive cab ride. We were seated in the lounge off the lobby, commiserating with each other over sarsaparilla. A young lady comes up to the table and she says, 'Hello, fellas, I'll do anything for $300.' "

"And I say, 'How about the pregame show?' "

Not only is Vin Scully an active broadcasting legend, he's a legend among active broadcasters. As proof, Houston television voice Bill Brown recounted a busy June 1989 weekend that included a 5-4 victory by the Astros in a game that lasted 22 innings and required 7 hours, 14 minutes to play.

"Scully was doing NBC Saturday afternoon games at that time," Brown said, "so he had been in St. Louis doing an afternoon game (Cubs at the Cardinals) on June 3 and then flew by private jet to Houston in order to be on time for the Astros-Dodgers game.

"Scully's second broadcast of that Saturday actually ended at 2:50 a.m. Sunday, after the Dodgers had used every active player and pitcher on their roster except for Sunday's starting pitcher (Tim Belcher). Los Angeles third baseman Jeff Hamilton was the final and losing pitcher, with Fernando Valenzuela finishing the game by playing first base.

"The next day, the Astros and Dodgers play a 13-inning game. So we're all just completely wiped out. Then I hear somebody say, 'Well, the Dodgers are headed to Atlanta where they play a doubleheader on Monday.' All I could think of was, 'Poor Scully.'

"He did both games on Saturday, including the 22-inning game, then Sunday's game. I couldn't imagine doing another baseball game. The Astros were off on Monday, so I just collapsed in a heap. But Scully had far more going than any of us did."

"He's sitting on 714..."

Milo Hamilton, the radio play-by-play voice of the Houston Astros since 1985, had a front-row seat when Hank Aaron broke Babe Ruth's all-time home run record. Hamilton, a member of the Radio Hall of Fame and the lead broadcaster for the Atlanta Braves that season, offers an insider perspective on events leading into one of the game's most monumental moments on April 8, 1974, at Atlanta-Fulton County Stadium.

"George Plimpton wouldn't let me forget it all winter," said Hamilton, who has been calling baseball for more than half a century. "He did the book and the feature on it for *Sports Illustrated*. After the 1973 season, we knew it was just a matter of time. Would it happen the first weekend? Would it happen the first week? We knew it was going to happen because (Aaron) only needed one to tie and one to break it. So Plimpton would call me over and over during the winter trying to get me to tell him what I was going to say. Spontaneity has always been my long suit, so I told him, 'I cannot plan this.'"

Not that Hamilton didn't give it a lot of thought—all winter.

"I'm kind of a nocturnal guy," he said. "I'm a big reader. When my family and my wife would go to bed, things would go through my mind like, 'Oh, they were the same age. Babe Ruth and Aaron were both wearing Braves uniforms (when they hit home runs No. 714). A lot of people forget that Ruth hit his final three home runs in the same game.' Then I thought, 'Well, maybe I can say one of those things when he goes to first, another when he goes to second.' Thank God I didn't do that! But I did have all of that on my mind. So, as they were gathering for a little ceremony at home plate, I was able to use all that. It's kind of an old saying: 'Don't cram it in if it doesn't fit; use it when it does fit.

"The pressure didn't get to (Aaron) really until maybe the last week or two, because he handled it well and the club handled it very well. They went to school on the really bad way that the Yankees handled it when Roger Maris hit 61. I won't say the Braves protected him, because they let him do a lot of interviews. But they did make sure he wasn't hounded."

As the season approached, the media horde multiplied in thickness.

"I think mainly because the interviews were involving people who were not in the sports business," Hamilton recalled. "For example, Tom Brokaw from NBC came and took up days and days doing all kinds of things. And Brokaw entered into the hate-mail situation, which really wasn't known to a lot of people, even those with the ballclub, until the last few days when Brokaw got into it and made it a big thing. What was almost lost in the NBC feature was why the feature was being done: Aaron was going to break Ruth's record. All of a sudden the racial thing took over as the theme.

"Plus, you had people interviewing him who didn't know him from a fence post. One writer interviewed Aaron and this writer took up an hour of his time while some of us were waiting to do the shows that we needed to do. At the end of this interview, this writer says, 'By the way, Mr. Aaron, do you hit righthanded or left-handed?' Silliness like that. I don't think the guys who were on the beats or the big national writers bothered Henry a lot, but when it got to people who were doing it because of the monumental moment, I think maybe that touched him a little bit."

Game on. No media. Just Aaron with his bat and Dodgers pitcher Al Downing with the ball.

"*Here's the pitch by Downing ... swinging. ... There's a drive into left-center field. That ball is going to be-e-e-e ... outta here! It's gone! It's 715! There's a new home run champion of all time. And it's Henry Aaron!*"

As the ball flew over the glove of Dodgers left fielder Bill Buckner and settled into history, Aaron circled the bases. At that point, Hamilton said, it got even stranger.

"Maybe it was crazy because of the time that it happened, but as everybody was watching him go around the bases and his teammates were waiting at home plate, then these two young men dashed out of the crowd and greeted Aaron at the shortstop position and tried to run around the bases with him. The fact that it was on a night when Babe Ruth's record was beaten—715 for Aaron—and all of a sudden here comes two guys from the stands to run around the bases with him. They greeted him right about shortstop, might have gotten to about third base, but then cooler heads prevailed.

" 'Henry Aaron's coming around third! His teammates are at home plate! Listen to this crowd!'

"Hardly a week goes by during the season, and a lot of times during the winter, that I don't hear (the call), so that means the fans are hearing it as well," Hamilton said. "So, I think that associates me with that moment. Aaron and I have done some card shows together over the years. Once in a while, when I see Al Downing, we always kind of kid each other and bump our hips and say, 'You know, we're kind of joined at the hip aren't we, with our association with 715.' "

Hamilton's on-air resume also includes the Western Union ticker recreation of Roger Maris' 61st homer, Ernie Banks' fifth grand slam of the 1955 season and 11 no-hitters—including Mike Scott's gem against the Giants that clinched the 1986 N.L. West title.

But among Hamilton's most cherished memories were a pair of doubleheaders that were played 18 years apart.

"I think fans who really know the game will get a kick out of this," Hamilton said. "When Stan Musial hit the five home runs in a doubleheader in 1954 at old Busch Stadium in St. Louis against the Giants, I was part of the Cardinals broadcast crew. Then in 1972, when the Padres' Nate Colbert duplicated that (at Atlanta), I was the announcer for the Braves.

"To have two guys hit five home runs in a doubleheader and to have one announcer associated with both events, I kind of relish that one because it's so different."

♦   ♦   ♦

His nine seasons as a player for the New York Yankees did not get Jerry Coleman into the Hall of Fame; neither did his one season (1980) as San Diego manager. But as a broadcaster, Coleman is a legend, known fondly as the Master of Malaprops. He has unloaded some unintentional classics over the years, including "he slides into second base with a standup double."

Coleman broke into broadcasting in 1963 with another pair of legends, Mel Allen and Phil Rizzuto. They helped make Coleman's transition from second base to the broadcast booth as smooth as a 4-6-3 double play—until the day they "turned two" and came away with one big blooper.

Before a June 1 doubleheader at Cleveland, Coleman asked Indians manager Birdie Tebbetts for his starting pitchers. "McDowell and Kralick," Tebbetts answered.

Coleman took that information to the booth and as the game proceeded, Allen, Rizzuto and Coleman gushed on the air about how impressive Cleveland lefthander Sam McDowell was throwing. McDowell tended to be wild, and so it was interesting to see him with great command. The gushing continued for several innings, until somebody finally burst into the booth to inform the Yankees broadcasters, "That's not McDowell, that's the other lefty, Jack Kralick."

"Mel handles it like a total professional," said Coleman, who, like Rizzuto, was literally rolling on the floor of the booth, unable to stop laughing. "I didn't come up for two minutes," Coleman said.

It's one thing to catch a broadcaster with his pants down. It's quite another to catch him with his pants completely off.

For Coleman, removing his pants was a desperate attempt to stay cool during a scorching midsummer game in Kansas City, where neither the radio nor television booths had a fan, much less air conditioning. Between innings, Coleman even stood on one of old Municipal Stadium's elevated catwalks with other Yankees broadcasters, trying to catch a breeze while still out of sight of Kansas City fans.

Coleman had returned to the booth when, "All of a sudden, I feel a hand on my shoulder. I turn around and there is a police officer and he says, 'Put your pants on!'

"Apparently, some woman had seen us and complained. I don't see what the big deal was. After all, I have beautiful legs."

◆　◆　◆

Coleman is not the only big-league broadcaster who has ignored fashion to beat the heat. Reds television analyst Chris Welsh recalled one of those hazy, hot and humid days in Cincinnati, when the mid-90-degree temperature made everyone feel like bacon in the frying pan and the sweltering Cinergy Field broadcast booth drove at least one person to extreme measures.

"The Cardinals have a broadcaster, Mike Shannon, who has been there for a long time," Welsh said. "If you've ever seen Shannon, you know he wears what you might call his own broadcaster's uniform to every game. It's essentially black. He looks like Johnny Cash when he shows up at the ballpark—black shirt, black pants, black shoes, black jacket. He wears this black jacket every day of the year, whether it's April or a hot Sunday in the middle of August in Cincinnati. He had it with him on this Sunday, but he didn't wear it.

"We're all just sweating (during this Cardinals-Reds game) like we've never sweated before. It's so hot and so muggy and you can cut the air with the proverbial fungo bat."

At Cinergy, the visiting radio booth was adjacent to the home perch where Welsh and partner George Grande were set up for the Reds broadcast. They looked around the corner at Shannon.

"He's got a big white towel draped around his neck," Welsh recalled. "Maybe it's soaked in ice water, I don't know. As he's doing the game, you can see his black hair is now matted and his face is just dripping.

"A few innings later, we look over and he's got his shirt off. Now,

Mike Shannon's skin probably hasn't seen the light of day in several decades. So, the white of that skin was enough to set you off in the first place. Then, a few innings later, we look over and he's got his trousers off. He's sitting there in his boxers with a towel around his neck calling the game. I'll tell you, if that wasn't a sight to put a good fright into you.

"It's an image I'd like to erase from my memory," Welsh said with a laugh. "We got him on camera, from the belly up, of course. He's not in shape like he used to be when he was a player. There was Mike Shannon, rolling all over the place. It was an ugly sight. I'll tell you what, he didn't a miss a pitch in the ballgame and I think he was the one guy who didn't have a fan in front of him.

"So God bless Mike Shannon for continuing on and bringing Cardinal fans their baseball."

Welsh, a Reds broadcaster since 1993, recalled his favorite road stop during a five-year pitching career (1981-86) that included stints with the San Diego Padres, Montreal Expos, Texas Rangers and Cincinnati.

"Before all the new stadiums were built in the early 1990s, I really enjoyed when we'd go to Los Angeles," he said. "L.A. was a big-league city and a big-league stadium in the National League. You always knew there'd be a full house. You never knew how many stars—actors and actresses—would be in the stands. You'd look up from the bullpen or the dugout and see a famous movie star and say, 'Wow, they're here to see us play. I can't believe it.'

"The other thing that was impressive about L.A. was when you stood on the pitcher's mound and you looked up and saw five different levels of stadium. It was the only stadium like that at that time. As a broadcaster now, I think the elevator at Dodger Stadium has eight, nine or 10 floors. I'm not sure how many stops, but it has more than any other stadium.

"As a player, it was just so impressive to stand on the mound and look up and see all five levels filled. You'd think, 'Wow, here I am at Dodger Stadium. And somewhere in front of me, on that third or fourth level, is Vin Scully.' "

◆　　◆　　◆

Bob Costas, a longtime broadcasting fixture for NBC-TV, has thrived in numerous sports and non-sports venues. But he always has expressed a special affinity for baseball. Not surprisingly, some of his best stories come straight from the booth, such as this delightful tale about an awkward moment for former Cardinals play-by-play man Bob Starr:

"It was the Cardinals against the Cubs, and at that time it was a three-man booth in St. Louis. Jack Buck was the lead announcer with Mike Shannon and the late Bob Starr, who was a terrific broadcaster, a very capable baseball announcer. But even the best of us occasionally have a moment and Bob Starr's moment happened in this game in 1977 or '78.

"It's National Dairy Day at Busch Stadium and as everyone knows, this is one of your huge promotional days. Fans flock from neighboring states for the colorful festivities so they have whatever ceremony it is you have on the field before National Dairy Day—cow-milking or whatever it may be. And then the game begins.

"The booth at that time in St. Louis was a two-tiered affair where the broadcasters sat kind of at the mezzanine level, and elevated two or three steps above them and behind them was an area where their friends or clients of the ballclub or the radio station could come and watch the game. If you were standing in that area behind them, the broadcasters would be sitting Buck on the left, Shannon in the middle and Starr on the right.

"So the game moves along, nothing particularly interesting happening. Bottom half of the fourth inning, Rick Reuschel on the mound for the Cubs, and as Ken Reitz steps to the plate and takes a curve outside for ball one and Buck is calling the action, the president of the National Dairy Council appears in the booth. And Buck, who liked to schmooze a visitor now and then, beckons him down to start talking to him between pitches.

" *'And Reitz fouls one back to the screen, he's hitting 286.'*

"And Buck says, 'So, have you enjoyed your trip to St. Louis?' And the guy from the National Dairy Council says, 'Oh, sure Jack, it's been great. Don't see much of the National League up in Milwaukee since the Braves went to Atlanta. Good to see the Cardinals and the Cubs.' Buck says, 'Drop my name in any restaurant in town. You'll get a good seat.' The guy from the National Dairy Council thanks him.

" 'Reitz bounces to short. He's thrown out at first. One out in the Cardinal fourth.'

"And at that point, a woman appears in the booth who is accompanying the president of the National Dairy Council and the woman is billed as 'Miss Cheesecake.' And Miss Cheesecake is dressed as if she were in a beauty pageant. She's in a one-piece, white bathing suit with white high heels and a sash going across her that, instead of saying 'Miss Wisconsin' or something, actually says 'Miss Cheesecake.' And so she's drawing a lot of attention all around.

" 'Keith Hernandez steps to the plate and fouls one back to the screen.'

And Miss Cheesecake comes sashaying down the steps from the back of the booth, bringing with her a goodwill offering from the National Dairy Council. Three individual-size cheesecakes, one for each broadcaster. And she places one in front of Buck, a second in front of Shannon and a third in front of Starr before, to much attention all around, she makes her way to the back of the booth.

" 'Hernandez pops it up. ... Two up and two down in the Cardinal fourth.'

"And as Ted Simmons makes his way from the on-deck circle toward the plate and Miss Cheesecake makes her way to the back of the booth, Buck leans across Shannon, eyes Starr and says, 'So Bob, what do you think of Miss Cheesecake?' And Starr, who was apparently distracted, thinks he said, 'What do you think of this cheesecake?' And he says, 'I'll tell you, Jack, I'd like to try a piece of that right now!'

"And Starr had no idea why everyone was convulsed in laughter. He had no idea what he had said, or why it was so funny, because he had misheard what Buck said."

From observer to victim, the words of a broadcaster always balance precariously on the edge of a steep cliff. Costas remembers his "moment" from an NBC *Game of the Week* telecast that pitted the

Oakland Athletics against Toronto.

"I'm doing the *Game of the Week* with Tony Kubek," Costas recalled, "and at that time Tommy John is bouncing from team to team, just trying to hang on. The Yankees have released him. The Angels have released him. And Oakland has signed him, but the A's haven't officially activated him for their roster. They're going to send him out on a minor league assignment to get ready and then bring him back. But he worked out with them in uniform before the game that day, and he was sitting in the dugout in uniform, although he wasn't eligible to play.

"So they come out of a commercial and the camera focuses on Tommy John and I try to think of the appropriate verbal caption to put beneath the picture, and I say to Kubek, 'Tony, there's Tommy John. The great lefthander, closing in on 300 wins but also closing in on the end of his storied career. Twenty-game winner in both leagues, pitched in the World Series for both the Dodgers and the Yankees, and the A's think he can eke a few more wins out of that tired left arm of his. He does, too, but he's not quite ready yet. So he'll be pissing in Appleton on Monday.'

"I knew what I had intended to say, and I was pretty sure what I had said. And I looked at Kubek, and he looked back at me with this expression of, 'You know, you're on your own. I don't know what the hell you're gonna say next, but I can't get you out of this.'

"So he's looking at me and I'm looking at him. And you begin to realize how long 10 seconds of dead air is on national television. So then I say, 'Well, come to think of it, Tony, he'll probably do both if he stays in Appleton long enough.' At which point, Kubek starts to laugh, and he can't help himself.

"And so, we just go on with it. I figured if the audience gets that reference, that's fine, but I'm not going to explain the whole thing or apologize for it. And then, on the following Monday or Tuesday, I'm walking down the hall at NBC, and here comes David Letterman in the other direction. It's a long hallway. So we see each other from probably 30 yards away. And as the gap between us closes as we walk toward each other, Letterman says, 'Bob, do you have a tape of Saturday's game? I need it for my archives.' "

◆ ◆ ◆

Philadelphia broadcaster Chris Wheeler offers this story about a game he worked on television one night with Richie Ashburn when the Hall of Fame center fielder surprised Wheeler by saying: "We'd like to send our best along to former Phillies owner Ruly Carpenter. Ruly was in an automobile accident today, but we understand he's doing just fine."

"Then," Wheeler said, "Ashburn proceeds to get on Carpenter's father, Bob, who ran the club before Ruly. He jokes about the elder Carpenter being cheap and says Carpenter still owes him $500, which is now worth about $5,000. It is a funny bit, except that is the first any of us has heard about Ruly's supposed accident. We wonder how Ashburn knew."

When the inning ended, Wheeler turned to Ashburn to ask about his revelation, but before he could even get the words out of his mouth, Phillies publicist Larry Shenk burst into the booth. "Whitey! Where did you hear about Ruly being in a car accident?" Shenk asked.

Ashburn confidently replied, "Well, I had dinner with some guy in the press room tonight and he told me about it."

"Whitey," Shenk said, "you had dinner with ME in the press room tonight and I told you my wife, JULIE, had been in a car accident."

Ashburn got this funny look on his face and said, "Oh, that's right."

"By this point, we are about to come back on the air," Wheeler said, "and I ask Ashburn what are we going to say to get out of this one? 'Let me handle it, pal,' Ashburn says.

"We are back on the air and Ashburn calls a few pitches, then in his dry, Nebraska twang says, 'I'd like to make a correction on something I said last inning. I was given some misinformation. It was Phillies publicist Larry Shenk's wife, JULIE, who was in that car accident today and not Ruly Carpenter. ... And, Larry Shenk needs to work on his enunciation.'

"It was beautiful, and only Ashburn could have dug himself out of that mess so eloquently."

◆ ◆ ◆

When Jon Miller began his broadcasting career with the World Series champion Oakland Athletics in 1974, he was 22 years old and still naive to the ways of his business. He recalled his first visit to Boston and the first interview he conducted at historic Fenway Park.

"You'd go down for the postgame interview," Miller said, "and I wanted to get (Boston's Carl) Yastrzemski. He had had a big night against the Oakland A's. Ordinarily, I would have interviewed Yastrzemski in the dugout, but we had a union issue. We would have needed two engineers and had to pay them full scale to do the interview in the dugout. We had only one engineer.

"The old broadcast booths were above the screen that ran from the top of the backstop to the back of the broadcast level. We ran a cable down when the game was all over. All I had to do was plug the microphone into the cable.

"We walk over to the backstop and he says, 'Where are we going?' I say, 'We have to do it by the backstop.' There are still hundreds of fans in the vicinity. Monte Moore was cueing me up in the booth. He throws his arms to tell me I'm on.

"I introduce Yastrzemski and all the people cheered, like we had a studio audience. We do the interview, go four or five minutes, he never gets impatient. He never signals, 'Can we wrap this up?' When it's over, the fans cheer again. There were all these people asking for autographs.

"He definitely could have blown me off when he saw where we were going to do the interview. I was always a huge fan of his from that point on."

By 1985, Miller was expanding his broadcasting niche by calling games for the Baltimore Orioles. But not even his golden voice and eloquent game descriptions could shield him from the inevitable bloopers and uncomfortable moments that every baseball broadcaster experiences from time to time.

One memorable faux pas occurred in a game at Memorial Stadium, when the Orioles were staging a ninth-inning rally against the California Angels. Down 5-2, Miller said, Baltimore got a home run and had a couple of men on base when righthanded-hitting Lee Lacy stepped to the plate.

"Lacy hits a deep fly ball down the right field line," Miller recalled. "It's going to go, but it's a question of whether it's fair or foul. I say, 'It's hit down the line. If it's fair, it's gone. It's hooking, hooking. ...,' then I think no, he's a righthanded hitter, it's slicing. But when the ball is in mid-flight, you've got no time to say, 'I beg your pardon, it's a righthanded hitter, it's slicing ... slicing off the foul pole for a game-winning home run.'

"Now the game is over. We're recapping and putting together some of the highlights. We get to the big moment. I set it up. I'm hearing the play for the first time. 'Deep down the right field line ... hooking, slicing, gone.' We come back and I say, 'I've never seen that kind of action on a fly ball before. That's my story and I'm sticking with it.' I had a laugh on the air about my own faux pas."

But to Miller's surprise, that wasn't the end of the story. Orioles games were being carried that year on WFBR, a rock-and-roll station. Typically, after a great Baltimore rally, someone would edit the play-by-play of the big finish with some rock-and-roll music and play it the next day and night leading up to the game. Miller's hooking-slicing call was heard again ... and again ... and again—with a musical backdrop.

"That call got played a hundred times," he said. "Every time I went around town the next day, everyone said, 'Which one was it, hooking or slicing?' People would try to help me out, saying, 'If it's a right-handed hitter, it's slicing.' I felt like I was getting a public flogging.

"In this business, screwing up a game-winning homer is about as bad as it can get."

Miller currently is the "Voice of the Giants" and the play-by-play man for ESPN's *Sunday Night Baseball* telecasts. His face and voice are recognized everywhere baseball is played, his congenial personality is welcomed into living rooms across the nation. So just how powerful is he? Well listen to this story:

During a typically intense Giants-Diamondbacks game in May

2003, the teams entered the bottom of the ninth inning at Pacific Bell Park tied, 2-2. Ruben Rivera, a pinch runner, was at first base when Marquis Grissom hit a drive into right-center field, the Death Valley area of Pac Bell that opens to the 421-foot marker. David Dellucci went back on the ball and appeared to have it under control. But when he reached up at the last second, the ball went over his glove and rolled to the wall. Game over ... or was it?

"I'm doing the play-by-play on radio," Miller said, "and I pick up Rivera and he's coming around second base. He had rounded second and for some reason he thought the ball had been caught. He turns around and re-touches second base and starts back to first.

"As he's going back, Marquis Grissom is screaming at him, waving at him, 'Get going, c'mon.' Rivera immediately turns back around and breaks for third. But he cuts across the infield without touching second base. Then he turns back around and touches it again—the third time he had touched second base.

"Now the throw is coming back. He's going to be out by 40 feet at third base. But the third baseman can't handle the throw. He sort of knocks it back toward shortstop. Rivera is safe. It's a miracle. They've got runners on second and third base. Except Rivera sees it roll to short. He gets up and heads for home. He's not satisfied that he's received a miracle and is safe at third base. Well, Tony Womack makes a nice pickup at short and throws home, and Rivera is out by 10 feet.

"I'm on the air. I'm incredulous. Has he gone completely stark-raving nuts? I've never seen anything like that. At the moment, I didn't have the slightest idea what he was doing. I sum it all up by saying, 'That was the worst baserunning in the history of the game.' It turns out to be a happy ending for the Giants—they do win the game in extra innings, and Marquis Grissom ends up driving in the winning run. There's a certain justice there.

"But now there are all-sports stations all over the country. ... By the next day, my semi-hysterical call of that play has been played all over. I start getting phone calls from people who want to do interviews. I feel bad. They play it on the air while I'm talking. When I get to the ballpark, all the players are kidding me about it. Nobody is upset with me. They all know it was the worst baserunning play they had ever seen. But two or three days later, Rivera gets released.

"He was about to get released, anyway. But I'd hear from some players about it, how I got Rivera released. I knew they were kidding me about it. On the other hand, maybe enough feel that I did get him released that they kind of talk softly around me, just in case I do have that kind of power.

"You're describing something while it happens. You don't know what's going to happen. But most of the stuff you describe, you've described many times before. You know the proper verbal shorthand that people can translate into mental images. Occasionally, there is a play that you've never seen before. But usually, it's not as outrageous as that."

◆　◆　◆

A baseball broadcaster can never be too prepared. That's why Jose Mota always comes to the ballpark packing, strictly as a defensive measure.

"When foul balls come in the booth, it's hilarious," said Mota, a former major league infielder who broadcasts Anaheim games for the Angels' Spanish radio network. "I keep a glove on when I'm in my booth. People say, 'Why do you keep a glove? You're a former player.' That's exactly why I keep a glove in the booth with me. I trust my hands more with a glove.

"Once you're on the field, you have this respect for balls flying in and out. Just because you were a player, you don't lose the fear of getting smoked in the head by a foul ball."

Twice while working Angels games, either on television or radio, Mota has put his leather where his mouth is.

"Where we sit in Anaheim, we get a lot of shots, especially from lefthanded hitters," he said. "Oh, my goodness, they fly in there and I'm always looking down calling the game and taking notes. Ray Durham of the A's hit a line drive. This was a bullet. I stick my hand out, boom, catch it. So my call was, 'Here's a foul ball and ... Hey! Right into my hands. Thank you very much.'

"It was like a reaction. If I had not been looking, it would have hit me square in the face. I had no time to think. It was like boom, catch it, here it is."

Mota's next foul ball opportunity was provided by Minnesota outfielder Bobby Kielty. "I had a little more extension on my arm for that one," Mota recalled.

Next time you see Mota going to a game, you know he is working because, "My glove is right there with me. It's a Mizuno with my name on it. I used to play some outfield with it in my playing days. Don't leave home without it. Are you kidding me, a ballplayer without his glove? I'd feel naked."

Anaheim was eight outs away from losing Game 6 and the 2002 World Series to the San Francisco Giants. So why was Mota struggling to fight off laughter?

"People see me in the booth and I'm laughing, even as the team is losing," said Mota, who seemingly had no reason to be happy as the Angels trailed, 5-0, with one away in the bottom of the seventh inning. "I don't want people to think I'm not taking this seriously, but I could not take my eyes off the guy who represents our station. It was one of the funniest things I've ever seen."

During a season filled with Rally Monkeys, amazing comebacks and the first championship in franchise history, the radio station rep refused to mess with the team's karma. It was his habit to stand in one spot when the Angels trailed.

"If the Angels were winning, he'd just roam around the booth saying, 'Hi' to people and so forth," Mota said. "But on this day, I had to hit the mute button on my microphone a couple times (to hide the laughter) because this guy was turning red in his spot.

"He kept saying, 'I can't believe it's going to come to an end like this. I can't believe it.' Then just to see within four or five batters how his expression changed. He was running around the booth yelling and saying, 'I knew we could do it! I knew we could do it!' He was just out of his mind.

"He was like a little kid. I was nervous myself. But I had to keep hitting the mute or cough button so people wouldn't hear me laugh because I was having just as much fun watching him."

◆   ◆   ◆

The Ted Williams legend is built around his consummate skills in three areas: hitting a baseball, flying a fighter plane and fishing. Longtime Boston Red Sox broadcaster Curt Gowdy adds a fourth category: talking.

"He was the best interviewee that I ever had," Gowdy said. "He had a great voice. He was very frank, honest and open. He didn't dodge anything. He was very glib and just a great person to interview."

Fishing and baseball were the genesis of the lasting friendship between Gowdy and Williams. Gowdy was there when the Splendid Splinter rounded the bases for the last time on September 28, 1960, in a game at Fenway Park against Baltimore.

"I remember that it was a lousy, gray, cold day in Boston," said the Voice of the Red Sox from 1951-66. "Only about 11,000 or 12,000 people showed up, although there were 300,000 people there according to fans later on.

"Before the game, I had gone into the Red Sox clubhouse and the clubhouse boy, Johnny Orlando, called me over and he said, 'Listen, don't say anything, but this is The Kid's last game ever.' I said, 'Well, we've got a series in New York over the weekend.' He said, 'Mr. Yawkey's excused him from that. He's got a chest cold. But don't tell anybody.' I said, 'Don't worry, I won't.'

"I broke my word. Ted's next-to-last time up he hit a long drive to right field that backed the right fielder up against the bullpen. But he caught it. So he came up his last time and on the count of 1-1, he hit a home run. A big soaring drive into the right field grandstand.

"So, as he's rounding the bases, I say, 'Ted Williams has hit a home run (No. 521) in his last time at-bat in the major leagues.'

"He rounded third, came into home and ducked into the dugout," Gowdy remembered. "The fans stood, applauded and begged him to come back out and tip his cap, but he never did. That was typical Ted Williams."

Gowdy also had a fascination for Red Sox center fielder Jimmy Piersall, who was better known for his unpredictable behavior than his playing.

"About as good a defensive outfielder as I ever saw," Gowdy said. "You wondered about all his antics and everything. It was sort of a tragedy what happened to him, but he gave me a lot of thrills in broadcasting with the catches he made in the outfield. I mean they were just unbelievable. I think of the five greatest catches I ever saw—he made two or three of them."

Gowdy remembered telling Williams, "You play in the kookiest outfield that ever played in baseball."

Williams said, "What do you mean?"

"You got Jackie Jensen, who had to fly with a hypnotist," Gowdy said. "Then there's Piersall and you."

"Hey," Williams demanded, "why am I included in there?"

"Well," Gowdy said, "you're just different."

Here's Gowdy, commenting on notoriously cement-handed first baseman Dick Stuart, who played for the Red Sox in 1963 and '64.

"A good home run hitter," Gowdy said, "but he picked up a gum wrapper one day at first base and they gave him a standing applause, he was such a terrible fielder."

◆   ◆   ◆

When the great Dizzy Dean retired from his pitching career after one last fling with the St. Louis Browns in 1947, he headed for the broadcast booth, where he immediately began throwing curveballs at the English language—to the delight of listeners and the horror of school teachers throughout the Midwest.

The English Teachers Association of Missouri was so appalled at Dean's grammatical faux pas, it filed a complaint with the Federal Communications Commission. Students, they argued, were being influenced by such colorful Dean colloquialisms as "it ain't braggin' if'n you can do it," "the runner slud into second" and "the runner was throwed out at home."

At the height of the controversy, Ol' Diz was invited to New York to explain his side of the story to a national audience on a popular radio show called *We the People*. Speaking to millions of listeners and a jam-packed studio audience at Radio City, Dean delivered the following message:

"I'm sorry I ain't had no real good schoolin'. I only went to the third grade. I didn't do so good in the second grade, either. Y'see, if I'd gone to the fourth grade, I'da passed my father and gotten one helluva whippin'. But I guarantee you folks one doggone thing. There's lots of teachers out there now who ain't gettin' 300 bucks for just bein' on the air for three minutes like I am. And there's lots of people out there who don't say ain't who ain't eatin', either."

The teachers quickly rescinded the complaint.

Another Dean classic: A scientist once locked himself in his laboratory and emerged weeks later with the shocking announcement that there was no such thing as a curveball. It was, he said, nothing more than an optical illusion.

When Dizzy heard this proclamation, he furrowed his eyebrows and offered to perform an experiment that would prove otherwise. "You tell that scientist feller," Dean said, "to go hide himself behind a tree and I will stand 60 feet, 6 inches away and whomp him one with an optical illusion."

◆ ◆ ◆

On their way to a near-record 119 losses during the 2003 season, the Detroit Tigers unintentionally challenged the ability of broadcaster Jim Price to put it all into words.

"We were losing, 7-1, or something like that," said the former Tigers catcher and member of their 1968 championship team. "We have a pinch runner at first and he gets picked off on the first pitch. I scream on the air, 'You gotta be kidding me! You GOT-ta be kidding me!' And then I stand up and scream again, 'You GOTTA be kidding me!' To see things like that, it just drove me crazy."

Price and Hall of Famer Al Kaline, another former Tiger, often wondered, "What did we see tonight that we've never seen before?" Three other incidents topped Price's list:

■ Three straight Detroit batters with bunt singles during one of the Tigers' 43 wins.

■ Three straight errors—on different plays—during a game at Yankee Stadium.

■ The Tigers had a runner on first with two out and a 3-2 count on the batter. The runner, of course, was off with the pitch—ball four. The runner, however, over slid second base and was tagged out. As Price said, "That was something else."

◆　◆　◆

September 1969 was a magical time for the New York Mets and broadcaster Ralph Kiner, the former Hall of Fame outfielder for the Pittsburgh Pirates. The once-lowly Mets had clawed their way back into the National League pennant race, and the Chicago Cubs were in town for a showdown series at Shea Stadium.

"The Mets were making their move on the Cubs and getting ready to take over first place," Kiner recalled. "A black cat comes from underneath the stands and goes right out in front of the Cubs' dugout. I remember the cat sort of looked in at (Cubs manager) Leo Durocher. And, as always, it put a curse on him.

"Of course, we made that a focal point of the broadcast. It was almost an omen that the Mets were going to win. As it turned out, it came true. It was like a movie you see and say, 'Well, that couldn't happen on the field.' In reality it did happen, just like it would in a movie.

"The whole season was that way."

◆　◆　◆

Colorado Rockies television analyst George Frazier tells this story about an atypical day at the office several years ago:

"We're in Dodger Stadium. The Rockies are not playing well and not winning. My producer says, 'Hey, let's get Pamela Anderson and Kid Rock in the booth.' From the very beginning, I'm saying to myself, 'Oh boy, I don't know if that's a good idea or not.' My partner, play-by-play man Dave Armstrong, is a very straight-laced guy, goes to church five nights a week. So he's panicking. I just keep thinking, 'Oh boy. ....'

"Pamela walks in with her two young children and (the kids) sit down on my lap. Kid Rock's kid stands up right behind me. As Kid Rock walks into the booth, church-going Dave says, 'Hi, Mr. Rock. How are you?' I just start laughing and laughing, because that's not the guy's real name. Most people call him 'Kid' or they say, 'Hey Kid Rock, how ya doin'' and all that stuff. It's funny at the time and even Pam starts laughing about it. But I still just keep thinking, 'Oh boy, something bad is going to happen here. I can just feel it.'

"We're on the air when Kid Rock asks, 'Why do guys always grab their crotches?' That didn't go over too good. He keeps going about his point and says, 'Do they just have an itch there all the time? What's the deal?' Right after Kid Rock says that—wouldn't you know it—a guy gets a foul tip right in the crotch. Pam says, 'Oh, that's gotta hurt.'

"In the meantime, I have a telestrator in my booth and Kid Rock's son circles Pam's breast on the screen. I'm trying to kill the telestrator. I can't get it shut off. I'm telling the truck, but they're all laughing so hard they can't get a straight face long enough to kill my telestrator.

"This insanity goes on for two innings and I finally just say, 'Pamela, it was great to have you and Kid Rock here in the booth with us. We appreciate that you came by.' "

◆　◆　◆

Before arriving at his current gig as radio play-by-play man for the Anaheim Angels, Terry Smith worked his share of games in the minor leagues. He was calling games in 1981 for Memphis of the Class AA Southern League when Chicks relief pitcher Stu Livingstone provided one of his most unforgettable moments.

Livingstone, the team's closer, came into a game at Birmingham's

Rickwood Field with Memphis leading 1-0 in the bottom of the ninth inning. He retired the first two Barons he faced, then walked a batter on four straight pitches. Tigers prospect Mike Laga launched a tape-measure two-run homer to right on Livingstone's next pitch and, just like that, boom—Memphis lost the game, 2-1.

"I can remember how crushing of a loss it was for our club," Smith said. "After the game, I was on the bus and we were getting ready to go to our next town. The bus was kind of quiet when Livingstone gets on. To break the ice, a couple of the guys start razzing him a little bit by saying, 'Hey, Stu, why don't you put some more fuel on the fire.' They started to laugh.

"Some of the lines from Livingstone's teammates were so funny it was hard not to laugh, but I didn't want to laugh at this guy because of his misfortune. I tried to turn my head because I was starting to chuckle, but apparently he saw me laughing. So he looked at me and said, 'Smith, you just wait until the next time I'm in a game with two outs and nobody on base. You wait and see what happens. You hear me?' "

Smith replied, "Yes, I hear you," as Livingstone continued walking to his seat on the bus. And that was that. Until, that is, about a month later, when the team was in Savannah, Ga.

"I hadn't really thought about that incident from a month earlier," Smith said. "Sure enough, there is a game that Livingstone comes in for the bottom of the ninth inning. He gets the first two batters out. I think it was a 4-0 lead, so it wasn't like the lead was really on the line.

"I say, 'Here's the pitch. …' The next thing I knew, he threw the pitch right up to the press box. It hit right near my broadcast position. On the radio I say, 'It's a wild pitch, but luckily nobody is on base.' Then, all of a sudden, it dawned on me what he had said a month earlier. I continue to describe the rest of the game, but in the back of my mind I'm thinking, 'He threw that pitch at me!' "

When the game ended, Smith hustled down to the clubhouse. "I can't wait to see him," he said. "He comes out of the clubhouse and he's got a big smile on his face. I confront him, 'Stu, did you throw that ball at me up in the radio booth?' "

Livingstone: "What did I tell you about a month ago in Birmingham?"

Smith: "You threw that ball at me!"

"And," Livingstone added, "you'll never forget this story for the rest of your life."

◆　◆　◆

It was a hot night in Pittsburgh and everybody's concentration was a little overcooked. Bill Brown, the current television voice of the Houston Astros, was a broadcaster for the Reds at the time and described a complicated Pirates double play that involved a rundown for the second out.

"It took several throws to complete the play and the runner kept himself alive for a while," Brown said, "When they finally tag the guy out, all the Pirates run off the field to their dugout and we go to a commercial.

"Then I look down at my scorecard … and it was only the second out. All the Pirates are off the field, in the dugout and we're in a commercial. I mentioned it to the TV truck and we all realize, oops! But we're not alone. I check it out and everybody who is broadcasting the game assumes it is the third out and they also are in commercials. I would have thought somebody would catch it.

"Fortunately, they don't figure it out in the dugout fast enough. We have plenty of time to run all our commercials, come back and wipe the egg off our faces before the umpires go to the Pirates and say, 'Hey, boys, you can't call that an inning yet. It's only two outs.'

"It was so weird that the entire Pittsburgh team ran off the field. I would have thought somebody with the Reds would say, 'Wait a sec, guys, we've got another out coming here.' It was just one of those dog days of summer lulls that seem to influence everybody on the field."

Brown offers this tidbit from the 1975 World Series, when the Reds were forced to endure three straight postponements in rainy Boston between Games 5 and 6.

Needless to say, the stir-crazy Reds—and Brown—were itching to get out of their hotel rooms. So Brown rode with the team to Tufts University in the Boston suburb of Medford, where the Reds were invited to use the gym for some throwing and hitting. Unfortunately, the team's charter got lost in a little neighborhood.

Sparky Anderson told the bus driver to stop at a gas station and the silver-haired manager got off, dressed in full uniform, cleats included, to ask how to get to the college. Hey, what's a manager to do if not provide a little direction?

◆　◆　◆

St. Louis Cardinals and FOX-TV broadcaster Joe Buck recalled, with a rueful chuckle, his initiation into the baseball fraternity at a young age, when his father, Hall of Fame broadcaster Jack Buck, took Joe on a Cardinals road trip.

"When I was 10 or 11 years old," he said, "my dad took me with him to San Francisco. He had arranged it so I could play catch with the guys warming up on the field before the game and be the bat boy. It was a little hard for me at that age to stand up to the peer pressure, so when one of the guys—and I really don't remember who it was now—offered me a pinch to place between by lip and my gum, I said OK.

"I didn't feel any effects for about the first 40 seconds, but after that … oh, man! I couldn't even walk in a straight line to get from the dugout to home plate to pick up the bats. I was quite a source of amusement to the players. Finally, I went into the smallest bathroom in the history of indoor plumbing, right in the far corner of the visitors' dugout, and threw up.

"It was only after that I was able to handle my duties the right way. I guess in the long run, it wasn't such a bad trick. I have never been tempted to try tobacco of any sort again."

Ask Buck for the defining moment in his still-blossoming career and he does not hesitate: the record-setting conclusion to Mark McGwire's great 1998 home run chase.

"It's fun to talk about going through the 1998 season," Buck said. "All the signs pointed to some time in September when the single-season home run record was going to fall. From both an announcer standpoint and from a father-son standpoint, my dad and I wondered where the roulette wheel would stop and which one of us would be behind the microphone at that moment.

"During his career, my dad had been involved in moments that were captured and lived over and over again. There was the Kirk Gibson home run in Game 1 of the 1988 World Series. There was the 'Go crazy, folks, go crazy' call on Ozzie Smith's home run in the 1985 National League Championship Series against the Dodgers. He learned that you never get away from those calls, that you are always attached to that moment. So he understood what was to come.

"As home run No. 62 approached, I was continually asked the question, 'How will you call it?' I woke up in the morning thinking about what I was going to say. I went to bed at night thinking about what I was going to say. My wife heard about 65 fake record-setting calls and they were usually met with snores, so I knew I had work to do. The pressure was on.

"One thing I did learn is that you can't write out what you're going to say during a time when every other moment of the broadcast is spontaneous. FOX broadcast the game that night (September 8 at Busch Stadium) and I had a miniscript written out in my scorebook. I never used it. I couldn't because of the type of home run that it was—a low line drive that barely got up and over the fence and stayed fair.

"I have never concentrated on anything more than on the flight of that ball, because you can't blow that call. You cannot blow that call. But I realized Mark McGwire was so excited he jumped over first base and that became part of the call. '*Touch first base Mark McGwire. You are the new single-season home run champion.*' Obviously, I never dreamed that would find its way in there. Just goes to show what happens.

"As it turned out, Mike Shannon had the call on the Cardinals radio network. My dad had (called) No. 61. To go through all of that with my dad, with both of us just waiting for that moment, is very special to me. I don't remember a lot of calls in my career, but I'll always remember that one."

◆　　◆　　◆

Another blown lead by the Angels bullpen. Another moment to celebrate for the Cleveland Indians during a 1999 run of good fortune against Anaheim. No need for a weather report because Angels broadcaster Rex Hudler saw the storm clouds looming.

"Being a former player," Hudler said, "I could tell something was going to happen because tempers were at a boiling point on the Angels' side."

After a three-run Richie Sexson home run off Angels closer Troy Percival leapfrogged the Indians into an eighth-inning lead, David Justice was the lucky next hitter. Justice stepped into the box and went down like a shot, courtesy of a Percival pitch to the back of the neck. Justice jumped up and charged Percival as players from both dugouts spilled onto the field.

Viewers on the Angels television network heard Hudler say, "Go ahead! Get it out of your system and get after it!" At the first station break, Steve Physioc told his rookie broadcast partner, "You can't say that. There are kids watching."

"He scolded me a little bit," Hudler said. "I was all worked up. I wanted to go next door and fight Rick Manning, the Indians broadcaster. It was my first year in broadcasting. I was so passionate. I hadn't been off the field that long. The passion from the field came up to the booth and it spilled over."

Once back on the air, Hudler tried to explain his reaction to viewers. He tried to spin it again during the postgame show. "The game was over and I had my final summary," he said. "We're talking about the fight and I got all choked up. This was live TV and I kind of wept and I felt bad."

Hudler's baseball buddies who saw the telecast were not impressed with his tearful recant. The next day, Clyde Wright, a former player now working in community relations, handed him a box of tissues and said, "Here, this is for your next broadcast."

"That was an embarrassment to me to weep on the air like that," Hudler said. "They kind of got on me a little bit, but a lot of people liked it, too."

That was not the last time Hudler would find himself in hot water over an on-air observation. Later in the 1999 season, the Angels were playing Tampa Bay and legendary slugger Frank Howard, the Devil Rays' bench coach and still a mountain of a man, came to the Wonder Dog's attention.

"Frank is a big guy and really proud of himself," Hudler said. "He's big, he's fun, he's strong and he's genuine. He used to work out in the gym with just his underwear on. I was talking to him before the game and he was telling me about how he loves training, loved being a ballplayer and loves spreading the game to young people."

During the broadcast that day, the camera stopped on the 6-7 Howard, who was standing on the top step of the dugout and looming over the field like a skyscraper over a city. Hudler's intentions were good, even if his delivery was flawed.

"There's Frank Howard," he said. "He's a big man and he's proud of his big unit."

"What?" was the quick response of partner Physioc, who picked his disbelieving jaw off the floor of the booth and then cleaned out his ears. "I can't believe you just said that!"

"Said what?" Hudler answered.

"It sounded like you were talking about a certain part of his body," Physioc said.

"No. I was talking about his body. He's proud of his big unit," Hudler explained later. "When I said that, I didn't mean it to sound like I was talking about his genitals, but I was talking about his entire body. I didn't get any mail on that, but that was an embarrassment to me and a lot of people heard it and they just laughed. I didn't mean anything by that."

As a player, Hudler was known for his quirky personality, hustling style and a willingness to do anything. As a broadcaster, he brings the same enthusiasm to the plate. The wildly popular

Hudler offered a unique view of a 2002 Cincinnati Reds-Angels interleague game at Anaheim.

"I got all miked up and I put an Angels uniform on and I was a batboy," he said. "I had a microphone on my lapel. I had an IFB in my ear so I can hear what they're saying (up in the booth and in the production truck). And I basically analyzed the game for three innings from the field."

Angels manager Mike Scioscia was not enthusiastic about Hudler becoming an imbedded journalist.

"He is a little superstitious," Hudler said, "and he didn't want me down there. I sat where the batboys sit. When I ran out to pick up the first bat, I covered home plate with dirt. I just covered it up by kicking dirt on the plate. The umpire looked at me once, then twice and then said, 'Hud? What are you doing down here?'

"I went from the broadcast booth to the field for three innings. I loved it. I had a blast. I was able to do commentary from right outside the dugout as a batboy and that was spectacular."

And the Angels even won the game, which meant that "Mike Scioscia was happy."

◆　　◆　　◆

Denny Matthews has been Kansas City's radio play-by-play broadcaster since Day 1 of the franchise's expansion season in 1969. He long has cherished that distinction and the experience of being the first person to say, "The Royals win." Matthews also cherished his relationship with the man he called his all-time favorite player.

"Dan Quisenberry had a way with words," Matthews said, referring to the Royals' submarine-style closer from 1979-88. "He was a wordsmith. He loved words. He wrote a couple of books of poetry that were very good. He and I kind of hit it off immediately upon his joining the team.

"On the bus to the ballpark, we would trade a word for the day. He would come up with a word that I would have to incorporate into the broadcast. And then he would have to incorporate my word of the day into his postgame commentary to the writers or the TV people. This went on for a number of years. We had great fun with it.

"One April night I gave him 'gelid.' We were on our way to play the Tigers at the old stadium. I think the game-time temperature was about 37 degrees with a wind out of the northwest. It was just damn cold. Gelid means extremely cold. (Quisenberry) comes into the game, gets the last two or three outs for the save. In the clubhouse after the game, he tells the media, 'A pitcher never knows what he is going to have under such gelid conditions.'

"I'm sure some of the reporters were scratching their heads."

◆　◆　◆

A shuttle explodes. A man walks on the moon. A president is shot. Where were you when history occurred? For New Englanders—or at least those who prefer white chowder and Red Sox—one particular sports moment is so unforgettable and painful that they remember where they were when a ball rolled through a man's legs.

What did Red Sox radio broadcaster Joe Castiglione see and say about the fateful bottom of the 10th inning in Game 6 of the 1986 World Series at New York's Shea Stadium? Nothing. What about Mookie Wilson's bouncer slipping through the wickets of Bill Buckner to give the Mets a stunning 6-5 victory? "Never saw it," Castiglione said, not out of denial, but duty.

"I called the top of the 10th, when Dave Henderson hit the home run to put the Red Sox ahead and Wade Boggs doubled and scored an insurance run on Marty Barrett's single," Castiglione recalled. "So I said to my radio partner Ken Coleman, 'Do you want to go to the locker room or stay up here?' He left it up to me. I figured he's been with the club longer than me, so I thought he should be the one to call the last out when the team wins its first World Series since 1918."

Castiglione hurried down into the bowels of the Flushing Meadows ballpark and was standing in the hallway outside the Red Sox locker room "watching them bring in the champagne" while NBC workers hurried to assemble a postseason trophy presentation platform and others draped protective plastic throughout the Boston locker room in anticipation of the champagne to come.

"I was listening on a security guard's radio to the voice of (Mets broadcaster) Bob Murphy as the ball gets away from Gedman back to the backstop and the tying run comes in," Castiglione said. "Then I was on my way hurrying back up the ramp for more innings when I heard the crowd go wild and I knew the Mets had won. I never saw it."

Actually seeing disaster unfold might be a worse fate, said Castiglione, who was still throbbing with disappointment in November after the abrupt and shocking finish to the 2003 Red Sox's season a month earlier.

"This year, I got to say those awful words, 'The Yankees win the pennant.' That was very, very painful," said Castiglione, referring to Aaron Boone's 11th-inning home run that ended Game 7 of the A.L. Championship Series and dashed Boston's pennant hopes for another season. "Actually, the eighth inning was much more painful, especially on (Jorge) Posada's hit because at first it looked like a catchable pop and then it dropped in."

Posada's bloop single to center field off Red Sox ace Pedro Martinez scored two runs and capped a three-run, game-tying rally. Boone took care of the dramatics in the 11th.

"I tried not to sound like the guy reporting when the Hindenburg blew up," Castiglione said, "but I don't know."

From a less historical perspective, Castiglione can regale listeners with stories about former Red Sox manager Joe Morgan, the hunch-playing former snowplow driver who guided the team from July 1988 through the 1991 season. One tale from 1989 gets right to the essence of this regular Joe.

Morgan handed the umpires a lineup card for a May 3 game at Chicago with righthanded-hitting Rick Cerone listed as the catcher against White Sox pitcher Shawn Hillegas. Perhaps because of his Yankee background, Cerone never was a popular player in Boston, even among teammates and broadcasters. The lefthanded-hitting Rich Gedman, on the other hand, was a native New

Englander and usually a sympathetic figure, even during the late 1980s when he struggled with the bat.

Before this game, Castiglione asked Morgan about the curious choice of Cerone starting against a righthander.

Morgan: "Isn't Hillegas a lefty?"

Castiglione: "No, Joe, he's a righthander."

Morgan: "Oh, (bleepity-bleep), I (screwed) up."

After Morgan apologized privately to a ticked-off Gedman, Cerone went out and hit a three-run homer to win the game. During the postgame broadcast, Castiglione interviewed the manager and gave him the chance to accept credit for his "stroke of genius."

"Well, Joe," Castiglione said, "that hunch to play Cerone certainly paid off."

"No," said the brutally honest Morgan to everyone in Red Sox Nation, "that was no hunch. I thought that pitcher was a lefty. I just screwed up."

◆　◆　◆

This story about a 1973 St. Louis-Philadelphia game at Veterans Stadium, supplied by ESPN analyst Dave Campbell, is enough to warm any broadcast booth:

"I kind of kid with Tim McCarver about it. We call it the 'All-Broadcast Play.' I was playing second base for the Cardinals, McCarver was catching, Tommy Hutton was the hitter and Danny Ozark put in Ken Brett to pinch run—you know, one of his pitchers.

"And Hutton hit a line drive and I didn't think I had the chance to catch it. There were two out, bottom of the eighth, tie score and, with a dive to my left, the ball somehow hit right in the webbing of my glove and kind of hung there until I hit the ground. I landed on my chin and the ball came loose. And so, I started crawling on my hands and knees, turned around on the AstroTurf and threw the ball on my knees to home plate.

"McCarver got the ball, blocked the plate, Brett tried to run him down and wrecked his shoulder. I call it the 'All-Broadcast Play' because we all went into broadcasting after that."

◆　◆　◆

Steve Physioc was the play-by-play television broadcaster for the Cincinnati Reds in 1985 when two major events converged to make for an especially exciting and stressful late summer and early fall. At work, Physioc was expected to say something meaningful when Pete Rose completed his pursuit of Ty Cobb's all-time hits record. At a more personal venue, Physioc was expected to say something meaningful at the altar as he completed his pursuit of Stacey's hand in marriage.

Physioc and his fiance planned a September wedding, even though they knew it could conceivably conflict with one of the great moments in baseball history. So before the season, Physioc asked Rose, "When do you think you'll get the record?"

Without hesitation, Rose said, "August 23."

Physioc: "What?"

Rose: "Yes, I'm only playing against righthanders now. So I take the percentage of righthanders and percentage of lefthanders and what I think I'll bat this year and it will be August 23."

Physioc: "Great, I'll make the wedding for September 7."

As the projected date got closer and closer, Rose fell off pace. "He doesn't break the record on August 23 and the television station says, 'You can't go on your honeymoon until Pete gets the hit,' " Physioc said.

"So I had Pete sign a baseball for Stacey. On one side I wrote, 'Stacey will you marry me ...' and on the other side, he wrote down, '... but not until I get the hit. —Pete Rose.' "

Rose was drawing close when Steve and Stacey got married, as scheduled, on September 7—a Saturday in St. Louis—then raced to Chicago where the Reds were playing the Cubs. Rose got one hit on Sunday (September 8) to tie the record. On Monday, Rose didn't play against San Diego lefthander Dave Dravecky in the opener of a series at Cincinnati. On Tuesday, with the newlyweds still waiting for their honeymoon, he went hitless against LaMarr Hoyt. On Wednesday, Rose finally broke the record.

"It was just a wonderful story," Physioc said, "and I turn to my wife and say, 'Now aren't you glad we waited.' And she says, 'Yes.' Simply because it was just such a great story."

Physioc, who was doing play-by-play for an ESPN game in 1993, invited former Los Angeles Rams wide receiver-turned-broadcaster Jack Snow to "stop by the booth." The hook: Snow's 25-year-old son, J.T., was playing first base for the California Angels.

"Up comes Jack's son," Physioc recalled. "Jack is talking about their history together and growing up when J.T. hits a home run. Jack goes crazy. He's practically jumping out of the booth. He just jumped out of his chair. We practically had to grab him or he would have fallen out of the booth. He was so excited and was saying, 'That's my boy! What a job! Look at the way he drove that pitch!'

"I think Dave Campbell was my partner in the booth and we were just laughing and having a great time with it. I'm thinking, 'What a wonderful moment for the fans to hear a dad watching his son play major league baseball and hit a home run.

"It was like Jack didn't realize there was a microphone attached to his head. Even though Jack is a wonderful broadcaster, at that moment he was just being a dad."

Snow was just being a dad. Sparky Anderson was just being a manager.

"He knew every single time the pitcher was going to throw to first base. It was like he had mental telepathy," Physioc said, recalling his first on-air experience with Anderson in the late 1990s when they partnered in the Anaheim Angels' booth. "But he wouldn't tell me how he knew because he was afraid he would give it away to the opponent."

During a commercial break, the veteran play-by-play man pressed the manager emeritus for some tutoring.

Physioc: "Sparky, how are you doing this? You know every time they're going to pitch and every time they're going to throw a pickoff move."

Anderson: "Just watch the catcher's back. When he relaxes his shoulders, he knows the ball is not coming to him. When he tenses up, he knows the pitch is coming."

Physioc: "Awesome! That's great stuff. Now, why don't you say it on the air?"

◆　　◆　　◆

Harry Caray, the Voice of the Cardinals for the first quarter century of his legendary broadcasting career, told a story that columnist Bob Verdi related in a 1989 issue of *The Sporting News*:

"I'm in Memphis one winter, early 1960s, to do a basketball game, the St. Louis Hawks, back on TV to St. Louis," Caray said. "They played a series of games in Memphis. I'm in my hotel room the afternoon of the game. The phone rings.

" 'Harry,' a voice says, 'been listening to you for years. How are the Cardinals gonna be this season?'

"I think we're gonna be OK," Caray said. "We've got a good ballclub. Uh, who is this?

" 'Elvis,' the voice says.

"Elvis who?" Caray responds.

" 'Elvis Presley,' " the voice answers.

"C'mon," Caray says, "don't give me that. You're not Elvis Presley."

" 'You're a sporting man,' the voice says. 'If you don't think it's me, be down in front of the hotel in 10 minutes.' "

Curious, Caray went down and watched a Cadillac pull up. Elvis Presley, indeed, was inside.

"Well, he took me to his mansion," Caray said. "We talked baseball, music, what have you. Then he dropped me off at the arena so I could do the basketball game and picked me up 15 minutes after the game. We went back to his house and wound up eating ribs and drinking Budweiser and shooting the bull until the wee hours.

"I'll never forget that phone call."

Caray was known for his colorful play-by-play descriptions, as well as his on-air enthusiasm and unrestrained overstatement. Caray offered this typical optimistic assessment in a 1964 game after a St. Louis pitcher had driven in two runs with a double.

"I can't believe it," Caray exhorted. "Roger Craig hit the left-center field wall. The Cardinals are going to win the pennant."

The game was played April 17—the Cardinals' fourth of the season. But true to Caray's prediction, the Cardinals did go on to win the National League pennant—and the World Series.

Caray built up a huge following during his years in St. Louis. That celebrity loomed big about 3 a.m. one night in 1972, three years after he had been fired by the Cardinals.

Caray, now a fixture in the broadcast booth for the Chicago White Sox, was making a winter visit to St. Louis and had spent a long evening at an old haunt in the Chase Park Plaza Hotel. When he finally departed in the wee hours of the morning, his car wouldn't start. So he phoned for roadside assistance.

When headlights appeared later behind his car, Caray got out to greet the emergency truck. But instead of help, he found himself face to face with two young men who pointed revolvers at him.

Caray started a panicky spiel, encouraging the men not to do anything foolish and telling them they could have anything they wanted. Suddenly one of the gunmen blurted, "Holy Cow! You're Harry Caray. How about that?"

The revolvers went down.

"Hey, Harry, you're with the White Sox now," he said. "You've got Richie Allen. Boy, do we miss you here, but we get your broadcasts. ... What are you doing here?"

Caray explained the problem and the would-be robbers offered to give him a push. He declined, telling them help was on the way.

"Well, OK, Harry," the man said, "if we can't help you, we'll see you around."

And they drove off into the night.

THE GREAT MOMENTS, REVISITED

It was one of the most memorable scenes in baseball history. Kirk Gibson, barely able to walk much less run, hobbling slowly and painfully around the bases after hitting a two-run, ninth-inning home run to give his Los Angeles Dodgers a 5-4 victory over the Oakland Athletics and closer Dennis Eckersley in a dramatic conclusion to Game 1 of the 1988 World Series.

Gibson's shocking blast and triumphant trot have become well-documented pieces of baseball legend. But NBC-TV broadcaster Bob Costas offers a unique perspective of the Gibson moment, an insider's view from the corner of the Dodgers dugout.

"Vin Scully and Joe Garagiola are calling the game and I'm hosting the pregame and any postgame stuff," he recalled. "It was Saturday night and once the game ended on the East Coast, they wanted to quickly get to local news and then to *Saturday Night Live*. So they wanted me to be close enough to literally jump on the field once the game ended and interview somebody."

Costas had made an arrangement with Marv Albert, another member of the NBC team. Costas would take the Dodgers after the game; Albert would handle the A's. It appeared Albert would be front and center with either Jose Canseco, who had hit a grand slam, or Eckersley, who had been nearly untouchable all season in his closer role. Costas was leaning toward asking Dodgers manager Tommy Lasorda about his pitching plans for the remainder of the Series.

"So I go down through the catacombs of the stadium," Costas said, "and I come up though the tunnel that connects the clubhouse to the dugout. And, technically, non-uniformed personnel are not supposed to be in the dugout while the game is being played. But the players knew me, and they didn't seem to have any objection, so I hung at the very corner of the dugout in the ninth inning.

"Lasorda had gone down the hallway to get a drink or something. And he saw me—now, Tommy has always been great to me—and he goes, 'What the (bleep) is your little ass doin' here? They think the (bleepin') game is over already? Why don't you just (bleepin') do the interview now?' So I'm like, 'Hey, Tommy, I hope you score 10 runs, I don't care. I'm just standing here.'

"So the inning starts to unfold and I can hear Gibson, down at the other end of the tunnel. A bat boy was down there with him, and they were putting a ball on a tee and he was trying to loosen up. And you could really hear him grunting in pain. It would be, 'thwack, Aaahhh, thwack, Aaahhh!' It was very difficult for him to swing the bat and try to get loose with the injuries he had.

"And then Ben Hines, who was the Dodgers' hitting coach, came walking up the tunnel and walked past me, and I could hear him say to Lasorda, like a line out of a B movie: 'He thinks he has one good swing in him.' I'm thinking, 'Who writes this script?' And then eventually, Gibson comes hobbling up the corridor. No question he was hobbling. I mean, none of that was done for effect. He could hardly drag himself from the locker room to the dugout. I mean he was really hurting.

"And his own teammates were surprised to see him. Their best hope seemed to be, after Mike Davis got a walk, that maybe he could bloop a hit somehow, somewhere, and they could get the tying run.

"Now in great theatrical fashion, here comes Gibson, hobbling out of the dugout. You know, the crowd goes nuts, it's a melodramatic scene, and as the count goes to 3-and-2, Davis steals second. And then, Eckersley tries to throw the backdoor slider, and to this day, I still don't know how with that swing Gibson hit the ball out of the park. An almost flat-footed swing, he completed his stride, and he just kind of flicked his wrists at it and somehow jerked it out to right field. And one of the great scenes, as that ball goes out in right field, you can see the red taillights of a lot of cars leaving the parking lot already.

"So now, by the time Gibson hits second base, I've jumped on the field and I'm waiting for him. And he crosses the plate and his teammates are all over him and it's this unbelievable scene. And we pull Gibson over and it was a genuine, spontaneous thing. Vin threw it right down and I don't even remember the content of it. But the whole place was abuzz, and he was on the air, literally, 15 seconds after he crossed home plate.

"I did the interview with him, and then I noticed that, very unlike a Los Angeles crowd, the people who had been there at the end were still there. Tens of thousands of them were in their seats, not wanting to move, not wanting to relinquish the moment.

"And I looked up and saw a guy walking down toward the railing. It was Tom Brokaw and he just wanted to see someone he knew, in this case me, and just say to somebody, 'Isn't that one of the greatest things you've ever seen? Can you believe this?' "

Later that night, Costas was discussing the Game 1 events with NBC producer David Neal and commented about the similarities between Gibson's home run and another at-bat that remains prominent in baseball lore.

"I said to him, 'You know, this is like what Robert Redford did in *The Natural*,' " Costas said. "And *The Natural* had come out only a few years before that (1984), so it was kind of fresh in people's minds. I said it was like Redford's last at-bat, except (Gibson) wasn't bleeding from a bullet wound.

"And that set off a light bulb in Neal's, head and he went and got the film of *The Natural* and he intercut Redford's last at-bat with

Gibson's last at-bat, and that's how we came on the air at the start of Game 2. And it was uncanny how what they did mirrored each other.

"You were able to cut from Redford grimacing on a swing to Gibson grimacing on a swing, and the best part was Wilford Brimley, who played the manager in the movie. When Roy Hobbs hits one out and it hits the light standard and all the lights go off, Brimley tries to jump up in the air and thrust his hands over his head and gets like about 2 inches off the ground. And Lasorda did exactly the same thing. He looked so much, in terms of the body, like Brimley jumping up and thrusting his hands in the air that it was like the whole thing was scripted.

"We ended with Redford going around the bases and Gibson going around the bases. It was just uncanny. And everybody had goosebumps again before Game 2 after seeing that."

◆　◆　◆

Relief ace Goose Gossage pitched in three Division Series games, eight Championship Series games and eight World Series games for the New York Yankees and San Diego Padres. But nothing could match the pressure he felt on October 2, 1978, when he was asked to close out the Yankees' 5-4 victory over Boston at Fenway Park—the one-game playoff to determine an East Division winner after a bitter and exhausting pennant race.

"As far as the pressure—the World Series pales in comparison," Gossage recalled two decades later. "It's by far the biggest game I ever pitched in. When you play 162 games and it comes down to identical records and you have to play one game for all the marbles, it just doesn't seem fair."

Gossage still shudders when he thinks about the tense ninth inning, when he had to protect a shaky one-run lead in a hostile ballpark with a runner on third base and two out.

"It was one of those things where the night before I went to bed and I can see myself tomorrow facing Yaz for the final out," Gossage said, referring to Red Sox slugger Carl Yastrzemski. "And here it is: ninth inning, two out and who's up? Yaz. ... My legs were shaking, I was shaking all over, I was just trembling. It was like nothing I had ever faced to that point. I never faced another game like that in my career.

"When Yaz came up, I backed off the mound and I said, 'Well, here it is.' I was holding a great conversation out there with myself and I said, 'What's the worst thing that can happen to you, that I'll be home in Colorado tomorrow elk hunting?' I was putting a life-or-death tag on that thing. ... What happened after that conversation with myself, it was like the weight of the world had been lifted off my shoulders. I just put the game in perspective. ... For the first time in that ballgame, I relaxed."

After throwing a first-pitch ball, Gossage threw Yastrzemski a fastball that rode in on his hands. Yaz popped it up to third baseman Graig Nettles, and the Yankees took a major step toward a second straight World Series championship. "Oh my God, that was beyond description," Gossage recalled. "You just had to feel this feeling that went through my body. I had never felt it before and I never felt it again."

◆ ◆ ◆

On May 2, 1939, New York Yankees great Lou Gehrig delivered the pregame lineup to the umpires, returned to the dugout and sat down, never to play in another major league game. The emotional moment, the official end of Gehrig's historic 2,130-game playing streak, was witnessed by teammate Tommy Henrich in stunned silence.

"The memory I have more than any other one," Henrich recalled six decades later, "was a sad situation when he came back and he sat down in the middle of the dugout and Lefty Gomez and I are standing on the righthand side on the top steps, looking at the field. We looked back and Lou was crying. Believe me, he was sobbing.

"And the great Gomez walked past Lou Gehrig and says, 'What the heck, Lou. Now you know how pitchers feel when they get knocked out of the game.' And Gehrig laughed. And I thought, 'Thata boy, Lefty.' That broke the whole thing."

♦ ♦ ♦

Former right fielder Don Mueller was a key performer in what many regard as the greatest moment in baseball history—Bobby Thomson's homer that won the 1951 pennant for the New York Giants. But Mueller didn't even see the three-run, ninth-inning blast that gave the Giants a dramatic 5-4 victory over the Brooklyn Dodgers in the third game of a pennant playoff at the Polo Grounds.

"I was in the clubhouse, on the trainer's table," Mueller said. "I had pulled the tendon in my ankle and they carried me to the clubhouse."

The Giants entered the ninth inning trailing the Dodgers and ace righthander Don Newcombe, 4-1. But Al Dark opened the inning with a single and Mueller followed with another single. One out later, Dark scored on Whitey Lockman's double and Mueller jammed his foot sliding into third on a close play. Clint Hartung was brought in as a pinch runner when Mueller was carried off on a stretcher.

"I didn't see it. I didn't hear it," Mueller said, referring to Thomson's game-ending blow off Dodgers reliever Ralph Branca. "All I heard was the crowd roar and the game was so close to being over I didn't know who had won. I didn't know until the team started coming into the clubhouse. They were all full of pep.

"Up to that point, all I had heard was the roar of the crowd. There were probably as many Dodger fans there as there were Giants fans, so you couldn't tell by that. That was a dandy day. They sent me straight to the hospital."

♦ ♦ ♦

Mueller wasn't the only player to miss out on one of baseball's classic moments. St. Louis catcher Joe Garagiola was in the Cardinals clubhouse when teammate Enos Slaughter made the eighth-inning Mad Dash that decided Game 7 of the 1946 World Series against the Boston Red Sox.

"I did not see it," Garagiola said. "Ted Williams had fouled a pitch off and broke my finger. It was a high curveball and I reached up and he fouled it off my finger. I was in the clubhouse being treated and I heard it—and I was part of the celebration. But I did not see it."

Neither did Garagiola witness the tense ninth when Cardinals reliever Harry Brecheen tried to protect a 4-3 lead. The game ended when Boston pinch hitter Tom McBride hit what appeared to be a routine ground ball to second baseman Red Schoendienst with runners on first and third. It was anything but routine.

"That was the toughest play I ever made in baseball," Schoendienst said. "It didn't look that tough, but I charged it, it took a bad hop and just went up my arm to my left shoulder. I blocked it, smothered it on my chest, reached in with my right hand and flipped to (shortstop Marty) Marion. My heart was beating fast on that play."

◆ ◆ ◆

Dave Henderson was not exactly thinking home run when he stepped to the plate in the ninth inning of Game 5 in the 1986 American League Championship Series. The Boston center fielder, batting with a man on base and the Red Sox trailing, 5-4, at Anaheim Stadium, was the only obstacle between the California Angels and their first World Series appearance.

"In those days, I was primarily a defensive replacement for Tony Armas late in the ballgame," said Henderson, who was forced into action when Armas twisted his ankle in the fifth inning. "So I wasn't getting that many at-bats. You're looking basically at a defensive replacement who is supposed to go in there, make outs and we can go home. So I was at a great disadvantage and (Angels reliever) Donnie Moore had a devastating forkball."

Henderson, who also was hobbled by torn cartilage in his right knee, quickly fell into an 0-2 hole against the Angels righthander. "There were 64,000 people all in their starting blocks to run out on the field," he recalled. "The guards at the stadium were like 64 years old and above so I knew they had no chance of stopping these people from running out on the field. Basically, I was looking for a way to get back to our dugout after striking out."

But Henderson took two balls and evened the count at 2-2. Then he fouled two pitches straight back and suddenly decided, "I had a chance." Moore threw a forkball and Henderson committed early, making solid contact with a ball he muscled out of the park with a one-handed follow-through.

"There was a deafening loudness before I hit the home run," he said. "Then you could hear a pin drop after it."

The Angels tied the game at 6-6 in the bottom of the ninth, but the Red Sox won in the 11th on Henderson's sacrifice fly. Boston went on to win Games 6 and 7 at Fenway Park.

The old superstition that no-hitters should never be acknowledged until the final out is recorded got a stern test on October 8, 1956, when New York Yankee Don Larsen, a free-spirited journeyman righthander, provided one of the most memorable performances in baseball history—his 2-0 perfect game victory over the Brooklyn Dodgers in the fifth game of the World Series at Yankee Stadium. No-hitter protocol was broken that day by none other than Larsen himself.

"After the seventh inning, I came into the dugout and I was smoking a cigarette and I bumped (Mickey) Mantle," Larsen recalled. "I told him, 'Look at the scoreboard. Wouldn't it be something? Two more innings to go.'

"Mantle looked horrified. He didn't say anything. He just walked away from me. Then it got like a morgue. Nobody would talk to me, nobody would sit by me—like I had the plague."

When New York lefthander Dave Righetti created his own brand of fireworks with a Fourth of July no-hitter against the Boston Red Sox in 1983—the first Yankee Stadium no-hitter since Larsen's in '56—his teammates remained true to convention and did not acknowledge the magic he was creating. But the pitcher heard a lot more than he wanted when he returned to the clubhouse before the ninth inning and a television announcer delivered all of the exciting details.

"I went back to change my gum, as I always do, and I heard it," Righetti said. "I could have killed him."

Yankees manager Billy Martin might have saved the day. Martin tried to give his 24-year-old lefthander a little divine inspiration as he neared completion of his gem.

"I did something I've never done in baseball before," admitted Martin, who was the Yankees' second baseman during Larsen's perfecto in 1956. "I've never said a prayer for myself during a game, not even in the World Series.

"But when that last guy (Wade Boggs) was up, I said a Hail Mary for Righetti. I wanted so much for him to get the no-hitter because he's such a good kid and such a competitor."

Righetti struck out Boggs to complete his 4-0 victory and while the pitcher celebrated and answered questions from the media, Martin placed a telephone call to his father—Leo "Pinky" Righetti, who had played with Martin in the Yankees farm system in the early 1950s. According to Martin, "His old man chewed him out for walking four batters."

◆　◆　◆

Lefthander Don Liddle remembers the intensity of the moment, he can describe the pitch he threw, and he never will forget the way Cleveland's Vic Wertz crushed it toward the wide-open center field pasture of New York's Polo Grounds. But he did not see what happened next—the incredible, over-the-head catch turned in by New York Giants teammate Willie Mays in Game 1 of the 1954 World Series.

"I didn't see him catch it," Liddle said. "My duty was to back up a base. With runners on first and second and a ball hit that deep, I didn't know whether to back up home or third base. So I ran over and got between third and home, over by the Cleveland dugout, to see which way the throw might go. When I turned and saw the runners, I knew Willie had caught it."

Liddle, like everybody in the ballpark who actually had witnessed the catch, was amazed that Wertz's 460-foot drive would go down in history as nothing more than a long out. He was even more shocked when Mays told him a little secret after the game.

"I was strictly a low-ball pitcher. I got a lot of ground balls," Liddle said. "But Willie didn't know that we had switched, that we weren't going to pitch Wertz low. So he sneaked in a couple of steps. He thought he might be able to throw that runner at second out at the plate.

"I've looked at (the catch) on TV a thousand times since and, my God, what a catch! But Mays told me, 'I had it all the way.'"

One person who did see the catch was Joe Garagiola, a late-season Giants acquisition who was not eligible for inclusion on the team's postseason roster. Garagiola, in fact, witnessed Mays' incredible catch from an unusual perspective.

"If you look at that famous Mays catch photograph," Garagiola said, "you'll see a bald head in the window of that center field clubhouse at the Polo Grounds. That was me. I had an angle on that catch that nobody else had, kind of a bird's-eye view. And I'll tell you, it was a great catch no matter what angle you saw it from."

Mays saved at least two runs with his catch and the game moved into the bottom of the 10th inning with the Giants and Indians tied 2-2. That's when Giants pinch hitter Dusty Rhodes hit a pop fly toward the inviting 260-foot foul pole down the right field line with two runners on.

"The wind blew it out of there," Rhodes recalled. "(Cleveland pitcher) Bob Lemon threw his glove farther than I hit the ball. Wertz hit a ball 460 feet and I hit one 260, but who cares. We won the game."

Game 7 of the 1962 World Series ended when San Francisco Giants slugger Willie McCovey, facing New York righthander Ralph Terry with runners on second and third and two out, hit a vicious line drive that perfectly positioned Yankees second baseman Bobby Richardson snared to preserve a 1-0 victory and a championship.

Years later, Richardson recalled an interesting exchange with shortstop Tony Kubek while Yankees manager Ralph Houk talked with Terry about the prospects of pitching to McCovey or on-deck slugger Orlando Cepeda.

"I really thought they were going to walk him," Richardson said. "Ralph Houk came out to talk to Terry and when he did I walked over to second base. Tony and I roomed together for 10 years and he kids a lot. He says, 'I hope he walks McCovey.' I said, 'Why?' And he says, 'If he hits the ball to you, you've already made two errors in this Series. I'd hate to see you blow one now.' And that's sort of what I was thinking before he hit the ball."

♦ ♦ ♦

That Game 7 victory was sweet vindication for Terry, who had been victimized two years earlier by Pittsburgh second baseman Bill Mazeroski's stunning World Series-ending Game 7 homer against the Yankees. Many pitchers wilt under the glare of such an infamous moment, but Terry pulled through, thanks to some wise counsel from manager Casey Stengel.

"After the game, I went in and talked to Casey," Terry said. "I felt bad for Stengel, more than myself or anyone else. I loved Casey Stengel. He was a great inspirational manager to me. ... We pretty well knew it was his last year, so I really felt bad for Casey.

"I said, 'Casey, I really feel bad it ended this way. He said, 'How were you trying to pitch him?' I said, 'Breaking stuff, low and away, but I couldn't get the damn ball down.' He said, 'As long as you pitch, you're not always going to get the ball where you want to.

That's a physical mistake. But if you went against the scouting report with high, hard stuff, then I wouldn't sleep good at night.' Then he said, 'Forget about it. Don't let it worry you.'

"And you know what? The Yankee fans are the greatest in the world. They never, ever came down on me for that. They never held that against me. I never got any bad response from those people and I love those Yankee fans for that."

◆ ◆ ◆

Kansas City closer Mark Littell had a different opinion of Yankee fans in 1976 after surrendering an A.L. pennant-deciding home run to New York first baseman Chris Chambliss, who was leading off the bottom of the ninth inning in Game 5 of the A.L. Championship Series. Littell was distracted during warmups by Yankees grounds crew members clearing debris from the the grass in right field—beer cans, bottles and batteries fans had directed at teammate Hal McRae.

"I remember Buck Martinez, who was catching, came out and I said, 'Hey, let's get off this mound. Let's get the hell off the field. Anything can happen,' " Littell recalled. "He said, 'They're going to get it cleared up quickly. Don't worry about it. They're already getting it pretty much cleared.' There probably was a four or five-minute delay."

Littell stood and watched. When the debris finally was cleared, he turned his attention to Chambliss.

"When I threw that first pitch, a fastball, and the ball went up in the air, I thought, 'Whoa. That ball's going to come down.' But it's carrying, carrying. And the next thing I know it's out. It went out by about 2½ feet."

McRae raced for the bullpen tunnel and safety from the delirious fans who were rushing the field. Chambliss fought through the thickening horde as he tried to complete his home run trot.

"I didn't know what to do," Littell said. "I just headed toward our dugout. There were so many fans coming at me, but not one touched me. I got down into the dugout and there weren't many players in there. Somebody pulled my jersey and got me out of the dugout and into the runway. All I can remember is a couple of thousand people running around going crazy."

Crazy enough to do $100,000 worth of damage to Yankee Stadium, which had to be repaired before Game 3 of the World Series against Cincinnati.

◆　◆　◆

Reggie Jackson wasn't with the Yankees in 1976, but he was the following season when the spotlight focused squarely on his broad shoulders. Chambliss and the mob scene his 1976 ALCS home run triggered couldn't have been far from Jackson's mind as the sixth game of the 1977 World Series neared its dramatic conclusion.

"I had worked the plate the day before and I was in right field in Game 6, when Jackson hit his three home runs against the Dodgers," umpire Jim Evans recalled. "I'll never forget the final out. Jackson was positioned about 10 feet behind the infield, as close as he could get to the dugout, because he was expecting the fans to come rushing out.

"If a Dodger had hit the ball to right field, he could have run all day."

◆　◆　◆

When the Brooklyn Dodgers won their first—and only—World Series in 1955 with a 2-0 Game 7 victory over the dreaded New York Yankees, one key member of the Bronx Bombers found consolation in defeat.

"I really felt great for Pee Wee (Reese)," Yankees shortstop Phil Rizzuto said. "Pee Wee would come over every time after we beat them. I was one of the only guys who went over to their clubhouse to congratulate them. He had done it every time for us. I was born in Brooklyn so I have a little spot in my heart for them.

"Brooklyn was a town that lived and died with the Dodgers. When the Dodgers were playing, you could walk up and down the streets of Brooklyn and never miss a pitch. Everybody had the game on the radio. It meant so much to them."

◆　◆　◆

The baseball world rejoiced when Cincinnati player-manager Pete Rose passed Ty Cobb with hit No. 4,192 on September 11, 1985, at Riverfront Stadium. But the record-breaker almost came three days earlier in a game against Chicago at rainy Wrigley Field—a near-miss that tortured unsuspecting Reds owner Marge Schott.

Everything was set up nicely for Rose to catch and pass Cobb in front of fans in an upcoming homestand at Cincinnati. He was two hits behind, Steve Trout was scheduled to pitch for the Cubs in the Chicago finale, and Rose would not play, continuing his season-long pattern of sitting out against lefthanders. Schott returned to Cincinnati before the game, as did most of Rose's family.

But the scenario suddenly changed when the Cubs announced that Trout had hurt himself in a bicycle accident and rookie righthander Reggie Patterson would be pitching in his place. Rose inserted himself into the lineup, news that did not sit well with family, fans and one indignant owner who waited anxiously 300 miles away.

Rose's first-inning single sent shock waves through the Reds community. His fifth-inning single tied Cobb's hit record and even his players and coaches watched with trepidation.

"He almost broke it that day in Chicago," longtime friend and first base coach Tommy Helms recalled. "We were trying to get him to take himself out of the lineup, but he almost got another hit—he hit a shot right at (shortstop Shawon) Dunston. We even got his son down to the bench to talk him into taking himself out of the game, but he wouldn't do it. That's just Pete."

Rose went hitless in his final two at-bats and the game ended in a rain-shortened 5-5 tie. "I had 30,000 people yelling here and one lady (Schott) sitting back in Cincinnati kicking her dog every time I got a hit," Rose quipped.

◆ ◆ ◆

Rose also was responsible for a few kicked dogs on July 14, 1970, when he took center stage on one of the most memorable plays in All-Star Game history. The National League won that night in Cincinnati, 5-4, when Rose barreled into American League catcher Ray Fosse and scored the winning run in the 12th inning.

Not only did the Reds star separate Fosse from the ball in the bang-bang play, he separated the Cleveland catcher's shoulder and caused a slight fracture. Fosse never again played at an All-Star level in a 12-year career that ended in 1979. Was he bitter about the collision taking place in an All-Star Game? The final chapter to the Rose-Fosse story suggests not.

Fosse had met Rose for the first time the day before that 1970 All-Star Game. After their meeting at home plate the next night, their paths never crossed again ... until 1983.

"I was working for Oakland then and I noticed that Pete was going to be playing at Candlestick Park in San Francisco," Fosse said. "I thought to myself, 'Isn't it odd that you haven't talked to this man since 1970?' So I went over to Candlestick to renew acquaintances.

"I walked into the Philadelphia locker room and went up to him and, well, did Pete tell you what happened next? That I asked him for his autograph? He didn't mention it? All right, well I did. I got a ball for him to sign and it's in my trophy case right now."

The inscription on Fosse's souvenir reads: "To Ray: Thanks for making me famous. —Pete Rose."

◆ ◆ ◆

One of the game's legendary feats occurred on May 26, 1959, when little Pittsburgh lefthander Harvey Haddix pitched 12 perfect innings in a game against the Braves at Milwaukee's County Stadium. Haddix lost the perfect game, the no-hitter and the shutout in a memorable 13th inning, sealing his place as the ultimate hard-luck pitcher in baseball history.

The irony is that Haddix's effort would have made less of an historical impact if his team had scored a run, allowing him to finish with a regulation perfect game. And, in retrospect, it's amazing that Braves righthander Lew Burdette was able to keep the Pirates off the scoreboard. Burdette survived a three-hit third inning, got three double plays and was aided by intervention from the baseball gods.

"I remember a ball that (Bob) Skinner hit," Pirates center fielder Bill Virdon said. "There was no doubt in anybody's mind that ball was going over the fence. But in that inning, maybe at the end of the inning before, there was a storm brewing in the right field area. All of a sudden the wind came up. The storm might have blown right on by because we didn't get any rain. But that wind started blowing right prior to him hitting that ball and (Hank) Aaron went back to the wall and caught the ball looking up."

Teammate Dick Schofield remembers Skinner's near-miss the same way.

"Yeah, he hit a ball that was going out of the park," he said. "But somehow it just hung up there. The wind suddenly came up and stopped it."

◆　◆　◆

The tiny, low-ceilinged dugouts at Tiger Stadium produced many headaches over the facility's long history. But none came at a more inopportune moment than the one suffered by Detroit pitcher Denny McLain on September 14, 1968.

McLain, bidding to become baseball's first 30-game winner since Dizzy Dean performed the trick for the St. Louis Cardinals in 1934, trailed the Oakland A's, 4-3, entering the bottom of the ninth inning. But Al Kaline triggered a Tigers rally with a leadoff walk, advanced to third on Mickey Stanley's one-out single and scored the tying run when A's first baseman Danny Cater threw wildly to home on Jim Northrup's ground ball.

When left fielder Willie Horton lined a Diego Segui pitch over drawn-in left fielder Jim Gosger to give the Tigers a 5-4 victory, the celebration was on—sort of.

"As soon as I saw Willie smack that ball, I jumped in the dugout," McLain said. "So high, in fact, that I cracked my head on the dugout's concrete ceiling. You may have seen the picture taken of me and Kaline a moment or two later. I'm smiling, all right, but you'll notice that Al has both arms around me as we're coming up the dugout steps. I couldn't have made it onto the field without his help.

"Thanks to Kaline, it didn't take long for the cobwebs to clear and I quickly joined my teammates in a big celebration. But I'll never forget that my initial reaction to becoming the major leagues' first 30-game winner in 34 years was to nearly knock myself dizzy."

McLain also was front and center in another memorable 1968 "moment"—Mickey Mantle's 535th home run, the second-to last of his storied career and the one that moved him temporarily into third place on the all-time list. Was it a going-away gift from the Detroit pitcher? The person closest to the New York Yankees slugger at the moment of impact, Tigers catcher Jim Price, knows best what happened on that September 19 at-bat.

"We'd already clinched the pennant and McLain (leading 6-1) was going for his 31st victory," Price said. "Mickey was coming up and we knew it would be his last time up in Detroit, so I move out to the pitcher's mound to give Mickey the center stage, and the folks gave him a standing ovation.

"When I was out at the mound, Denny says, 'Hey, big guy, let's let him hit a home run.' I'm thinking: 'C'mon, get serious.' I look at McLain and he was very serious and I say, 'OK, good idea.' Then McLain says, 'Ask him where he wants it.' OK, so I went back behind the plate. Mickey was always great and as always he says to me, 'How ya doing, Jimmy?'

"I say to him, 'Mickey, he wants you to hit one out.' Mantle was kind of stunned. He looked back at me and he says, 'What?' I tell him, 'Yes, he wants you to hit a home run.' Then Mantle looks out to McLain who is shaking his head with a yes motion. So, Mickey says to me, 'High and tight, mediocre cheese,' which is an average fastball, high and tight.

"Mantle was a little skeptical at first, taking the first pitch for a strike. Mantle pulled the next pitch foul. Then McLain threw a high-and-inside, mediocre-cheese fastball that Mantle hit into the upper deck for a home run. I remember McLain kind of trotting with Mantle out by second base and clapping. As he comes across home plate, Mantle tells me, 'Thanks.'

"I didn't want to belittle anything Mantle did, so I never told that story until years later when Mantle began to tell people that McLain grooved it for him on that home run."

Longtime Tigers broadcaster Ernie Harwell takes the story from there:

"And then (Joe) Pepitone came up and he thought maybe McLain would groove one for him," Harwell said. "He put his hand out, like Mantle did, and asked for one. McLain knocked him down, knocked his wig off. That's a second climax to a great story."

◆　◆　◆

When Tiger Stadium ended its 88-year run more than three decades later, those tiny dugouts were but one of the many quirky nuances that lured 43,356 fans to the corner of Michigan and Trumbull for one final look at one of the game's most revered ballparks. Tigers reliever Todd Jones remembered the crazy scene as he recorded the final out and brought down the curtain on a baseball era.

"That was 1999," said Jones, who worked a hitless ninth inning in Detroit's 8-2 victory over Kansas City. "We were just coming off that incredible '98 season, all that McGwire home run stuff, and everyone came to the park with their cameras. Once I got the second out, all the cameras began flashing. It was incredible; I could hardly see a thing.

"It seemed like there were 55,000 people there and 30,000 of them had flashes going. But then I realized, if I couldn't see, then (Royals hitter Carlos) Beltran couldn't see the rotation on the ball. So with two strikes I threw him a curveball. He swung over the top of it and that was that."

◆　　◆　　◆

Carlton Fisk's 12th-inning walkoff home run in Game 6 remains the signature moment of the 1975 World Series, but a controversial 10th-inning Game 3 play involving Fisk and Cincinnati's Ed Armbrister was no less emotional.

The play occurred when Armbrister tried to move Cesar Geronimo, who had singled to open the inning, to second with a sacrifice. Armbrister dropped his bunt a few feet in front of the plate, lingered momentarily and then became entangled with catcher Fisk as he tried to field the ball. Fisk pushed Armbrister out of the way, grabbed the ball and threw wildly to second, allowing the runners to advance to third and second.

The Red Sox screamed for an interference call, which seemed in order. But home plate umpire Larry Barnett ruled the contact was "unintentional," a call supported by his crew and the 55,392 fans at Cincinnati's Riverfront Stadium. Moments later, Joe Morgan's single scored Geronimo with the winning run.

Few plays in history have generated a more stormy reaction from players in a postgame setting, as reported in the next issue of *The Sporting News*:

"(Bleep) the umpires," screamed pitcher Dick Drago as he heaved towels against the side of his locker. "Let's just do away with the rotten creeps and use the honor system. It couldn't be worse than anything you saw tonight. That (bleeping) slob of a plate umpire, Larry Barnett, has been (bleeping) the Red Sox all season long. He stinks, and they can fine me if they want to."

Relief pitcher Bill Lee called it the worst miscarriage of justice he had seen since his Little League days. He muttered, shouted and screamed at nobody in particular, his eyeballs rotating wildly as he made his feelings known. Pitcher Reggie Cleveland reiterated the sentiments of Drago and Lee.

"They stole this game from us," he said. "It was the most raw, unfair thing I have ever seen. Barnett is the most gutless slob who ever umpired a baseball game. Armbrister threw a block at Pudge (Fisk). The umpires' association now dictates who'll officiate the Series. They rotate their men. Maybe we ought to rotate teams, too. If they can put two or three of the worst, least-respected umpires in either league in the Series, why can't the San Diego Padres play the Minnesota Twins next year?"

Fisk screamed incoherently at reporters before finally calming down—relatively speaking.

"We should have had a double play on that ball," he said, "but the umpires are too gutless under pressure. We asked Dick Stello at first to rule on it, too, and he backed up his fellow thief. The umpires have been trying to put it to the Red Sox all year. Well, now they've (bleeped) us good. This is a game that would have given us the edge and now we're just (bleeped.)"

The immediate aftermath of the 1975 Series was not pleasant for Barnett, who received an extortion threat against his family from an irate gambler who said he had lost $10,000 on the game. The fear passed, however, and Barnett actually enjoyed his 15 minutes of fame—making national television appearances, doing TV commercials and earning considerable money from speaking engagements.

The umpire was inundated with letters, hundreds that weighed the merits of his Game 3 call. "At first," he said, "they ran 2-to-1 against me. Then, after I made a few television appearances, including one in which I debated with Tony Kubek, the letters started coming 2-to-1 in my favor.

"I got some wing-dingers, but the funniest was the one that came right after the Series. It was addressed, 'Larry Barnett, Home Plate Umpire, Third Game, 1975 World Series, Prospect, O.' The letter read simply, 'You stink!.'

"The second funniest letter came right after I was on TV. It was addressed the same way and read, 'You still stink!' "

♦ ♦ ♦

It wasn't a no-hitter and the Seattle Mariners even managed to score on a Gorman Thomas home run in the seventh inning. But everybody who watched 23-year-old Roger Clemens record a nine-inning-record 20 strikeouts in a 3-1 Boston victory on April 29, 1986, seemed to agree it was a performance for the ages:

Red Sox manager John McNamara: "I've seen perfect games by Catfish Hunter and Mike Witt and I've seen some great-pitched games by (Tom) Seaver. But I've never seen a pitching performance as awesome as that, and I don't think you will again in the history of baseball."

Red Sox pitching coach Bill Fischer: "I almost had tears in my eyes. It was the best game I ever saw pitched. The second best was by Jim Bunning, when he pitched a no-hitter for Detroit against the Red Sox in 1958."

Red Sox catcher Rich Gedman: "Rocket was unhittable. The thing that amazed me the most was that they had so many swings and weren't even able to foul the ball. It wasn't like he was trying to paint the corners or anything. He was challenging them and they weren't able to get a bat on the ball."

Home plate umpire Nick Voltaggio, who was unaware Clemens was closing in on the strikeout mark: "All I knew was that I was working the best pitching performance I'd ever seen. I told the batboy that after the seventh inning."

Mariners slugger Thomas: "Anything you say is an understatement. Clemens was overbearing. I think we should all be happy we were here. We'll never see that again."

♦ ♦ ♦

If Orel Hershiser had his way, he wouldn't have broken Don Drysdale's scoreless-innings streak in 1988. He just would have tied it.

"I really and truly didn't want to break the record," Hershiser said after working 10 shutout innings and stretching his scoreless streak to 59 in his final start of the season. "I wanted to stop after nine innings so that two Dodgers would be there on top."

Drysdale, the Hall of Fame righthander, had held the record since 1968, when he worked 58 consecutive scoreless innings—a streak that included six complete-game shutouts. Drysdale's streak ended on June 8 when the Philadelphia Phillies scored a two-out fifth-inning run. For years the record was listed as 58⅔ before finally being amended to 58.

"I wanted to stop at 58⅔," said Hershiser, whose streak included five complete-game shutouts and his 10-inning finale—a game the Dodgers lost to the Padres in 16 innings. "I wanted me and Don to be together. But the higher sources (manager Tommy Lasorda, pitching coach Ron Perranoski) told me they weren't taking me out of the game, so I figured, what the heck, I might as well get the guy out."

And what did Drysdale, a Dodgers broadcaster in 1988, think about Hershiser's grand plan?

"I'd have kicked him in the pants if I'd known that," he said. "I'd have told him to get his buns out there and get them."

◆　◆　◆

Where were you when Toronto's Joe Carter hit his World Series-ending home run against the Philadelphia Phillies in 1993? Umpire Dave Phillips was stationed at first base and didn't even see the historic Game 6 three-run blast off pitcher Mitch Williams.

"I never saw the ball leave the ballpark," Phillips said. "I saw him hit it—it wasn't a high drive, it was more of a line drive that didn't get over the fence by that much—but my head was down as I made sure he touched the first base bag. I never saw the ball leave the park.

"I didn't know for sure what had happened until I saw Carter begin jumping up and down. I knew it was over because of his jubilation."

That career-defining home run changed Carter's life. Suddenly the low profile he had been able to maintain through seven 100-RBI major league seasons was lost in the glare of a national spotlight. He knew his world had changed when, on his way to a charity golf event in his hometown Kansas City, he went through a McDonald's drive-through and was asked for an autograph by attendants.

"I'm like, 'Guys, I gotta go,' " he said. "It's definitely happened a lot here, maybe more than I thought."

But it could be worse.

"It's not anything like Toronto," Carter said. "In Toronto, it's impossible to go anywhere now. One thing I liked doing was just getting up and going and taking my kids to the science museum, or go to Canada Wonderland, things like that. Not anymore.

"I went last year to the science museum with my three kids. Usually we spend three or four hours there. After about 45 minutes or an hour I had to leave, because I was like the Pied Piper—everywhere I went it was like three or four thousand kids following you, and it got to the point where it wasn't even fun.

"It's not fair to my kids, because they weren't having fun. They were sharing me. It's like we were just running the whole time, trying to get away from the people."

◆　　◆　　◆

What Paul Molitor heard on the night of September 7, 1987, was both disturbing and humbling. He was disturbed when Milwaukee fans at County Stadium booed teammate Rick Manning for delivering a game-winning hit. He was humbled by the thunderous ovation he received moments later, saluting the 39-game hitting streak that he had failed to extend.

Molitor had gone 0-for-4 against Cleveland rookie righthander John Farrell through nine innings of a scoreless game. But anticipation was high as the Brewers' designated hitter knelt on deck in the bottom of the 10th, preparing to face reliever Doug Jones. Pinch hitter Manning eliminated that possibility when he hit a two-out single to score Mike Felder and give Milwaukee a 1-0 victory.

For a few moments after Felder scored, a strange silence blanketed County Stadium. Then a few fans began to applaud and many others let out groans that quickly turned to boos. Manning, they decided, had deprived Molitor of one last shot at extending his streak.

"Sorry about that," Manning told Molitor as they exchanged high fives in a spontaneous victory celebration.

"Sorry?" Molitor responded, incredulous over Manning's apology.

All was forgotten moments later when the crowd gave Molitor a standing ovation that subsided only when he took a postgame curtain call.

◆　　◆　　◆

St. Louis catcher Tom Lampkin, a teammate and close friend of Cardinals slugger Mark McGwire, was watching closely as the big first baseman tried to nail down the home run title in the final week of a magical 1998 season. Big Mac already had broken Roger Maris' single-season home run record of 61, but he could not shake Chicago challenger Sammy Sosa.

The Cubs outfielder even took a lead over McGwire on the Friday night leading into the season's final weekend. News of Sosa's 66th homer, a monster shot off Houston's Jose Lima that landed in the fourth deck of the Astrodome, sent shockwaves through a packed crowd at St. Louis' Busch Stadium, where the Cardinals were getting ready to start their game against Montreal.

McGwire quickly answered with his 66th homer, again tying Sosa for the major league lead. Then on Saturday, he blasted home runs 67 and 68 and followed with his title-clinching 69th and 70th homers on Sunday.

"He came into the dugout after he hit his (66th) home run, and he looked at me and just exhaled," Lampkin said. "It was like he just had the biggest weight lifted off his shoulder. He didn't say anything, but it was like he finally got over the hump. He tied Sammy again.

"And I came in (Saturday) and I never had as good a feeling as I did about him hitting two home runs. Because after he gave me that little sign on the bench, I had a feeling that he was going to explode.

"He was so locked in, so relaxed, as if he had no pressure on him at all. And he just crushed two balls."

◆   ◆   ◆

Fans were well-versed on the guile and cunning Gaylord Perry employed to become the 15th member of baseball's 300-win club on May 6, 1982. But few were aware of his sly off-field ingenuity, a trait Seattle owner George Argyros discovered the hard way in the days leading up to the historic moment.

Argyros, who had purchased the Mariners before the 1981 season, had extensive California real estate holdings in addition to owning Air California. That did not mean much for the team, however, which was expected to travel on less-expensive commercial flights that included frustrating layovers on virtually every trip east of Chicago.

The Mariners had played at Baltimore on May 4 and Perry was scheduled go after his 300th win in the next game, the opener of a homestand against the Yankees. Argyros was excited about the prospects of a large crowd.

The trip had been challenging. It started with an April 26 exhibition game. Then came visits to Cleveland, New York and Baltimore. May 5, a scheduled off day, would be used for travel.

When Perry, who had joined the team that spring, asked traveling secretary Lee Pelekoudas about the flight home from Baltimore, Pelekoudas explained it would be commercial. Argyros would not approve the extra expense for a charter.

Perry demanded to speak to the owner.

"George," Perry told him, "I'm having some back stiffness. I'm thinking after spending all day flying commercial on Thursday to get home, I probably won't be able to pitch again (until the Mariners went back on the road). It would be too bad if the people in Seattle didn't get to see me win the 300th."

The next thing Pelekoudas knew, Argyros was telling him to find a charter to get the team home.

Perry got his way—and Argyros got his crowd. With 27,369

cheering him on at the Kingdome, the 43-year-old righthander joined pitching's most elite club with a 7-3 victory.

◆   ◆   ◆

Hank Aaron's record-breaking 715th home run, hit on April 8, 1974, might have come sooner and under different circumstances if not for a lost home run he hit in St. Louis nine years earlier.

Aaron and his Milwaukee Braves were playing a game at old Busch Stadium, the renamed Sportsman's Park, on August 18, 1965, when Cardinals lefthander Curt Simmons threw one of those slow curveballs that he used to tantalize and often frustrate Hammerin' Hank.

"Henry Aaron is the only ballplayer I have ever seen who goes to sleep at the plate and wakes up only to swing as the pitch comes in," Simmons once said.

Aaron woke up just in time to flick his wrists and drive this Simmons curveball onto the right field roof. "He did a kind of hop, skip and double-shuffle," Simmons recalled years later.

So much so that plate umpire Chris Pelekoudas declared that Aaron was out. He had made contact, Pelekoudas ruled, when he "was a good step and a half or two steps" out of the batter's box. It is believed to be the only home run Aaron lost in that manner.

As a result, baseball's all-time home run king entered the offseason after 1973 with 713 home runs, one short of Ruth's record, and had to wait all winter before tying and then passing the Babe.

◆   ◆   ◆

Lou Brock was not sure what he heard moments before breaking Ty Cobb's career record of 892 stolen bases. But he knew he heard something.

Brock entered the August 29, 1977, game at San Diego Stadium one steal shy of Cobb's record and quickly took care of that in the first inning. Brock drew a leadoff walk off Dave Freisleben, a broad-shouldered righthander, and set sail for second base on his first pitch, tying the mark. Then in the seventh, Brock reached base on a fielder's choice and the crowd of 19,656 braced for a baseball moment. Here was Brock's chance.

A full moon hung over San Diego Stadium as the Cardinals left fielder called time and walked over to first base umpire Billy Williams.

"What?" he asked.

Williams told him he had not said anything.

Brock checked with Padres first baseman Gene Richards, who told him he had not said anything, either. How about St. Louis first base coach Sonny Ruberto? No, nothing.

"I know I heard something," Brock said later.

Marty Hendin, the Cardinals' public relations director, had a thought: "Maybe," he mused, "it was the ghost of Ty Cobb"—an intriguing theory given the ferocity of the wild-eyed, spikes-sharpening, egocentric former Tigers star.

Freisleben threw to first base and Brock got back easily. Then Freisleben tossed a pitch that didn't count because Brock had called time. He was asking everyone about that voice.

On Freisleben's next pitch, Brock was flying again toward second and he beat catcher Dave Roberts' throw for record-breaking steal No. 893.

Afterward, Shirley Cobb, one of Ty Cobb's surviving children, was contacted in Palo Alto, Calif. She said she did not begrudge Brock his accomplishment. "I don't think even the old man would object," she said.

Perhaps not. But we'll never know for sure. Brock didn't catch what he said.

◆　　◆　　◆

Garth Iorg found himself in left field on a boiling August 17 afternoon in 1980. The scene was Kansas City, where the artificial turf cooked players' feet and where George Brett's attempt to hit .400 heated the fans' ardor.

Iorg was an infielder for the Toronto Blue Jays, but several outfielders were injured and there he was in left when Brett ripped a bases-loaded double, his fourth hit of the game, to reach .401. Iorg watched helplessly as the ball screamed past him to the outfield wall.

Blue Jays righthander Mike Barlow, who was brought in to face Brett in the eighth, was angry that Iorg didn't catch that ball. But Iorg defended his reactions years later.

"I don't care if you have the best outfielder in the country playing that game," Iorg said. "By the time it got to me, it was 13 or 14 feet high. Nobody is going to catch that ball. It was just a rocket."

When the play was over, Brett, standing on second, doffed his helmet and raised his hands to salute the standing, cheering crowd of 30,693. Iorg remembered thinking: "This is just incredible. How cool it must be to be that talented. And what are these people doing out here in this incredible heat?"

Although Brett did not top the magic .400 plateau, he did finish at .390 and he never forgot that special moment in the Kansas City heat.

"Looking at the scoreboard and seeing .401. To this day, it still gives me goosebumps," he said.

Brett also might have had a few goosebumps 13 years later when he said goodbye to Royals fans with a most unexpected, yet appropriate, gesture in his final appearance at Kauffman Stadium.

After playing his final Kansas City game on September 29 of his career-ending 1993 season, Brett was driven around the stadium, waving to the crowd of more than 37,000 fans who gave him the last in a daylong series of ovations. The ride completed, he jumped out of the golf cart and, to the amazement of everyone, fell on his knees in the batter's box and kissed home plate.

The crowd loved it.

Most of the platoon of photographers assigned to capture the farewell were caught off guard. But, Cliff Schiappa of the *Associated Press* clicked off a shot—and captured the moment for posterity. Brett got the idea from Hank Bauer, the former manager, scout and Yankees outfielder.

"Hank Bauer used to tell Jamie Quirk that he should kiss home plate every time he comes to the ballpark," Brett said. "So I figured that the last time in uniform, I'd kiss home plate and tell Jamie what he was missing."

So how was the kiss?

"Nothing special," Brett said with a grin.

◆　◆　◆

It was a surrealistic scene in pitch-black downtown San Francisco. People were wearing "space lights," those little eyeball-shaped red, blue and green bulbs that were clamped on their head and wiggled wildly like antennae.

An entrepreneur was selling his bagful of lights for $5 a pop outside the Westin St. Francis Hotel. They were worth it. There was no other source of light.

That's because at 5:04 p.m. on October 17, 1989, San Francisco was plunged into darkness by a terrifying earthquake, one that measured 7.1 on the Richter scale, killed more than 60 people, injured another 2,400, left thousands homeless and caused $8 billion worth of damage.

It also interrupted the World Series between the San Francisco Giants and Oakland Athletics for an unprecedented 12 days.

When the earthquake struck, more than 60,000 fans were packed into Candlestick Park, looking forward to the start of Game 3. It was instant chaos. One press box swayed down toward the field and snapped back up. Players called their families onto the field, away from the concrete hovering above them. Fans fled to the parking lot. Commissioner Fay Vincent quickly called the game.

Reporters trying desperately to file stories encountered a nightmare. Most phones were out of order. Workrooms were closed and officials tried to evacuate the stadium. Dark was falling and baseball writers hunkered under emergency lights, typing their reports.

Columnist Jonathan Rand and reporter Dick Kaegel of the *Kansas City Times* got lucky. They happened on an ABC-TV truck where a helpful technician allowed them to file their stories over the one working phone line.

Others had to go the extra mile. Columnist Bernie Miklasz of the *St. Louis Post-Dispatch* ventured into the somewhat seedy neighborhood near the stadium. He gave a man $40 to find a residence with a working phone. He found the phone, but it would cost him even more to make a call. Miklasz typed out his story on a dining room table while people in the kitchen smoked crack. He filed his column, shared a beer with his friendly hosts and left—in a hurry.

Later, at the St. Francis, many baseball people were huddled in the darkened lobby, watching the horrifying scope of the tragedy on a TV operated by emergency power. Joe Torre, then a broadcaster, was there.

"You know what this is like?" he said. "It's like somebody dropped a bomb and you're looking for your relatives."

When the World Series finally resumed on October 27 amid a somber atmosphere, the A's won twice at hastily repaired Candlestick and completed their Bay Area four-game sweep. But that's not what people who were there will remember about the World Series of 1989.

◆　◆　◆

It was an unanticipated victory lap and Cal Ripken fought the idea right up to the last possible instant. But the moment was bigger than one man's determination on the night of September 6, 1995, at Baltimore's Camden Yards and a tidal wave of emotion carried him where no baseball star had gone before.

A nation was watching as the Orioles' ironman played in his record-breaking 2,131st consecutive game, breaking the longtime mark of New York Yankees first baseman Lou Gehrig. When Ripken casually trotted off the field after the California Angels had been retired in the top of the fifth inning, marking an official game, the celebration started.

It was overwhelming. Ripken stepped out of the dugout to tip his cap to the 46,272 fans. The ovation continued. He came out again ... and again ... and again—seven times in all—and the cheering would not subside.

"Cal wanted the game to continue," said first baseman Rafael Palmeiro. "He wanted the game to go on. It was only the fifth inning. We'd been sitting there forever, and the fans were still cheering."

Palmeiro finally turned to Ripken and said, "You're going to have to figure something out. You're going to have to do something to get the fans settled down and get the game going."

"Oh no, let's just get somebody up to bat," Ripken said.

"Why don't you just go and run around and take like a victory lap or something and see what happens?" Palmeiro suggested.

"No, I'm not going to do that," Ripken said.

Palmeiro and Bobby Bonilla came to a sudden decision. They pushed him out of the dugout. Ripken, who always avoided showy situations, finally resigned himself to the inevitable and began a slow, hand-slapping lap around the field.

"I tried to acknowledge the celebration and acknowledge the ovation," Ripken said. "But I was trying to get the game back on line, too. And the game didn't seem to want to go back on line. So when Bobby Bonilla and Rafael Palmeiro pushed me out of the dugout, I started the lap.

"The first part of the lap, I was thinking, 'OK, let's get this going and then maybe we can get the game back on. But as I slowly started to make my way around the stadium, I started to feel a more personal celebration. And by the time I got three-quarters of the way around, I could care less if the game started again.

"I don't remember anything that was said, specifically. It wasn't a time when you actually had verbal exchanges. There was a lot of eye contact. There was a lot of handshaking. It seemed like we were all communicating without the use of words. ... And I saw a few people I knew. I saw some faces I knew, but I didn't know their names. And I saw some people at the end, the guys with the Angels I knew very well."

The lap finally ended and, after one final curtain call, Orioles left fielder Mark Smith stepped to the plate. The game, at long last, continued.

THE BAT, THE BALL
AND OTHER THINGS

One August day in 1997, the Kansas City Royals did a little time traveling. Back to, say, about 1947.

The Royals skipped their typical fare, the airplane, and rode a train from Boston to New York for a weekend series. What better starting point than ancient Fenway Park to take a step into the past?

Johnny Pesky, the great Red Sox shortstop who began his career in the '40s, had fond memories of train travel.

"We'd sit around and talk about hitting, playing," he recalled. "Oh, we'd talk about girls, too. But there was more baseball talk. It was a comfortable feeling. Clickety-clack, clickety-clack, clickety-clack."

This was all new to the Royals, of course. Pitcher Kevin Appier never even had been on a train. He prepped himself by studying a Popular Mechanics article on the high-speed trains that zipped through their Boston-New York-Washington runs.

The train whooshed away from Boston's South Station.

"We're flying," pitcher Jeff Montgomery said. Then he grinned and corrected himself. "We're really *going.*"

For the four-hour trip, Amtrak outfitted the Royals with two club cars—their booster group, the Royal Lancers, was along for the ride—and a 74-seat coach.

The players settled into their usual airplane pursuits—cards, chess, computers, CD players—but also watched the seashore towns with bobbing boats and old train stations. It was a history lesson for pitching coach Bruce Kison, lounging in one of the club cars.

"For me, it's part of the reality of what baseball used to be like," he said. "It's a throwback that everybody needs to know, out of respect for the history of the game."

Amtrak provided champagne, Courvoisier and plenty of beer. Slugger Chili Davis passed out cigars from his personal stash. Smoke filled the car and time seemed to be moving backward. Before long, the players even forgot their games and computers. They gathered in the club car and began talking baseball—how to pitch this guy, where to play that guy. They threw phantom pitches and showed off batting stances.

"Hardball!" someone shouted. Then it became a chant.

"Hardball! ... hardball! ... hardball!"

Clickety-clack, clickety-clack, clickety-clack. You almost could smell the soot and see the cinders of old engines that carried ballclubs for ages.

The train eased into New York's Penn Station. Suddenly, it was 1997 again. Too soon, much too soon.

Baseball secrets can be difficult to keep. Especially if they are the product of whirlwind activity that often accompanies trade talks. Roland Hemond, currently an executive advisor in the Chicago White Sox organization, recalled his days as head of baseball operations in Baltimore and the 1988 trade that sent Orioles superstar first baseman Eddie Murray to Los Angeles.

"We made the deal in December, at the winter meetings," Hemond said, "but the talks had started in September. I went with our club president, Larry Lucchino, and my assistant, Doug Melvin, to a meeting in Chicago with Dodgers general manager

Fred Claire. It was at a hotel near the airport. After we were done, Fred checked out. But we didn't have a room. He said, 'I've paid for the suite for tonight, anyway.' So we just stayed there.

"One of the sportswriters from Baltimore called Fred's room, and Larry Lucchino picked up the phone. The writer said, 'I'd like to speak with Fred Claire.' Larry said, 'He's not here!' and hung up. We then had meetings during the World Series. To Fred's credit, despite the fact that the Dodgers were playing in that Series, he gave us undivided time. (The negotiations) went on during the winter meetings in Atlanta, and finally we agreed on a deal.

"We were handicapped in consummating this trade. Eddie Murray was a 10-and-5 player and wanted to be traded strictly to a club in California. Unfortunately for us, Mark McGwire was the first baseman at Oakland. Will Clark was playing in San Francisco. Jack Clark was in San Diego. And Wally Joyner was with the Angels.

"We had our sights set on pitcher Bob Welch and first baseman Mike Marshall. But that didn't get off the blocks. Other names were bandied about. Finally, we settled on shortstop Juan Bell and pitchers Brian Holton and Ken Howell. A day or two later, we traded Howell to Philadelphia for outfielder Phil Bradley.

"At the winter meetings, the Dodgers were staying on our same floor. We agreed that we would head to the press room together and announce the deal. Tommy Lasorda was there. Fred Claire. Their scout, Ed Liberatore. They had about five or six people. We had about four or five. But then we got stuck on a glass elevator at the Marriott Marquis, directly above where the writers had gathered. They could see us. We were waving at them.

"It started getting so hot in there, the glass was getting steamed. Tommy Lasorda was drawing profanities on the steamed glass, directed to the writers. I started kidding around, choking Fred Claire, saying, 'Before you expire, I need one more player!' Our scout, Birdie Tebbetts, said, 'This is the biggest story of the meetings, except that we won't be alive to read about it!'

"It was 44 minutes before we got out, I recall. Hilarious."

Hemond also remembered a trade he had engineered four years earlier when he was general manager of the White Sox. This one did not have that "hilarious" twist, but Hemond does recall getting an ego-boosting last laugh.

Desperate for a shortstop, his scouting staff had zeroed in on a young minor leaguer who was progressing quickly in the San Diego organization. Garry Templeton was entrenched at short with the Padres, so Hemond figured the youngster, Ozzie Guillen, might be available.

He was right, but he had to part with veteran righthander LaMarr Hoyt, a 24-game winner in 1983 who had faded to 13 wins in '84. Hemond also got three other young players in the seven-player deal at the 1984 winter meetings.

"He was 20 years old," Hemond said, referring to the flashy young Guillen. "But he had played in the Pacific Coast League. I made the deal at the meetings in Dallas, and from there I went to Mexico to see some winter ball. Then I went to California for the holidays; we were living there at the time. When I came back to Chicago, all my friends were asking me, 'Are you OK?' I asked why. And they said, 'You've been taking a beating for trading LaMarr Hoyt. The talk shows have been ripping you. There haven't been favorable articles in the paper.

"It didn't hurt me a bit. I had been in Mexico and California. I hadn't heard anything about it. But when Guillen reported to Sarasota for spring training, I went down to meet him in the clubhouse. He was sitting in the trainer's room. He had his shirt off. I see a skinny kid who weighed 150 pounds. My first reaction was, 'Oh my gosh, we traded for a jockey!'

"It did scare me to see how little he was. But he justified the judgment of the scouts. The very next year he was Rookie of the Year. And he went on to have a very fine career."

◆　◆　◆

By the early 1950s, Ted Williams was well known for his baseball heroics. But he spent most of the 1952 and '53 seasons playing a different, more dangerous kind of game.

Grounded during World War II, he became an active participant in the Korean conflict, flying 38 combat missions and barely escaping with his life.

On February 19, 1953, the Marine Corps captain, flying an F-9 Panther jet over enemy territory, was hit by small-arms fire. He perilously flew his burning plane back over enemy lines, crash landed it on an allied airfield and escaped from the cockpit, seconds before the plane exploded into flames.

◆　◆　◆

The great Joe DiMaggio led by example—quietly, professionally and always with grace and dignity. Respect was returned to the Yankee Clipper in much the same way.

"As long as I can remember, when the Yankees took the field, they all waited for Joe to make the first break," former New York pitcher Joe Page said in 1951. "Nothing was said about this ritual, but everybody held back and waited for Joe to lead us out."

That DiMaggio dignity and pride extended to his non-playing days, even to the Old-Timers Day games that once were a staple of baseball's promotional efforts. One night in the 1970s, the Atlanta Braves assembled quite a lineup of former stars.

DiMaggio came out to take some swings against Bob Feller, the Cleveland fireballer. But instead of grooving one for DiMaggio to smack as was the custom, Feller reached back for some mustard and struck him out.

The crowd was disappointed and DiMaggio was steamed. Returning to the dugout, DiMaggio growled, "I'll never play in one of these again."

And as far as we know, he never did.

◆　◆　◆

Gaylord Perry already was notorious for his spitballing tactics when baseball's elite attended a White House reception before the

1969 All-Star Game in Washington, D.C. So notorious, in fact, that the San Francisco Giants righthander drew special notice from the President of the United States.

The nation's No. 1 fan conversed briefly with each player. But Richard Nixon seemed particularly interested in all those allegations about Perry's sneaky fidgets on the mound and his affinity for "foreign" substances.

"When he got to me," Perry recalled, "the President gave me one of those Paul Bunyan handshakes that wins elections. Then he lightly jabbed his elbow in my ribs and whispered, 'Gaylord, tell me, where do you get it?' "

Always prepared for such questions from less prominent citizens, the pitcher showed he also could play in the diplomatic big leagues.

"There are some things," he replied, "you just can't tell the people —for their own good."

Diplomacy was the furthest thing from the mind of St. Louis righthander Danny Cox late in the 1985 season. First he knocked out the New York Mets with a 4-3 victory that put the Cardinals in position to clinch the National League East Division. Then, a few hours later, he knocked out a different kind of adversary with two well-aimed punches 600 miles away in Warner Robins, Ga.

Cox's 18th win in an October 3 game against the Mets at Busch Stadium gave the Cardinals a two-game lead over the Mets with three to play. The next morning, he flew home to Georgia and punched out his former brother-in-law, whom he said had made threatening remarks to Cox's sister and parents, who lived in Warner Robins.

After taking care of his personal business in Georgia, the 6-4, 230-pound Cox returned to St. Louis in time for a game against the Chicago Cubs. He was greeted at the airport by reporters and camera crews who had heard about his whirlwind trip and altercation with Richard Diebold, a sports coordinator at Warner Robins Air

Force Base.

"I started it. I finished it," Cox said later. "It took only two punches. I think anybody in that situation would have done the same thing. If you wouldn't have, then you're not a man and you don't love your family."

"That was an amazing story," former Cardinals teammate Rick Horton recalled. "He flew home, knocked out his former brother-in-law and flew back. All he would say was, 'You gotta do what you gotta do.'"

◆　◆　◆

Keith Bodie is a baseball lifer, a man who has spent almost three decades in the game. In 2001, he managed Class AA Wichita into the Texas League playoffs and was invited that September to join the parent Kansas City Royals for the final month of the season.

Shortly after the September 11 terrorist attack in New York, Bodie received news that his cousin, firefighter Nicholas Chiofalo, was lost while helping people as the first tower at the World Trade Center collapsed.

Word got around the Royals' clubhouse. Quietly, players reached into their wallets and pulled out checkbooks. Quickly, an envelope for Chiofalo's wife and son contained $20,000.

The Glass family, owners of the team, learned of the players' gesture and matched their donation. The envelope swelled to $40,000.

"I don't know if there are words to describe how you feel," Bodie said. "It's a tremendous gesture of love and support."

Bodie was a fringe member of the team, but he was part of a baseball family. When a family member is hurt, others respond.

The next June, when the Royals traveled to Shea Stadium for an interleague series against the New York Mets, Nick Chiofalo Jr. was invited to join them. Nick, 14, was given a "No. 1" Royals jersey autographed by the players. He took batting practice and hung out in the clubhouse.

"I never thought I'd be out here with Mike Sweeney and Chuck Knoblauch," Nick said. "It's just so cool."

The Royals just hoped it would be another day that Nick Chiofalo would never forget.

◆　　◆　　◆

David Gaines will never forget the day he sang the national anthem for the 1992 season opener between the Angels and Chicago White Sox at Anaheim Stadium. Gaines, the star of a Los Angeles production of *Phantom of the Opera*, finished his performance and then waited for a helicopter that would whisk him to his theater about 35 miles away.

The game already was underway when Gaines became airborne. On a whim, he asked his pilot to take one final swing over the ballpark, just as Angels newcomer Von Hayes was coming to bat in the bottom of the first with a man on base. Hayes, who did not hit a home run in 77 games with Philadelphia in 1991 and had not homered in his last 336 plate appearances, took a cut at the first delivery from White Sox starter Jack McDowell and drove it over the right field fence.

Gaines got a bird's-eye view of the home run—and the pyrotechnic display that celebrated it. Last seen, the chopper was taking evasive action from skyrockets that whizzed dangerously close to its rotor blades.

◆　　◆　　◆

To call Hall of Fame knuckleballer Phil Niekro relaxed is something of an understatement. The longtime Atlanta Braves star has always valued his rest—to the point of being able to fall asleep anywhere and snooze through the wildest of commotions.

Former teammates still marvel at Niekro's ability to sleep through one infamous airplane flight during which teammates Hank Aaron and Rico Carty engaged in a loud altercation. Niekro learned of the headline-generating incident secondhand.

By his own account, Niekro has slept through Super Bowls, World Series games, movies, boxing matches and many other events that typically keep viewers on the edge of their seats. He even admitted falling asleep one time while he was standing up.

"Yeah," he said, "it happened when I was a senior in high school. I was playing football for the first time, and we were standing around watching a scrimmage. All of a sudden, I found myself on the ground. Somebody ran over with smelling salts. ... They thought I had fainted. But I had fallen asleep."

◆　◆　◆

There was no sleeping for Los Angeles ace Orel Hershiser in 1988. The Dodgers righthander was on a major league roll and couldn't afford to close his eyes for fear of missing another opportunity.

Hershiser compiled a 23-8 record for the N.L. West champions, finished the regular season with a major league-record 59 consecutive scoreless innings and earned the league's Cy Young Award. He also won three postseason games, including Game 7 of the NLCS against the New York Mets and World Series-deciding Game 5 against the Oakland Athletics.

According to veteran catcher Rick Dempsey, Hershiser's incredible 1988 success was not limited to the field. He recalled a side trip that several Dodgers took to Atlantic City on an off day for a little gambling and relaxation.

"We are all going in there and playing $5 or $10 on the crap table," Dempsey said. "But Orel just heads right to the baccarat table and puts all of his $5,000 on one hand. I couldn't believe it."

So what happened?

"The SOB won," Dempsey said. "He wins at everything he does."

◆　◆　◆

Another pitcher in the Hershiser vein is Greg Maddux, who constantly amazes teammates with his unyielding obsession with studying hitters and the incredible memory that allows him to put his studies to work on the mound.

Former Chicago first baseman Mark Grace recalled going to dinner with Maddux when they were Cubs teammates in the late 1980s. They had to wait for a table so they sat at the bar watching the Atlanta Braves play on television.

"Except Greg didn't really watch the game," Grace said. "He zeroed in on the hitters. He watched to see if they were changing their stance during the count, if they gripped their bat differently. And then, when the maitre d' finally tells us our table's ready, Greg doesn't budge.

" 'Wait a second,' he says. 'Pendleton's up. I wanna watch him.' And he stays glued to the TV until Pendleton's at-bat is over. Later, when I ask him why he wanted to watch Pendleton so badly, he says, 'Because I may have to get him out in a big situation someday.' "

◆   ◆   ◆

Many major league stars long for the peace and quiet of pre-baseball life, but anonymity sometimes comes like a slap to the face. Larry Phillips, Nolan Ryan's longtime ranching friend in his hometown of Alvin, Texas, told this story about the then-Houston Astros righthander:

"We had been at a cattle sale, and people had been bugging Nolan all day. We go to this restaurant that's got good barbecue and great onion rings. We're sitting there eating and this table full of girls just start looking at us. Then one of 'em can't take it any longer. She gets up and comes over to our table with a camera.

"She says, 'I'm sorry to bother you, but we're from New York and I've never seen onion rings as big as those. Do you mind if I take a picture of the onion rings?' They didn't know Nolan from Joe Blow. I said, 'You should have held them up so when the pictures were developed somebody would say, "Hey, isn't that Nolan Ryan with the onion rings?" ' It was great to see him get shot down by onion rings."

More typical of Ryan's dealings with demanding fans was this story told by Kevin Kennedy, who managed the Hall of Fame pitcher in his final big-league season—1993 with the Texas Rangers.

"We drove to a concert one day early in spring training," Kennedy said, "just after we got down (to Port Charlotte, Fla.). It was Nolan, myself and my coaches, and we all went to see Wynonna Judd.

"We were pulling out of Charlotte County Stadium after a workout and Nolan was driving. We had guys chasing him down. We were getting some gas, we were all in Nolan's car, and there was a guy running up at him. He'd run after us all the way from the stadium. I mean, you don't know if it's somebody trying to hurt him, or what.

"But Nolan stopped. He actually stopped and was going to sign the guy's card, except the guy didn't have it with him. It was his buddy's card, who was still back at the stadium. And the guy gets mad when Nolan won't go back. I mean, I don't think people understand what he goes through. Here he's making a concession and he gets chased down in the parking lot of a Circle K when we stop to get gas. And that has to happen to him every day of his life."

◆ ◆ ◆

Tom Gamboa has had some tough times in Chicago's Comiskey Park. In 2002, father and son thugs came out of the stands to attack him as he was coaching first base for Kansas City. Gamboa suffered some hearing loss from the blows they delivered.

The next season, Gamboa was on the field during batting practice when a line drive struck by Royals catcher Mike DiFelice drilled him in the left side. After being attended by trainer Nick Swartz, Gamboa was taken to a hospital for an overnight stay and tests.

"My urine was wine-colored," Gamboa reported. "It went from burgundy Monday night to white zinfandel when I woke up Tuesday morning. I told Nick that I'm almost to Chablis."

◆ ◆ ◆

Former Oakland A's owner Charlie Finley told this story about the trip he took to the Hertford, N.C., backwoods in 1964 to meet Hall of Fame righthander Jim "Catfish" Hunter:

"I'll tell you about the day I signed him back in June '64," Finley said. "My scout in North Carolina, Clyde Kluttz, had told me about this kid and recommended we pay him $75,000. No other club was willing to offer more than $50,000. So I flew down there and watched Jimmy pitch in this high school tournament. I saw his curve and I couldn't believe it. It was better than any of the pitchers on my own team had.

"So I go over to his house, which was like everything you'd read about in *Tobacco Road*. It had a tin roof, and his momma was out hoeing weeds in the peanut patch, wearing a sunbonnet, and his dad was in the smokehouse rearranging the hams and bacon.

"The inside of the house was immaculate. I had dinner there two nights—hog jowls, black-eyed peas, okra, squash and peanuts.

"I go inside to see Jimmy and within minutes, he is taking off his boot to show me his right foot, which was filled with buckshot from a hunting accident. He had me feel the shotgun pellets. There were about 30 of 'em. The little toe was gone, and so was part of the bone. Here I am, about to offer him $75,000, and he's telling me he's damaged goods.

"That's Jimmy Hunter."

◆   ◆   ◆

Everybody knows about the tough, sometimes-harsh, business-first side of New York Yankees owner George Steinbrenner. But peel away the hard exterior and you discover a diehard baseball fan, rooted in a childhood spent cheering for his hometown Cleveland Indians.

"I'll never forget it," Steinbrenner told Joe Falls in a 1984 column in *The Sporting News*. "Mel Harder was a great pitcher for the Cleveland Indians, a great man. My uncle got one of his caps and gave it to me. It was too big, and so I bunched it up in the back and put a safety pin on it. Wherever I went, I wore that cap. I was Mel Harder, even when I went to bed."

He was Mel Harder, that is, when he wasn't Bob Feller or Hal Trotsky.

"Oh, Bob Feller," he said. "I used to be Hal Trotsky, and then I was Jeff Heath. But I was always Bob Feller. We were all Bob Feller when we were growing up in Cleveland. A friend of mine, Dalton Dagg—he lived behind us—he'd come over to my backyard and he'd have a catcher's glove and he would catch and I would be Bob Feller. I'd give it that big windup, that big kick—and I'd just shoot the ball in there. Then it would be his turn, and I'd catch and he'd be Bob Feller. Those were the best days of my life."

Contrary to popular opinion, Steinbrenner also could be interactive with Yankee fans. For weeks during his early years as the team's principal owner, he got letters from Joe's Bar in Astoria, Queens—complaints about the Yankees, always the same ones, with the same signatures.

One day, when Steinbrenner was returning to his office from LaGuardia Airport, he told the cab driver to take him to Joe's Bar in Astoria.

"It was a typical neighborhood bar," he said. "These big, burly guys with their bellies flopping over their belts, sitting at the bar drinking quart bottles of beer. At first they didn't believe who I was. But I finally convinced them and I bought a few rounds and we had a good talk.

"When I left, they were my friends."

◆　　◆　　◆

Chewing gum magnate Phil Wrigley had plenty of money during the years he owned the Chicago Cubs, but he rarely felt compelled to spend much of it on improving the ballclub. One year, when Wrigley attended an organizational meeting, the Cubs' scouts tried to impress him by building up the minor league players to the point of exaggeration.

"This guy is a helluva player. ..."

"It won't be long before he's in the majors. ..."

"You should see how this fella hits. ..."

Wrigley sat there listening to the scouts' reports. When they were finished, he said, "Gentlemen, after listening to what all of you had to say about the players in our organization, we have so many good ballplayers that I don't think we're going to need to spend any money in the next few years on young talent."

Some players mug shamelessly for the camera. Others are not even aware it's there. As the time approached for the American League's 1982 Most Valuable Player to be announced, Milwaukee Brewers favorite Robin Yount was at the grocery store with his wife.

It took Brewers public relations director Tom Skibosh 10 frantic phone calls to reach his star shortstop. When Yount finally picked up the phone, Skibosh told him, "You're gonna get a call any minute from New York."

"OK," Yount replied. "Do I have time to bring in the rest of the groceries first?"

Los Angeles Dodgers righthander Don Drysdale, who won 209 career games and teamed with lefthander Sandy Koufax to form one of the most devastating 1-2 pitching combinations in history, told reporters he did not subscribe to any baseball superstitions. His first wife, Ginger, however, begged to differ.

"I have to cook just the right meal at the right time for him at 3:30 every afternoon," she said. "And when we get in a winning streak, it has to be the same each day, even to the salt.

"One season, I fixed him a nice steak before going out to the park and he won his first game. From that time on, you know, I had to fix one of those big steaks every afternoon and Don won 24 more."

Drysdale also won the 1962 Cy Young Award with his 25-9 record and 2.83 ERA.

"At the end of the season," Ginger said, "our butcher was driving a Cadillac, along with the home run hitters."

◆　　◆　　◆

Ken Rosenthal, a senior writer for the *Sporting News*, tells this story from his days as a columnist for the *Baltimore Sun*:

"I had my head down, typing away, when the foul ball came straight toward my seat in the press box at Camden Yards. I should have tried to catch it, or at least flipped down the screen on my laptop. But I just stood up and waited, figuring the ball would land harmlessly. Naturally, it crashed into my Gateway 2000, knocking it to the press-box floor and sending it to the permanent disabled list.

"The ball was hit by Cal Ripken Jr. And if he wasn't quite targeting my laptop, he sure seemed delighted by his aim. I had occasionally written critically about Ripken. Twice after he broke Lou Gehrig's consecutive-games record in 1995, I questioned the wisdom of his continuing The Streak.

"Alas, Ripken had strange powers on a baseball field. He hit his fateful foul ball shortly after one of my unfavorable columns. When informed of my loss, Ripken reacted with one word: 'Sweet.' "

◆　　◆　　◆

This had all the makings of an explosive situation.

On a steaming July 17, 1988, at Fenway Park, the Boston Red Sox completed a four-game sweep of Kansas City. The final loss came less than 24 hours after Royals manager John Wathan had called a team meeting and scorched his players for their lack of a "killer instinct."

Pitcher Ted Power was shelled, yanked in the second inning and angry, riled enough to engage in a dugout argument with Wathan. Then, in the eighth, Wathan was ejected for arguing ball-and-strike calls on Wade Boggs, the league's leading hitter.

"A woman will be elected President of the United States before an umpire calls Wade Boggs out on a third strike at Fenway Park," the Royals' George Brett grumbled.

Things did not get any better after the game. The bus taking the Royals to the airport in 99-degree heat did not have air conditioning. The plane booked to Milwaukee was small and the Royals filled every seat. A storm was rolling in over Logan Airport and as the plane waited in a long line for takeoff clearance, the pilot asked everyone to take their seat.

Willie Wilson, the Royals' sometimes moody center fielder, decided instead to sit on a flight attendant's jump seat. He might have gotten away with it on a charter flight. But this was technically commercial, even though the Royals had booked the entire plane. And the pilot was going by the book.

Wilson ignored the crew's entreaties and the pilot warned there would be no takeoff until every passenger was sitting in a passenger seat. Finally, an incensed Brett got up and approached Wilson, yelling for him to get in his seat.

The shouting match quickly escalated into a shoving, pushing and pulling skirmish in the rear of the plane. No punches were thrown before coaches jumped up and separated the team's stars. But the incident prompted the pilot to pull the plane out of line, and security officers came aboard to conduct an investigation. The plane returned to the back of the line, the rainstorm hit, and the departure was delayed for about two hours while the Royals steamed inside.

Two *Kansas City Star* reporters also were on the flight. Bullpen coach Jim Schaffer leaned over and growled: "I better not see anything about this in the paper tomorrow."

Of course not!

Since there was no place for the combatants to hide, the reporters quickly got their interviews and started banging on their little Radio Shack computers. Because of the delays, the flight landed in Milwaukee right on deadline. The reporters swooped into a vacant office and filed their stories with minutes to spare.

Later, at the Milwaukee hotel, Wathan tried to look at the bright side.

"I guess it could be a positive sign," he said. "It shows the aggressiveness of our team."

Or not. The Royals lost seven of their next 10 games and fell out of the A.L. West race.

◆　　◆　　◆

At first glance, former New York Yankees catcher Thurman Munson did not look athletic. His pudgy 190-pound body made him appear slow-footed, and his gruff exterior projected intensity over athleticism. But Munson in reality was a fast runner with quick, sure hands and the ability to perform well in any sport he chose.

In high school, he excelled in football, basketball and baseball. He also was a highly ranked handball player in his Canton, Ohio, hometown. Yankees Hall of Fame shortstop and broadcaster Phil Rizzuto, who was known to spend considerable time on the golf course, discovered the hard way that Munson had a knack for that sport as well.

"Phil invited me to play golf with him the first year I was up," Munson said. "When I got to the course, he offered to play even and I agreed. Then I smoked him pretty good. I think I shot about a 73 that day."

"Yeah, and you should have heard Rizzuto talk about it on the air that night," said Munson's wife, Diane. "He couldn't understand how he was taken by that 'Huckleberry Munson.'"

Rizzuto, indeed, was impressed. "If that guy practiced for a month, he could make the pro tour," he said. "The first time I played him I thought he was a huckleberry on the course, but it cost me money to find out how wrong I was."

In addition to superior athleticism, Munson also had supreme confidence. One day, in jest, a writer told him that the free-spending Yankees were close to making a deal for superstar Cincinnati catcher Johnny Bench.

"Great," Munson said without the hint of a smile, "but where are they going to play him? Designated hitter?"

◆ ◆ ◆

Former Orioles pitching great Jim Palmer was adopted two days after birth by Moe Wiesen, a wealthy New York dress manufacturer, and wife Polly. His first address was Park Avenue, a revelation that led former Baltimore teammate Frank Robinson to dub him "Reginald Van Palmer."

Wiesen died when Palmer was 9 years old and his mother remarried Hollywood actor Max Palmer and moved into a Beverly Hills, Calif., home previously owned by actor James Cagney. It was an exclusive neighborhood that included Frank Sinatra and Peter Lorre. Tony Curtis and Janet Leigh lived just across the lane.

"I would set my alarm clock every morning," Palmer said, "so I could be at the window when Janet came out in her pink peignoir (negligee) to pick up the paper."

◆ ◆ ◆

In January 1972, Gordon Lakey, Philadelphia's director of major league scouting, got a first-hand look at the bulldog mentality that would help Pat Gillick rise to prominence as a general manager for the Baltimore Orioles, Toronto Blue Jays and Seattle Mariners. Both were scouts for the Houston Astros at the time.

"Pat called me early one morning and asked, 'What are you doing?' " Lakey recalled. "I said, 'I'm not doing anything.' He said, 'Can you meet me in Minneapolis tonight? We're going to fly to Winnipeg. Bring the warmest clothes you have.' I didn't have any warm clothes. I was born in the South. I was living in Houston, working for the Astros. I had never been in cold weather before in my life.

"Pat had gotten word that Montreal was going to try to sign Bobby Bourne, who would later play in the NHL. I had not been a part of it, but Pat had signed Clark Gillies in 1969. Like Bourne, he went on to become a member of the Stanley Cup-champion New York Islanders. And he later got inducted into the Hockey Hall of Fame.

"We were really active in the western part of Canada. In 1970 and '71, we had a lot of tryout camps in the summer in Canada. I flew to Minneapolis and met Pat there. We got on a plane to Winnipeg. It was going to stop in Grand Forks, N.D. But we got the sense something was wrong when the pilot came to the back of the plane and pulled the rug up to look at the periscope and make sure the wheels were down. Well, we got to Grand Forks. But sure enough, we couldn't take off. This was about 10 o'clock at night.

"Nobody was at the airport. We contacted the rental-car agency and they had only six or seven cars. There were probably 30 people on the plane. So, we all paired up and drove in those cars to Winnipeg. I'm freezing. And the first thing we do is go to a gas station and put alcohol in the gas tank to keep the gas line flowing. I had never seen anything like that.

"Now we drive to Winnipeg. We get there at 3 or 4 o'clock in the morning and sleep at the airport. Then we take a flight that morning to Saskatoon. We get to Saskatoon and the temperature is minus-40 and the wind-chill factor is minus-80. We get a rental car and Pat takes off, spinning in the parking lot. There's ice all over the place.

"We get to the hotel, get in contact with Bourne. Bourne and Gillies were playing against each other for teams in the same junior-hockey league. We're going to go see them play. That night, we go to the arena. The arena is not heated, but it felt like we were in the tropics compared to what it was like outside. It was so cold that we had to stop every 50 feet to duck into a building because our bodies were freezing. We sat with Clark Gillies' dad and watched them play. The next day, we contacted Bourne and signed him to a Rookie League contract.

"After he signed, we stayed on a day or so, watched the Super Bowl in Moose Jaw with Clark Gillies. We ran into a scout for the Montreal Canadiens. He said, 'You guys are wasting your time. Both of those guys are going to be first-round picks in the NHL.' The next year, they both played in the Appalachian League. But neither got out of the league.

"Finally, we start home and take a bus back to the United States;

the air-traffic controllers are on strike. We get on the bus, and the bus catches fire. I don't even remember how we got back, probably by another bus. It was one of those trips where everything went wrong. But we accomplished what we wanted to. It was a testament to Pat's perseverance. We were going to sign two hockey players to baseball contracts in the middle of January."

◆　◆　◆

When the Chicago White Sox traded pitchers Goose Gossage and Terry Forster to the Pittsburgh Pirates for Richie Zisk and Silvio Martinez at the 1976 winter meetings in Los Angeles, writers scrambled to get news of the blockbuster deal to their publications. *Chicago Sun-Times* columnist Jerome Holtzman wrote about his fortunate timing in *The Sporting News*:

"I was on the telephone in the lobby of the L.A. Hilton at midnight, calling my office with the news about the big White Sox-Pirates trade. I looked up and realized that (new Pirates manager Chuck) Tanner was using the next phone, telling the operator he wanted Colorado Springs, Colo., which is the home of pitcher Rich Gossage.

"I listened carefully. Here's exactly what Tanner (Gossage's former Chicago manager) said:

" 'Goose, is that you? Goose, this is Chuck. Chuck Tanner. I've got great news. You've been traded to the Pirates—you and Terry Forster. That's right, Goose, we're going to be together again. Great! Now listen, Goose, don't make any plans for October. We're going to be in the World Series!' "

◆　◆　◆

Not all trades require reporters or players to do any scrambling. Such was the case on April 14, 1997, when baseball's wacky schedule brought three teams—the Dodgers, Angels and Giants—together for a little quality time at the same New York hotel.

Resurrecting memories of the old-style winter meetings, the

Angels and Giants even made an intra-hotel exchange, San Francisco sending righthanded pitcher Rich DeLucia to Anaheim for a player to be named. DeLucia may have changed teams and leagues, but he didn't even have to trade rooms. The only question was who would pay his hotel bills.

"We picked up breakfast," said Ned Colletti, the Giants' director of major league administration, "and they picked up dinner."

◆   ◆ / ◆

The holdout of Boston righthander Roger Clemens was big news around Florida in the spring of 1989. And *Boston Globe* sports-writers Steve Fainaru and Dan Shaughnessy thought they had stumbled onto a scoop.

When they spotted a luxury rental car parked at a Holiday Inn in Clearwater, Fla., their reporter instincts took over. They were convinced the vehicle belonged to the Hendricks brothers, Randy and Alan, who represented Clemens. So Fainaru and Shaughnessy rented a room and staked out the car. They watched through the drapes to see when it left, planning to tail it and find Clemens.

The Red Sox were playing Toronto that day just up the coast in Dunedin. Phyllis Merhige, the American League's public relations director, happened to be in town for that game and spotted *Boston Globe* columnist Mike Madden on the field during batting practice. She asked if he knew where Shaughnessy might be.

Madden pulled Merhige aside and quietly told her of their "find" at the Holiday Inn. There's one problem with their theory, Merhige told Madden. The Hendricks brothers were inside the hospitality trailer at the Dunedin ballpark, eating lunch.

◆   ◆   ◆

As the St. Louis Cardinals got off their plane and entered the airport, smiling waiters handed them frozen daiquiris. Spring training had never been like this.

But this 1978 trip was special. The Cardinals and the

Philadelphia Phillies were to play three exhibition games in the Dominican Republic.

Both teams were ensconced at an Americanized hotel in Santo Domingo. One game was scheduled to be played there, two others in the Dominican hinterlands—games that would require long bus rides to San Francisco de Macoris and Santiago.

Not only were the rides long, they were wild trips of terror on wheezing buses over narrow roads with one fearless motorcycle cop clearing the way. He sent trucks laden with green bananas fleeing to the roadside. One truck dodged into a ditch and the workers riding in the back were clotheslined by tree branches. Transportation was a highlight of the Dominican adventure.

During the game at San Francisco de Macoris, Cardinals manager Vern Rapp decided to give four of his biggest stars a break. So, he pulled left fielder Lou Brock, catcher Ted Simmons, first baseman Keith Hernandez and shortstop Garry Templeton after a few innings and sent them by "taxi" back to Santo Domingo. Without a change of clothes, the players piled into a battered Ford Galaxy.

But, alas, on a remote highway, the car died. And much later, when the team bus came roaring along, there stood Brock, Simmons, Hernandez and Templeton—in full Redbirds regalia—hitch-hiking.

They clambered onto the bus, their short day now just as long as everyone else's.

◆　　◆　　◆

During the 2003 World Series, 23-year-old Florida righthander Josh Beckett got his first introduction to the mystique of Yankee Stadium. Among the highlights of that grand adventure was a tour of Monument Park, the area beyond the left-center field fence where New York baseball immortals are memorialized by special monuments and plaques.

The brash youngster with the high-90-mph fastball was quizzed by reporters after the tour. "Ruth, Gehrig, DiMaggio, Mantle—don't you feel intimidated?" he was asked.

"Why should I be?" Beckett shot back. "I'm not pitching to them."

♦   ♦   ♦

Red Schoendienst was nearing the end of his Hall of Fame playing career in 1958 when routine X-rays revealed that the veteran second baseman was suffering from tuberculosis. Part of his right lung was removed in February 1959 and any thoughts of a comeback were premature—and unrealistic.

"He was flat on his back for four months," said Mary Schoendienst, Red's wife. "The first day they got him up, I went down there (to the hospital). The bat company had sent him some bats and they were over in the corner.

"When the nurses got him out of bed, I thought he would come over and shake my hand or do something, but he went over to the corner and picked up a bat. From that moment on, I figured this guy was going to play ball again. He was going to play ball and to heck with me and the rest of the world."

Schoendienst did play again—including five games at the end of the 1959 season. He concluded his 19-year career with Milwaukee in 1960 followed by three more years in a career-ending return to St. Louis.

♦   ♦   ♦

In 1987, San Diego's Tony Gwynn was well on his way to the second of eight career batting titles. He told an interviewer one of the secrets to his success:

"I had my wife, Alicia, tape my at-bats when I was on the road," Gwynn said, recalling his early season struggles in 1983, his second big-league campaign. "Nobody else told me the right thing to do, so I looked at the tapes and for the rest of the year I batted .333 and finished the season with a 25-game hitting streak.

"From that point on, I knew I could become a better player, so now you're looking at a man with eight video machines in the house, a satellite dish and a closetful of tapes. Actually, I'm surprised everybody doesn't do it."

Tony was not the only member of the Gwynn family who paid

close attention to baseball detail. Alicia was both a fan and critic, as was son Anthony. Alicia recalled a memorable conversation between father and 6-year-old Anthony after a game in the late 1980s.

"We were watching the game on TV in New York," she said, "and Tony called. Anthony jumps on the phone and says, 'Dad, was your arm hurting or something? That was a terrible throw.'

"Tony said, 'What, no hello dad? No how are you doing, dad? Come on, can't you say hello before busting my chops?'"

◆ ◆ ◆

Morganna, known throughout baseball circles as the "Kissing Bandit" during her heyday in the 1980s, once was arrested for her kiss-and-run tactics during a 1985 game at Houston's Astrodome. The busty and gregarious exotic dancer, who already had claimed such victims as Steve Garvey, George Brett, Mark Fidrych, Mike Schmidt and Johnny Bench, added Astros pitcher Nolan Ryan and shortstop Dickie Thon to her list in a first-inning assault that resulted in her being hauled off to jail by police.

That was only the start of a long ordeal for Morganna, who was prosecuted for criminal trespassing in Harris County Criminal Court at the insistence of Astrodome officials. She was represented by lawyer Richard Haynes, who asked that the charges be dropped because of the "insufficiency of the accusation." Haynes offered this scientific explanation for Morganna's actions.

"It was the law of gravity," he said, explaining that Morganna was leaning over the boxseat rail when "the laws of gravity took over. She ran onto the field and saw police chasing her, so where else would she run but to the safety of the pitcher?"

Morganna, who had been arrested for previous kiss-and-run episodes but never jailed, said she did not want to go to the slammer. "Stripes make me look top-heavy," she explained.

◆ ◆ ◆

Ron Guidry, "Louisiana Lightning" to New York fans who

remember his blazing fastball and the incredible 25-3 record he carved out in a spectacular 1978 season for the Yankees, was a bona fide outdoorsman and the subject of many unfounded tales. According to Roland Guidry, Ron's father, most of those stories were a product of his son's sense of humor.

Guidry was not one of 12 children. He did not hunt alligators with a bat. He did not get into baseball to feed his starving family. He did not raise three struggling sisters. He did not run down rabbits as a young boy.

Guidry was, however, an avid hunter who sought dove, geese, duck, rabbit, quail and any other quarry that could be found near his Lafayette, La., roots.

"Ron tells such tall tales to his teammates," said Roland. "I don't know if they'll ever come down for a hunt. He's got Goose Gossage scared to death of alligators."

◆　◆　◆

Most disabling injuries take place on the diamond. But some of the darndest things happen elsewhere, too, as the Kansas City Royals can readily attest.

Hall of Famer George Brett once broke a big toe while running up steps at his home to watch a television replay of a home run by Bill Buckner. Catcher Brent Mayne missed nearly a month of another season when he strained his lower back while crossing a mall parking lot in Detroit. Mayne turned to look at something and … ouch!

Pitcher Kevin Appier injured his shoulder in a fall while carrying baby-shower gifts to a car at his farm. Pitcher Bret Saberhagen suffered a cut forehead when he fell over an ottoman heading for the bathroom of his New York hotel room. Pitcher Luis Aquino missed spring training time after burning his hand on a plate of fajitas at an Orlando restaurant.

And while in Mike Sweeney's garage, designated hitter Jeremy Giambi suffered lacerations when a tool box fell on his head.

Or so the stories were told.

When veteran righthander Jim Slaton jumped out to a 4-1 start for the California Angels in 1986, he inspired a rush of enthusiasm from his brother Frank. But by early June, excitement had faded into concern as Slaton slumped to 4-6, prompting Frank to take rash action.

He vowed to eat no food that required chewing until Jim recorded another victory. But 16 pounds later, Jim was demoted to the bullpen and Frank added an addendum to his vow—"Make it a win or a save."

Frank even tried to get his dad to join the fast, but in the Slaton family, Father knows best. "I love my son," he said, "but I'm not crazy."

On June 30, Jim was released by the Angels and Frank decided to forego his pledge. Slaton was later picked up by Detroit and appeared in 22 games. He did not get a win for the Tigers, but he did record two saves.

◆   ◆   ◆

Old-school baseball writers were famous for their nocturnal escapades. None was better at this pursuit than Neal Russo, the zany, joke-cracking, lovable beat writer for the *St. Louis Post-Dispatch*.

Years ago, when the Post-Dispatch was an afternoon newspaper, writers had more leeway in filing their stories. The Post-Dispatch deadline was 7 a.m.—at the latest.

One night, after a game against the Giants, Russo decided to sample the famous cuisine and cocktails of San Francisco before filing his game story. He finally cruised into the lobby of the Sheraton Palace Hotel in the wee hours, just as Cardinals publicist Jim Toomey was coming through another door.

"Well, Neal, what did you write about today?" Toomey inquired.

Russo looked at Toomey with a blank stare and smacked himself on the forehead.

"Oh, write! Write! Write!" Russo groaned.

Given the time difference, he was right on deadline.

Russo rushed to a nearby Western Union office and began typing his story. He had it transmitted page by page, perhaps the only time an afternoon game story was written in "takes" for the next afternoon's paper.

◆　　◆　　◆

Clint Hurdle learned the hard way that nothing is definite.

Hurdle, a 1983 non-roster invitee to spring training with the Seattle Mariners, enjoyed a good spring and impressed manager Rene Lachemann with his ability to play outfield, first base, third base and catcher. Lachemann told Hurdle before camp broke that he had made the team.

Hurdle worked out with the Mariners the night before the season opener at Seattle's Kingdome. Then he called his father and asked him to load his pickup and drive it from his home in Merritt Island, Fla., to Seattle.

But things suddenly unraveled an hour before the opener. Mariners president Dan O'Brien told Lachemann he wanted to cut Hurdle and put Ken Phelps on the roster instead. O'Brien called Hurdle into the manager's office, where he thought he would be signing a contract.

O'Brien gave him the bad news.

Hurdle moved quickly to track down his father. He went so far as contacting the Missouri and Kansas highway patrols, who put out a watch for Hurdle's truck so they could tell his father to turn around and head back to Florida.

◆　　◆　　◆

Cheaper by the dozen. Or, in this case, free by the dozen.

Baseball clubs are always looking for good promotions and the Kansas City Royals came up with a doozy in 2003. Every time the Royals got 12 or more hits in a home game, each fan could turn in their ticket stub at a Krispy Kreme shop for a dozen free doughnuts.

As the season went on, fans began whooping it up whenever the Royals got close.

"As soon as we get 11 hits," said second baseman Desi Relaford, "they get hyper—and hungry."

By season's end, the Royals had reached the dozen-hit mark 27 times and the number of doughnuts that could have been claimed by hungry fans was 6,796,152. Of that total, 2,241,660 were actually picked up. That's a .330 batting average, pretty tasty by anybody's count.

Krispy Kreme was delighted. The chain received national publicity —a promotion without holes.

◆　　◆　　◆

Hall of Fame player Ralph Kiner on the influence of another Hall of Fame player in his life:

"Hank Greenberg came over to the Pirates in his last year in baseball (1947). He became a very close friend of mine. He helped me tremendously. It was my second season in the league and he was one of the great people in baseball history.

"Of course, 1947 was also the year of Jackie Robinson coming into baseball. Robinson went through hell and endured a lot as the first black player in the league. The first time Greenberg saw Robinson in uniform with the Dodgers, they were playing in Pittsburgh. Greenberg went up to Jackie. He told Jackie about how he went through hell as a Jewish player when he broke into the major leagues. Then he told Robinson, 'Hang in there and keep doing it right.'

"Greenberg was by far the biggest influence on my life. He was the biggest man I knew and more than one of the greatest players of all time. He went through the war and lost four years in the service and came out to lead the Tigers to the pennant. He was great for the game of baseball and a great leader. He was a big inspiration to me.

"I looked up to him as a big brother image. I believed everything he told me. As Yogi Berra would say, Greenberg 'really learned me his experience.' "

Steve Physioc, the television play-by-play voice of the Anaheim Angels since 1996, got a premonition the Disney-owned team would successfully complete its amazing 2002 World Series championship run on the morning of Game 7.

"They (the Angels) had the unbelievable comeback in Game 6," he said. "They were down, 5-0, and came back to win the game. Well, the next morning I go into my office, where I have this little Rolodex with great quotes from some of the top people in history. It could be a quote from Jesus Christ or Thomas Edison or Albert Einstein.

"For October 27, the quote is from Walt Disney, and the words are: 'If you can dream it, then you can do it.' I yell to my wife, 'Honey! There's no way the Angels are going to lose today!' "

The Angels beat the San Francisco Giants, 4-1, that day and won the franchise's first championship.

Jackie Autry, the widow of longtime Angels owner Gene Autry, watched with both pride and sadness when Anaheim defeated the Giants in that memorable 2002 fall classic. Pride because of the Autry dream that finally was fulfilled; sadness because the "Singing Cowboy" was not around to be part of the festive victory celebration.

She also was touched by the tribute paid to her husband by Anaheim outfielder Tim Salmon, an Angels fan favorite since his debut in 1992.

"Everybody has favorites on their team," Autry said. "I know that Tim Salmon, our right fielder, played with a commemorative patch that the team wore in 1999, after Gene passed away, in his right pocket.

"He played with it (to show respect and gain inspiration) throughout the Division Series, the Championship Series and the

World Series. And that's one of the reasons I gave Tim Salmon one of Gene Autry's hats."

◆   ◆   ◆

In 1980, a group of baseball writers gathered at Orlando's Tinker Field, spring home of the Minnesota Twins. Stories were exchanged and *St. Paul Dispatch-Pioneer Press* writer Bob Fowler told about former *Minneapolis Star* competitor Dan Stoneking, who one spring in the early 1970s decided to work out with the Twins and give readers a first-person report.

In his first workout, players running sprints in the outfield left the ample-bellied Stoneking far behind, where he kept pace only with Harmon Killebrew and Tony Oliva, both of whom were nursing leg injuries. Twins owner Calvin Griffith was watching with concern from a dugout.

"I know two of those fellows," Griffith said, "but who in the hell is that third man?"

Griffith, when advised what Stoneking was doing, patted his heart and smiled. "Thank God," he said. "I thought he was one of ours."

◆   ◆   ◆

Back in 1988, it sounded like a great idea. The new spring training home of the Kansas City Royals would be anchored by a theme park called Boardwalk and Baseball.

Nestled right next to the new Baseball City Sports Complex, with its stadium and practice fields, the amusement park had a baseball theme and a mile-long boardwalk. The site formerly was the home of Circus World, and it was not far from Orlando, Fla., where the Disney empire sprawled.

"Tinker Bell came over from Disney World," pitching coach Frank Funk said, "and waved a little wand."

There were exhibits from the Hall of Fame, batting cages, a spot where fans could get their own baseball cards made and a rollercoaster that clattered past the stadium with joyful cargo. But, alas, not enough folks followed Tinker Bell over from Disney World. The magic dust did not last.

Crowds at the team's exhibition games were usually small and attendance at the theme park was sparse. The anticipated spillover between Disney World and Baseball City never developed.

Years later, Royals general manager John Schuerholz, who supported the idea, became general manager of the Atlanta Braves and helped develop the Braves, new spring complex in a hotter entertainment spot—on the outskirts of Disney World. The Braves had no trouble drawing crowds.

And Boardwalk and Baseball?

After a couple of years, the property was sold to Anheuser Busch and the beer giant's entertainment division shut down the theme park. John Wathan, Royals manager in 1988, mused: "It became Boarded-Up and Baseball."

In 2003, the Royals departed Florida for a new training facility in Surprise, Ariz.

◆   ◆   ◆

After his 17-11 season with Cleveland in 1983, pitcher Rick Sutcliffe made the banquet-circuit rounds and took this lighthearted jab at Indians president Gabe Paul and general manager Phil Seghi:

"I dreamed I was in heaven," Sutcliffe told listeners, "and Phil Seghi was there with the ugliest woman I ever saw. I asked St. Peter why and he said, 'Phil lived a bad life, and he's going to be punished.'

"Then I saw Gabe Paul with Bo Derek, and I said, 'Gabe must have lived a good life, huh?' And St. Peter said, 'No, he's Bo Derek's punishment.' "

Was it a coincidence that Sutcliffe was traded to the Chicago Cubs the following June?

INDEX

A

Aaron, Henry "Hank"   114, 190-191, 240, 250, 264
Adams, Glenn   96
Adcock, Joe   87
Aikens, Willie   105
Albert, Marv   225
Allen, Mel   193
Allen, Richie   223
Alomar, Roberto   120
Alou, Felipe   178
Alou, Jesus   8
Alston, Walter   48, 173
Amalfitano, Joe   57, 129
Anderson, Brian   62
Anderson, Pamela   208-209
Anderson, Sparky   18, 105, 149, 162, 212, 221
Andrews, Shane   100
Andujar, Joaquin   34
Appier, Kevin   257, 281
Aquino, Luis   281
Argyros, George   23, 163, 249
Armas, Tony   95, 231
Armbrister, Ed   243
Armstrong, Dave   209
Ashburn, Richie   99, 146, 199

Ashford, Emmett   148
Ausmus, Brad   159
Autry, Gene   39, 285
Autry, Jackie   285

B

Baird, Allard   9
Bamberger, George   47, 49
Banks, Ernie   70, 99, 192
Barlick, Al   143
Barlow, Mike   252
Barnett, Larry   95, 179, 243-244
Barrett, Mac   43
Barrett, Marty   144, 217
Bauer, Hank   77, 252
Bavasi, Buzzie   20
Baylor, Don   35, 67
Beane, Billy   91
Bearnarth, Larry   7
Beck, Rod   118
Beckert, Glenn   108
Beckett, Josh   278
Belanger, Mark   139
Belcher, Tim   189
Bell, Buddy   98
Bell, Juan   259
Belle, Albert   44

Beltran, Carlos   130, 243
Bench, Johnny   18, 105, 116, 123, 168-169, 273, 280
Benson, Vern   25
Berra, Dale   94
Berra, Yogi   165, 285
Blyleven, Bert   71, 173
Bochte, Bruce   93
Bochy, Bruce   98
Bodie, Keith   263
Boggs, Wade   172, 217, 233, 271
Bolick, Frank   10
Bonds, Bobby   69
Bonilla, Bobby   255
Boone, Aaron   218
Boone, Bob   9, 82
Boone, Bret   90
Bordagaray, Frenchy   59
Bourne, Bobby   274
Bowa, Larry   88, 107, 150, 171
Boyd, Dennis "Oil Can"   34, 82
Boyer, Ray   172
Bradley, Phil   259
Bradley, Scott   81
Branca, Ralph   230
Brantley, Jeff   131
Branyan, Russell   86
Brecheen, Harry   231

Breeden, Scott 122
Bremigan, Nick 139
Bresnahan, Dave 157
Bresnahan, Roger 158
Brett, George 10, 38, 82-83,
127, 136, 152, 165, 169, 251,
272, 280-281
Brett, Ken 219
Brimley, Wilford 228
Brinkman, Joe 117, 152, 160
Bristol, Dave 25-26, 168
Brock, Lou 97, 250, 278
Brock, Norman 183
Brokaw, Tom 191, 227
Brooks, Mel 68
Brown, Bill 61, 189, 211
Brown, Gates 31, 129
Brown, Joe 177
Bryant, Don 132
Bryant, Ron 50
Buck, Jack 32, 196, 212
Buck, Joe 212
Buckner, Bill 115, 144, 192,
217, 281
Budig, Gene 10
Buhl, Bob 99
Buhner, Jay 21
Bumbry, Al 93
Bunker, Wally 73
Bunning, Jim 245
Burdette, Lew 88, 240
Burke, Joe 12
Burke, Phil 49
Busch, Gussie 26
Butler, Brent 52
Byrd, Paul 98

C

Campbell, Dave 219, 221
Campusano, Silvestre 183
Canseco, Jose 63, 91, 226
Capra, Buzz 115
Caray, Harry 222
Cardenal, Jose 127
Carew, Rod 106
Carlton, Steve 87, 114, 166
Carneal, Herb 111
Carpenter, Ruly 199
Carter, Joe 85, 246
Carty, Rico 58, 93, 264
Cash, Dave 104
Cash, Johnny 194
Cash, Norman 188
Cashen, Frank 103
Castiglione, Joe 95, 217

Cater, Danny 240
Caudill, Bill 125
Cedeno, Cesar 104
Cepeda, Orlando 8, 108, 235
Cerone, Rick 218
Cerutti, John 91
Chalk, Dave 105
Chambliss, Chris 236
Charboneau, Joe 60
Chiofalo, Nicholas 263
Chiofalo, Nick, Jr. 263
Christensen, John 184
Chylak, Nestor 117
Claire, Fred 259
Clark, Jack 120, 259
Clark, Will 33, 259
Clemens, Roger 51, 151, 165
245, 277
Clemente, Roberto 90
Cleveland, Reggie 243
Cobb, Mickey 29
Cobb, Shirley 251
Cobb, Ty 220, 238,
250-251
Colbert, Nate 192
Colborn, Jim 96
Coleman, Jerry 63, 193
Coleman, Ken 217
Coles, Darnell 81
Colletti, Ned 277
Collins, Terry 10
Comiskey, Charles 66
Conlan, Jocko 143, 146
Connors, Jimmy 72
Cook, Murray 65
Cooney, Terry 151
Corrales, Pat 84
Costas, Bob 196, 225
Coughlin, Dan 60
Cowley, Joe 35
Cox, Billy 20
Cox, Bobby 142
Cox, Danny 262
Craig, Roger 108, 223
Crawford, Pat 181
Crawford, Shag 70, 127,
143, 153
Cubbage, Mike 106
Cuellar, Mike 14, 73
Cumberland, John 63

D

Dade, Paul 93
Dalton, Harry 47
Damon, Johnny 51

Daniels, Kal 65
Dark, Alvin 27, 85, 178, 230
Dascenzo, Doug 7
Davidson, Donald 86
Davis, Chili 258
Davis, Mike 84, 226
Davis, Ron 111-112
Davis, Storm 56
Davis, Tommy 42
Dawley, Bill 114
Dean, Dizzy 128, 206, 240
DeBerry, Hank 76
DeCinces, Doug 93
Dellucci, David 202
DeLucia, Rich 277
Demery, Larry 89
Dempsey, Pat 184
Dempsey, Rick 55, 94, 265
Denkinger, Don 84, 100
Dent, Bucky 137
DePastino, Joe 158, 176
Derek, Bo 287
Dibble, Rob 122
DiBiasio, Bob 71
Didier, Bob 108
Diebold, Richard 262
DiFelice, Mike 267
DiMaggio, Dominic 169
DiMaggio, Joe 259
Downing, Al 114, 191-192
Drago, Dick 243
Drake, Sammy 99
Dravecky, Dave 220
Drysdale, Don 143, 245, 270
Dunlop, Harry 28
Dunn, Jack 103
Dunston, Shawon 7, 238
Durham, Ray 203
Durocher, Leo 20, 57,
146, 208
Dykstra, Lenny 140

E

Eckersley, Dennis 93,
120, 225
Elia, Lee 147
Embser, Rich 183
Engel, Bob 150
Engle, Dave 172
Eskew, Alan 16
Essian, Jim 7
Estalella, Bobby 86
Evans, Darrell 120
Evans, Jim 60, 109, 139,
144, 237

Rice, Jim 53, 96
Richards, Gene 251
Richards, Paul 36
Richardson, Bobby 40, 235
Richman, Milton 28
Righetti, Dave 138, 232
Righetti, Leo 233
Rigney, Bill 17, 173
Ring, Joe 5-6
Ringolsby, Tracy 28
Ripken, Cal, Jr. 47, 52, 180, 254, 271
Ripken, Cal, Sr. 180
Rivera, Ruben 202
Rivero, Francisco 178
Rizzuto, Phil 193, 237, 273
Roa, Joe 176
Roberts, Dave 22, 251
Roberts, Leon 23
Robinson, Brooks 41
Robinson, Frank 24, 140, 274
Robinson, Jackie 284
Robinson, Wilbert 76
Rock, Kid 209
Rodgers, Andre 99
Rodgers, Buck 34
Rodriguez, Alex 52
Roe, Rocky 149
Rogers, Kenny 109
Romero, Ed 150
Romero, Ramon 184
Romo, Enrique 120
Roof, Phil 178
Rosario, Santiago 23
Rose, Pete 15, 57, 91, 114, 122, 168, 220, 238-239
Rosenthal, Ken 271
Rowe, Ralph 173
Royko, Mike 70
Ruberto, Sonny 251
Runge, Ed 41
Russo, Jim 14
Russo, Neal 282
Ruth, Babe 167, 190, 192, 250
Ryan, Nolan 51, 100, 109, 171, 188, 266, 280

S

Saberhagen, Bret 109, 281
Sabo, Chris 57
Sadecki, Ray 88
Sain, Johnny 129
Salazar, Luis 94
Salmon, Tim 285
Samuel, Mike 183

Sanguillen, Manny 24
Santo, Ron 50, 70
Sarmiento, Manny 22
Sarmiento, Wally 172
Sawyer, Eddie 11
Sax, Steve 41
Schaffer, Jim 272
Schiappa, Cliff 252
Schmidt, Mike 88, 104, 141, 280
Schmidt, Milt 177
Schoendienst, Red 21, 231, 279
Schofield, Dick 240
Schott, Marge 65, 238
Schueler, Ron 7
Schuerholz, John 287
Scioscia, Mike 216
Scott, George 73
Scott, Mike 192
Scully, Vin 189, 195, 225
Seaver, Tom 66, 70, 90, 245
Seghi, Phil 287
Segui, Diego 241
Seitzer, Kevin 97, 109
Selkirk, George 46
Sells, Dave 126
Sergio, Michael 144
Sexson, Richie 45, 128, 214
Sferrazza, Matt 183
Shannon, Mike 194-196, 213
Shaughnessy, Dan 277
Sheffield, Gary 162
Shenk, Larry 199
Sheppard, Bob 107
Shirley, Bob 108
Shopay, Tom 43
Short, Bob 12
Showalter, Buck 106, 181
Simmons, Curt 88, 250
Simmons, Ted 127, 197, 278
Singleton, Ken 93
Sizemore, Ted 88
Skibosh, Tom 270
Skinner, Bob 240
Skizas, Lou 56
Slaton, Jim 282
Slaughter, Enos 230
Smalley, Roy 106
Smith, Lee 113
Smith, Mark 255
Smith, Mayo 129
Smith, Ozzie 213
Smith, Terry 209
Snow, J.T. 221
Snow, Jack 221

Soar, Hank 56
Soriano, Dewey 23
Sosa, Sammy 248
Spano, Steve 183
Springstead, Marty 142
Stanky, Eddie 153
Stanley, Mickey 240
Starr, Bob 196
Staub, Rusty 57, 85
Steinbrenner, George 39, 268-269
Stello, Dick 244
Stengel, Casey 8, 37, 40, 235
Stenhouse, Mike 184
Stewart, Art 82
Stewart, Dave 131
Stobbs, Chuck 83
Stone, Harvey 36
Stone, Jeff 23
Stone, Steve 13, 69
Stoneking, Dan 286
Stoneman, Bill 69
Stottlemyre, Mel 14
Strawberry, Darryl 174
Stuart, Dick 206
Summers, John "Champ" 72
Sundberg, Jim 52
Suppan, Jeff 9
Sutcliffe, Rick 287
Sutter, Bruce 123
Sutton, Don 150
Sveum, Dale 183
Swartz, Nick 267
Sweeney, Mike 97, 164, 263, 281

T

Tanana, Frank 96
Tanner, Chuck 56, 120, 179, 276
Taubensee, Eddie 171
Tebbetts, Birdie 193, 259
Tekulve, Kent 120
Templeton, Garry 26, 260, 278
Tenace, Gene 108, 116
Terrell, Jerry 106
Terry, Ralph 235
Thomas, Gorman 245
Thompson, Chuck 49
Thompson, Hank 21
Thomson, Bobby 187, 230
Thon, Dickie 280
Thornton, Andre 93
Thorpe, Jim 66
Tiant, Luis 43